Hagop Kevorkian Series on
Near Eastern Art and Civilization

The publication of this work has been aided by
a grant from the Hagop Kevorkian Fund.

PATTERNS OF STYLISTIC CHANGES IN ISLAMIC ARCHITECTURE

Local Traditions versus Migrating Artists

Michael Meinecke

NEW YORK UNIVERSITY PRESS
NEW YORK AND LONDON

NEW YORK UNIVERSITY PRESS
New York and London

Library of Congress Cataloging-in-Publication Data
Meinecke, Michael.
Patterns of stylistic changes in Islamic architecture : local traditions versus migrating artists / Michael Meinecke.
p. cm. — (Hagop Kevorkian series on Near Eastern art and civilization)
Includes bibliographical references and index.
ISBN 0-8147-5492-9
1. Architecture, Islamic. I. Title. II. Series.
NA380.M45 1995
720′.956—dc20 95-5508
CIP

New York University Press books are printed on acid-free paper, and their binding materials are chosen for strength and durability.

Manufactured in the United States of America

10 9 8 7 6 5 4 3 2 1

Contents

Preface by Jill N. Claster ix
List of Illustrations xi
Foreword by Priscilla P. Soucek xvii
Abbreviations xxi
Introduction 1

1. Forced Labor in Early Islamic Architecture: The Case of ar-Raqqa/ar-Rāfiqa on the Euphrates 5

1. Nikephorion/ar-Raqqa: Islamization of a Classical City 7
2. ar-Rāfiqa: The Early Islamic Metropolis 8
3. Hārūn ar-Rashīd at ar-Raqqa: The New Center of the Islamic World 16
4. Forced Labor versus Local Schools of Architecture 24

2. Buṣrā: From the Provincia Arabia to the Darb al-Ḥajj 31

1. Redevelopment by Amīn ad-Daula Kumushtakīn (Early Sixth/Twelfth Century) 35

2. Golden Age of aṣ-Ṣāliḥ Ismāʿīl (First Half of Seventh/Thirteenth Century) 38
3. Buṣrā in Eclipse: The Mamluk Period (Eighth/Fourteenth Century) 43
4. Limitations of Local Styles of Architecture 48

3. Hasankeyf/Ḥiṣn Kaifā on the Tigris: A Regional Center on the Crossroad of Foreign Influences 55

1. Artuqid Period (Sixth/Twelfth Century) 58
   Tigris Bridge (I) 58
   Great Palace of the Citadel 60
   Citadel Mosque (I) 61
   Ismāʿīl Ibn ar-Razzāz al-Jazarī 62
   Artuqid Coinage 63
2. Aiyūbid Revival (Second and Third Quarter of the Eighth/Fourteenth Century) 64
   Small Palace of the Citadel 65
   Sultan Süleyman Camii (I) 66
   Koç Cami 68
3. Aiyūbid Zenith: Reign of al-ʿĀdil Sulaimān 71
   Citadel Mosque (II) 71
   Sultan Süleyman Camii (II) 72
   Jāmiʿ ar-Rizq 73
   Small Mosque 75
   Mausoleum 76
   Citadel 77
4. Āq Qoyūnlū Period (Later Ninth/Fifteenth Century) 77
   Zeynel Bey Türbesi 77
   Mashhad Imām Muḥammad b. ʿAbd Allāh aṭ-Ṭaiyār 78
   Tigris Bridge (II) 80
5. Southwest versus East 80

4. Mamluk Architecture and the Ottoman Empire: The Formation of New Architectural Styles 89

1. Formative Period of Ottoman Architecture (Late Eighth/Fourteenth and First Half of Ninth/Fifteenth Centuries) 91

2. Ottoman Architecture after the Conquest of Constantinople 99
3. Ottoman Supremacy after the Conquest of Cairo 109
4. Patterns of Changes in Architectural Styles 111

Appendix 155
Index 157

Preface

It was with the deepest sadness that Professor Michael Meinecke's many friends and admirers at the Hagop Kevorkian Center for Near Eastern Studies learned of his sudden death on January 10, 1995. In our sense of the loss of an esteemed and influential historian of Islamic Art, we join his colleagues and friends worldwide who mourn his death.

This book, published posthumously, is based on the four lectures Professor Meinecke delivered at the Center in the spring of 1991, for the Hagop Kevorkian Lectureship in Near Eastern Art and Civilization. We remember the creativity and insight of his lectures as well as the great personal pleasure that he gave to those of us privileged to know him. We were honored by his presence at the Center and recall him as a lively, spirited human being—and as a gentleman and a scholar.

The manuscript, including the placement of photographs and illustrations in the text, had been completed at the time of Professor Meinecke's death. We owe an enormous debt of gratitude to Professor Priscilla Soucek, Hagop Kevorkian Professor of Islamic Art, for her help in shepherding the manuscript through to the end and ensuring that Professor Meinecke's wishes were carried out. It was truly a labor of love for Priscilla. The New York University Press, particularly Despina Papazoglou Gimbel, worked with infinite patience and great dedication to see the manuscript through to its present form.

The Kevorkian Center is proud to have been able to bring Professor Meinecke's manuscript for the Lectureship to fruition. In memory of Professor Meinecke, we dedicate this book to his wife, Dr. Viktoria Meinecke-Berg, as we believe he would have wished to do.

JILL N. CLASTER

List of Illustrations

FIGURES

Fig. 1. ar-Raqqa: location map 6
Fig. 2. ar-Raqqa/ar-Rāfiqa: fortification 10
Fig. 3. ar-Raqqa/ar-Rāfiqa, ʿAbbāsid Great Mosque: reconstructed ground plan 14
Fig. 4. ar-Raqqa/ar-Rāfiqa, Palace City—Excavation Site East: topographical map 20
Fig. 5. ar-Raqqa/ar-Rāfiqa, Palace City—Excavation Site East: East Complex 21
Fig. 6. ar-Raqqa/ar-Rāfiqa, Palace City—Excavation Site Northeast: Northeast Complex 22
Fig. 7. Darb al-Ḥajj: alternative routes in South Syria 32
Fig. 8. Buṣrā: location map of monuments 34
Fig. 9. Buṣrā, al-ʿUmarī Mosque: ground plan 36
Fig. 10. Buṣrā, Birkat al-Ḥajj: plan and sections 40
Fig. 11. (1) Buṣrā, Ḥammām Manjak: ground plan after excavation; (2) Damascus, Ḥammām at-Taurīzī, ground plan 45
Fig. 12. Buṣrā, Ḥammām Manjak: axonometric reconstruction 46

Fig. 13. al-Muzairīb, Khān: reconstructed ground plan 47
Fig. 14. Hasankeyf: location map of monuments 56
Fig. 15. Artuqid and Zengid bridges 59
Fig. 16. Hasankeyf, Artuqid mason marks 61
Fig. 17. Hasankeyf, Sultan Süleyman Camii/Madrasa of al-ʿĀdil Ghāzī: sketch plan 67
Fig. 18. Hasankeyf, Koç Cami/Madrasa of ʿAbd Allāh Ibn al-Mawardī: sketch plan 69
Fig. 19. Hasankeyf, Citadel Mosque: sketch plan 72
Fig. 20. Hasankeyf, Jāmiʿ ar-Rizq: sketch plan 74
Fig. 21. Hasankeyf, Small Mosque: sketch plan 75
Fig. 22. Hasankeyf, Mausoleum: sketch plan 76
Fig. 23. Hasankeyf, Mashhad Imām Muḥammad b. ʿAbd Allāh aṭ-Ṭaiyār: sketch plan 79
Fig. 24. (1) Manisa, Ulu Cami: plan; (2) Iznik, Yeşil Cami: plan; (3) Edirne, Üç Şerefeli Cami: plan 94
Fig. 25. Cairo Citadel, Mosque of an-Nāṣir Muḥammad: plan 95
Fig. 26. Selçuk, Isa Bey Camii: plan 96
Fig. 27. Damascus, Mosque of Yalbughā al-Yaḥyāwī: reconstructed ground plan 97
Fig. 28. Istanbul: (1) Mosque of Meḥmet Fātiḥ: plan; (2) Mosque of Bāyazīd II: plan 100
Fig. 29. Istanbul, Şehzade Cami: plan 101
Fig. 30. (1) Aleppo, Mausoleum of ʿUthmān Ibn Ughulbak: plan; (2) Balat, Ilyas Bey Camii: plan; (3) Cairo, Qubbat al-Fadāwīya: plan of upper story; (4) Istanbul, Davut Paşa Camii: plan 104
Fig. 31. Edirne, Mosque of Bāyazīd II: plan 106
Fig. 32. Istanbul, Mosque of Selīm I: plan 107
Fig. 33. Cairo: (1) Madrasa of Khāʾīrbak al-Ashrafī: plan; (2) Madrasa of Qānībāy Qarā ar-Rammāḥ: plan 108

PLATES *(All plates appear as a group following p. 117.)*

Plate 1. (a) ar-Raqqa/Nikephorion, Great Mosque: aerial view of 1942; (b) ar-Raqqa/Nikephorion, Great Mosque—Maʿdhānat al-Munaiṭir: minaret; (c) ar-Raqqa/ar-Rāfiqa, city walls and palace area: aerial view of 1929

Plate 2. ar-Raqqa/ar-Rāfiqa, city walls: (a) Aerial view of 1961; (b) North Gate after excavation
Plate 3. ar-Raqqa/ar-Rāfiqa, Great Mosque: (a) View of ruin in 1973 before excavation; (b) Stucco decoration of prayer niche
Plate 4. ar-Raqqa/ar-Rāfiqa, Palace City: (a) Central palace of Hārūn ar-Rashīd and adjacent residences: aerial view of c. 1930; (b) Excavation Site East-Eastern Palace, after partial reconstruction in 1989
Plate 5. ar-Raqqa/ar-Rāfiqa, Palace City, Excavation Site East-Western Palace: (a) View from southwest during excavation; (b) Stucco frieze; (c) Stucco frieze
Plate 6. ar-Raqqa/ar-Rāfiqa, Palace City, Northeast Complex: (a) Aerial view of c. 1930; (b) Main building, south façade
Plate 7. (a) ar-Raqqa/ar-Rāfiqa, Palace City: Excavation Site East-Western Palace; stucco friezes of central reception room; (b) Hiraqla near ar-Raqqa: aerial view of 1935
Plate 8. Buṣrā: (a) Citadel: Seljuq northwest tower, interior of upper part; (b) Madrasa of Kumushtakīn at the al-Mabrak Mosque: ceiling of main *īwān*
Plate 9. Buṣrā: (a) Madrasa of Kumushtakīn at the al-Mabrak Mosque: interior courtyard; (b) Citadel: Aiyūbid southwest tower, interior
Plate 10. Buṣrā, alʿUmarī Mosque: (a) Prayer hall; (b) Stucco decoration of *miḥrāb;* (c) Fragment of stucco frieze on *qibla* wall
Plate 11. Buṣrā: (a) al-Fāṭima Mosque: interior; (b) Dār al-Qurʾān of ʿAbd al-Wāḥid ash-Shāfiʿī: view from east
Plate 12. (a) Buṣrā, Ḥammām Manjak: reception room; (b) Damascus, mosque of Khalīl at-Taurīzī: mausoleum dome
Plate 13. (a) Buṣrā, Ḥammām Manjak: bath chambers; (b) Damascus, Ḥammām at-Taurīzī: central bath chamber
Plate 14. (a) Buṣrā, Ḥammām Manjak: fragment of corner transition in bath chamber; (b) Damascus, Ḥammām at-Taurīzī: stucco *muqarnaṣ* vault of bath chamber
Plate 15. (a) al-Kiswa, Zāwiyat Manjak: *qibla īwān;* (b) al-Muzairīb, Khān: entrance

Plate 16. Hasankeyf: (a) Tigris Bridge; (b) Citadel-Artuqid palace and Aiyūbid mosque
Plate 17. (a) Batman Su Bridge near Silvan; (b) Cizre, Bridge: general view; (c) Cizre, Bridge: mason marks on south pier
Plate 18. (a) Istanbul, Topkapi Sarayı Library ms. Aḥmet III: double page miniature of palace door at Diyarbakır by al-Jazarī; (b) Cizre, Ulu Cami: bronze door on middle entrance of prayer hall façade
Plate 19. Hasankeyf, Koç Cami: (a) Stucco *miḥrāb* in main domed chamber; (b) Stucco *miḥrāb* in central *īwān*
Plate 20. (a) Washington, D.C., Freer Gallery of Art: figural scene from a miniature page of a Mamluk copy of al-Jazarī's treatise; (b) Cizre, Bridge: zodiac relief of Saturn and Libra on south pier
Plate 21. (a) Istanbul, Topkapı Sarayı Library ms. Aḥmet III: door knocker of palace door at Diyarbakır by al-Jazarī; (b) Berlin, Museum of Islamic Art: bronze door knocker from Tiflis; (c) Berlin, Museum of Islamic Art: coins of the sixth/twelfth and seventh/thirteenth centuries from Southeast Anatolia and North Mesopotamia
Plate 22. Hasankeyf, Citadel: (a) Small Palace: exterior façade; (b) Second gate
Plate 23. (a–b) Hasankeyf, Sultan Süleyman Camii: minaret and base with inscription; (c) Aleppo, Madrasa aṣ-Ṣāḥibīya: window panel; (d) Hasankeyf, Jāmiᶜ ar-Rizq: minaret; (e) Aleppo, mosque of Mankalībughā ash-Shamsī: minaret
Plate 24. (a) Hasankeyf, Sultan Süleyman Camii: domed courtyard of three-*īwān* structure; (b) Aleppo, Dār al-Fakhrī: stucco ceiling of *īwān*
Plate 25. (a–b) Hasankeyf, Jāmiᶜ ar-Rizq: minaret shaft and base; (c) Mardin, Sultan İsa Medresesi: entrance porch
Plate 26. (a–b) Hasankeyf, Mausoleum: façade and window niche; (c) Aleppo, Jāmiᶜ ad-Darraj: window niche of façade
Plate 27. (a) Hasankeyf, Zeynel Bey Türbesi: building inscription on portal in cut tile mosaic; (b) Istanbul, Çinili Köşk: cut tile mosaic decoration of portico
Plate 28. Hasankeyf: (a) Zeynel Bey Türbesi: exterior view; (b) Mashhad Imām Muḥammad b. ᶜAbd Allāh aṭ-Ṭaiyār: entrance of mausoleum

Plate 29. (a) Manisa, Ulu Cami: lateral niche of north portal; (b) Selçuk, İsa Bey Camii: courtyard window; (c) Damascus, madrasa of Jaqmaq al-Arghūnshāwī: prayer niche; (d) Aleppo, mosque of Mankalībughā ash-Shamsī: east portal
Plate 30. (a) Manisa, Ulu Cami: courtyard; (b) Edirne, Üç Şerefeli Cami: courtyard
Plate 31. (a) Selçuk, İsa Bey Camii: window of façade; (b) Iznik, Yeşil Cami: door of exterior portico
Plate 32. Edirne: (a) Üç Şerefeli Cami: exterior view; (b) Mosque of Bāyazīd II: exterior view
Plate 33. Aleppo, Mausoleum of ʿUthmān Ibn Ughulbak: (a) Exterior view; (b) Interior dome
Plate 34. Cairo, Qubbat al-Fadāwīya: (a) Façade; (b) Interior
Plate 35. Cairo: (a) Madrasa of Khāʾirbak al-Ashrafī: interior; (b) Madrasa of Qānībāy Qarā ar-Rammāḥ: main *īwān*
Plate 36. (a) Gebze, Çoban Mustafa Paşa Camii: interior; (b–c) Berlin, Museum of Islamic Art: Mamluk brass chandeliers from the Mustafa Paşa Camii at Gebze

Foreword

In these essays, Michael Meinecke draws upon his remarkably detailed knowledge of Islamic architecture to investigate its evolution. Most conventional analysis has usually focused on the linear development of regional building traditions arranged either by dynasties or by typological categories. Many are often limited to monuments within the boundaries of a modern nation-state. Although the existence of broad regional traditions is undeniable, architectural development in all but the largest centers is frequently episodic and sometimes manifests clear shifts from period to period. Meinecke's essays offer a reconsideration of various features which have remained anomalous with traditional lines of investigation.

In four case studies, Meinecke explores how changes in the local workforce, such as the movement of skilled craftsmen, help to explain transformations in the development of Islamic architecture. In some instances the movement of artisans from one region to another is due to the action of a patron, but in other cases it appears to result from the initiative of the craftsmen themselves. Often these two factors interact to affect the character of buildings or their decorative programs.

Meinecke's first essay focuses on the city of Raqqa in the Euphrates Valley and draws upon the results of excavations carried out in recent decades. These demonstrate the critical role played by the Abbasid Dynasty in that city's development. Building programs expanded or contracted as the patrons' concern with Raqqa waxed or waned. The connection between Raqqa and metropolitan centers in Iraq was so intimate that some Syrian monuments can be used to reconstruct missing phases from the artistic development of the dynasty's heartland.

The architectural history of Buṣrā, located south of Damascus, provides a very different challenge. There, buildings of various periods share a number of features arising from the strong local building tradition, which used basalt slabs as a roofing material. Episodically, however, buildings were created that transcend the limitations of this technique. Meinecke explains these shifts through the actions of patrons who sought to raise the artistic level of local craftsmen through the importation of specialists from Damascus.

Perhaps the most challenging example Meinecke presents is his explanation for curious fluctuations in the architectural history of Hasankeyf, a stronghold overlooking the Tigris in southeastern Turkey. The architecture of this rather isolated center contains traces of several distinct traditions. It has in succession a local Anatolian phase in which structures were ornamented with figural reliefs; one where its buildings display simultaneously close connections with both the stoneworking practices of Aleppo and with the decorative traditions of Iran, particularly in stucco carving and the creation of muqarnas vaults; and finally a phase where both structural and decorative features replicate those of Iran. Meinecke links these fluctuations with both local and interregional developments.

His final essay focuses on broader questions, namely the ways in which the architectural traditions of the Mamluk and Ottoman dynasties are interconnected. Specifically, he examines the role of artisans from Syria and Egypt in shaping the evolving Ottoman architectural idiom. He explores the role of Syrian plans in those of Ottoman mosques and the impact of Syrian stone masons on Anatolian practice. As an example of how such forms could be transmitted he invokes the career of a specific Damascene craftsman, ʿAlī b. Mushaimish ad-Dimashqī, who worked on a mosque at Selçuk in ancient Ephesus, and the two generations of his descendants known to have been in Ottoman employ. Finally Meinecke examines how the Ottoman defeat of the Mamluks affected architectural practice in both Anatolia and Egypt.

These wide-ranging essays present eloquent proof of the need to approach the history of Islamic architecture with a broad historical and art-historical perspective. The methods Meinecke uses will no doubt inspire others to emulate his approach in studying other regions or areas. Few, however, will be able to attain his consummate mastery of the subject, which enlivens these essays.

—PRISCILLA P. SOUCEK
Hagop Kevorkian Professor of Islamic Art
Institute of Fine Arts
New York University

Abbreviations

The following abbreviations are used in the notes:

Altun (1978)	Ara Altun, *Anadolu'da Artuklu devri türk mimarisi'nin gelişmesi* (Istanbul, 1978)
Ayverdi I	Ekrem Hakkı Ayverdi, *Istanbul mi'mârî çağının menşe'i Osmanlı mi'mârîsinin ilk devri: Ertuğrul, Osman, Orhan Gaazîler, Hüdavendigâr ve Yıldırım Bâyezîd, 630–805 (1230–1402)* (Istanbul, 1966)
Ayverdi II	*idem, Osmanlı mi'mârîsinde Çelebi ve II.sultan Murad devri, 806–855 (1403–1451)* (Istanbul, 1972)
Ayverdi III–IV	*idem, Osmanlı mi'mârîsinde Fâtih devri, 855–886 (1451–1481),* 2 vols. (Istanbul, 1973/1974) [vol. V of the series by I. Aydın Yücel, 1983]
EMA I.1–2	K.A.C. Creswell, *Early Muslim Architecture* 2nd ed. I, 1–2 (Oxford, 1969)
EMA II	K.A.C. Creswell, *Early Muslim Architecture* II (Oxford, 1940)

Gabriel (1940)	Albert Gabriel, *Voyages archéologiques dans la Turquie orientale* (Paris, 1940)
MAE I–II	K.A.C. Creswell, *The Muslim Architecture of Egypt* I–II (Oxford, 1952 and 1959)
Meinecke (1976)	Michael Meinecke, *Fayencedekorationen seldschukischer Sakralbauten in Kleinasien* I–II (Tübingen, 1976)
Meinecke (1992)	Michael Meinecke, *Die mamlukische Architektur in Ägypten und Syrien (648/1250 bis 923/1517)* I–II (Glückstadt, 1992)
RCEA	Étienne Combe - Jean Sauvaget - Gaston Wiet, eds., *Répertoire chronologique d'Épigraphie arabe* I–XVII (Cairo, 1931–1984)
SPA	Arthur Upham Pope, ed., *A Survey of Persian Art* I–V (London/New York, 1938 and 1939)
Yücel	I. Aydin Yücel, *Osmanlı mimârîsinde II. Bâyezid, Yavuz Selim devri (886–926/1481–1520)* (Istanbul, 1983) [= vol. V in sequence of Ayverdi I–IV]

Introduction

The architecture of the Islamic world, systematically researched for about one century, is usually investigated along several well-established lines. In reference works the buildings are often described in a chronological sequence, and grouped according to political dynasties, resulting in a positivistic presentation of formal evolution. Another approach is based on subdivisions according to the various functions of buildings, which permits the definition of typological changes but obscures stylistic developments. In most cases, research on Islamic architecture tends to center on national characteristics, almost inevitably emerging from the classification according to the ethnic origins of Arabic, Persian, or Turkish patrons. The same is the case with studies defined by modern boundaries, devoted to the art and architecture of Turkey, Persia, or Egypt, to name only some of the most frequent options. Each of these methods was surely effective in enlarging our knowledge of Islamic architecture. Nevertheless, this book follows a different approach; instead of defining local variations, I will here emphasize the similarities resulting from interrelations among neighboring or far-away areas, with the aim of indicating basic patterns of stylistic changes.[1]

In this respect some general observations should at least sketchily be introduced, to explain the methodological approach. First, as defined by previous research, local characteristics are to be considered an undeniable, basic fact. The availability or the scarcity of building materials, for instance, determines the preference for different media such as mud brick, burned brick, stone, or wood, which not only require special skills in fabrication, but also determine architectural features. The resulting variations usually characterize larger cultural areas, as most Muslim cities could not maintain local schools of architecture long enough to formulate individual traditions. In contrast, these relatively few urban centers of a long-lasting political and cultural development in the Islamic world often exerted a decisive impact on architectural developments.[2]

The evident changes in the regional evolution of architecture often reflect the challenge posed by previous masterpieces. Among these influential world monuments at least two pre-Islamic buildings are of paramount importance: the Sasanian Tāq-i Kisra at Ctesiphon, and the Byzantine church of Hagia Sophia at Istanbul. Three Islamic monuments also exerted far-reaching influence: the Umaiyad Dome of the Rock in Jerusalem, the Great Mosque of Damascus, and finally the Saljūq Friday Mosque of Iṣfahān.[3] In addition, a score of architectural inventions in various locations also constituted models for a series of repetitive designs. The intellectual impetus for pursuing previous standards most often originates from the imperial patrons' intention to match, or even surpass, these admired older monuments. But the implementation, of course, depended on the skills of the artists and craftsmen in following the demands of the patrons.

It is in fact the role of the artists which constitutes the general topic of this book. Though all gifted artists are determined by their personal striving for perfection, they also depend on the availability of demanding tasks to improve their talents. Consequently in search of challenging assignments, artists and architects throughout all periods constituted, as K. A. C. Creswell once rightly remarked, "a migratory race."[4] From this viewpoint Islamic architecture can be interpreted on the basis of the transfer of experience, accomplished by migrating artists either working on their own or together with fellow specialists within a larger atelier, or joining regional schools of architecture for limited periods.[5]

The following chapters are devoted to individual case studies indicating four different patterns that artists employed, all resulting in decisive stylistic changes. At the early Islamic city of ar-Raqqa on the Euphrates (chapter 1) imperial intent was to create a new metropolis, implemented by forced labor. The medieval development of the Syrian capital Damascus, resulting in an influx of specialized artists, changed the local architectural tradition also in the provinces, as illustrated by the Muslim monuments of the Classical city of Buṣrā (chapter 2). At Hasankeyf on the Tigris (chapter 3), artists from changing backgrounds who passed through produced a series of strikingly diverse monuments dependent on distant traditions. And finally the artistic movement between political rivals, the Mamluk and the Ottoman empires (chapter 4), testify to shifting impacts according to the changing course of political development.

Notes

1. This viewpoint is also expressed in my monographs on medieval faïence decorations of Anatolia, and the Mamluk architecture of Egypt and Syria; Meinecke (1976 and 1992).
2. On regional architectural schools in the Aiyūbid period, see Terry Allen, *Five Essays on Islamic Art* (Sebastopol, 1988), pp. 91–110: "The concept of regional style"; for the following period Michael Meinecke, "Mamluk architecture. Regional architectural traditions: Evolution and interrelations," *Damaszener Mitteilungen* 2, 1985, pp. 85–105.
3. These influential world monuments have attracted much scholarly attention. As an example of far-reaching analysis one of the previous volumes of this series can be singled out: Oleg Grabar, *The Great Mosque of Isfahan* (New York and London, 1990).
4. Creswell, *MAE* I (1952), p. 163.
5. As indicated in a series of detailed studies, quoted in the notes of the following chapters; for a general survey on Muslim artists, see Michael Meinecke, "Zur sogenannten Anonymität der Künstler im islamischen Mittelalter," in Adalbert J. Gail, ed., *Künstler und Werkstatt in den orientalischen Gesellschaften* (Graz, 1982), pp. 31–45.

CHAPTER 1

Forced Labor in Early Islamic Architecture: The Case of ar-Raqqa/ar-Rāfiqa on the Euphrates

The first case study in this book is devoted to the early Islamic city of ar-Raqqa (fig. 1) on the Middle Euphrates, the traditional capital of the Diyār Muḍar of the Jazīra, the so-called Island between the Euphrates and the Tigris, now the center of a governorate of northern Syria. Though of outstanding political importance in the early centuries of Islam, ar-Raqqa was outlasted and overshadowed by the two urban antipodes of the region, Aleppo, the north Syrian capital over 170 km farther west, and Mosul, the north Mesopotamian capital c. 380 km farther northeast, both attracting much scholarly attention. First documented in 1907 by the German researchers Ernst Herzfeld and Friedrich Sarre,[1] systematic archaeological investigation by the Syrian Antiquities Organization started in 1944.[2] Despite the impressive results of a long series of excavations, knowledge about ar-Raqqa remained amazingly limited within the scholarly world.[3] Recently the German Archaeological Institute Damascus has actively been sharing in the efforts to investigate the glorious past of this early Islamic metropolis.

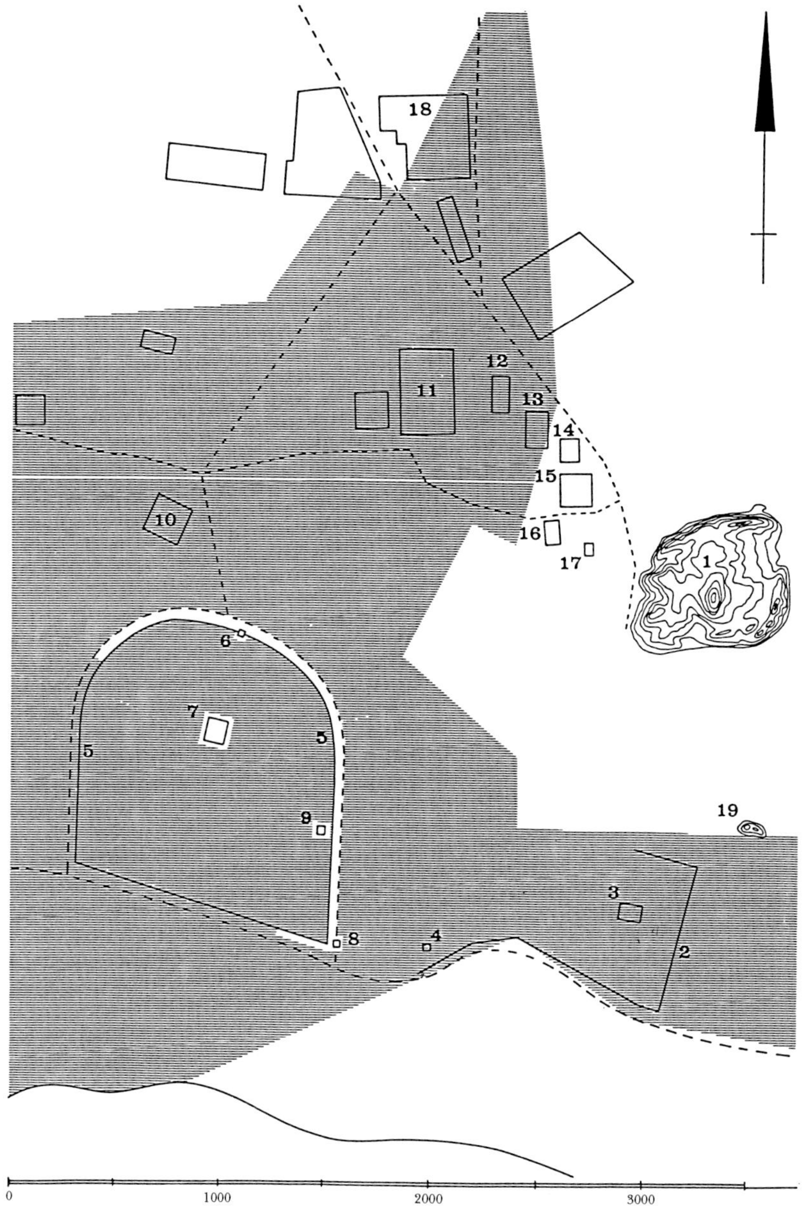

1 Tell Biᶜa
2 City walls of Nikephorion/ar-Raqqa
3 Umaiyad Great Mosque
4 Mausoleum of Uwais al-Qarani
5 City walls of ar-Rāfiqa
6 North Gate
7 ᶜAbbāsid Great Mosque
8 Baghdād Gate
9 Qaṣr al-Banāt
10 Palace A
11 Qaṣr as-Salām of Hārūn ar-Rashīd
12 Palace B
13 Palace C
14 Palace D
15-17 Excavation Site East
18 Excavation Site Northeast
19 Tell Aswad

Fig. 1. ar-Raqqa: location map, in scale 1:30,000, with extent of modern city indicated in grey (Norbert Hagen 1989).

1. NIKEPHORION/AR-RAQQA: ISLAMIZATION OF A CLASSICAL CITY

At the outset, this city was one of the many Classical urban centers of the eastern Mediterranean lands, transformed according to the needs of a steadily growing Muslim community.[4] Founded by Seleukos Nikator (301–281 B.C.) at a topographical point of far-reaching strategical importance, marked by the junction of the rivers Balīkh and the Euphrates, the Classical city covered an area of at least 1200 × 600 m. By origin and extension ar-Raqqa can be regarded as just another example of large-scale Hellenistic city foundations, paralleled for instance by Antiochia on the Orontes, or Dura Europos farther down the Euphrates. Demolished in 542 A.D. by the Sasanian emperor Khusrau I (531–579), the city was soon reconquered, restored, and refortified by the Byzantine emperor Justinian (527–565). Recently some parts of the Byzantine city walls (fig. 1, no. 2) on the original river bank were investigated archaeologically, revealing solid round towers of burned bricks set into extremely thick layers of mortar enriched by pebbles, a characteristic technical feature of military architecture in the time of Justinian.[5] Thus on the eve of the Muslim era this city matched other urban centers in importance, and it should be remembered that the ancient city of Damascus, the future capital of the early Islamic empire of the Umaiyads, at that time evidently was only slightly larger, having reached an extension of approximately 1400 × 900 m.[6]

Conquered in 18/639 by the Muslim forces on the order of the second "rightly guided" caliph ʿUmar Ibn al-Khaṭṭāb (13/634–23/644), the city received the name ar-Raqqa, "the Morass," reflecting its marshy surroundings. For some time the population remained predominantly Christian. The treaty concluded with the victorious general ʿIyād Ibn Ghanm expressly states that the churches should not be destroyed or occupied, but also stipulates that new Christian buildings would not be tolerated.[7] Only a few years later the first Friday mosque (no. 3) was founded by Saʿīd ibn ʿĀmir Ibn Ḥidhyam, who succeeded the conqueror as governor of Mesopotamia in 20/641. The ruins of this building (pl. 1a), one of the earliest mosque foundations on the territory of the modern state of Syria, were surveyed by Ernst Herzfeld in 1907.[8] According to his sketch drawing, the mosque, covering an irregular rectangle of about 75 × 108 m, depended heavily on architectural elements of the Classical periods. Unfortunately this building of far-reaching importance for the formation of mosque architecture has long been sacrificed to modern building projects without further investigation. Consequently no archaeological indications are available to clarify the process of subsequent enlargements reflecting the increase in the numbers of Muslim citizens, in evidence in several other contemporary mosque constructions[9] and surely also the case at the Raqqa mosque.

During the initial Islamic period, the region provided the stage for the battle of Ṣiffīn, a site about 45 km to the west, where the last of the orthodox caliphs, ʿAlī Ibn Abi Ṭālib (35/656–40/661), in 37/657 unsuccessfully confronted the rebellious governor of Syria, Muʿāwiya Ibn Abī Sufyān, who only four years later would found the Umaiyad dynasty of Damascus. Several of ʿAlī's followers were buried in the cemetery on the western side of ar-Raqqa, which thereafter remained a venerated place of pilgrimage.[10] The last of these *mashhads* (no. 4), identified with one of the companions of ʿAlī, Uwais al-Qaranī, survived until recently,[11] when the mausoleum, along with a surrounding cemetery, was leveled to the ground for the construction of a modern center of Shīʿite pilgrimage. In the local tradition this person is credited with the erection of the Maʿdhānat al-Munaiṭir, the minaret of the city's early Islamic mosque.[12] Fortunately documented by earlier travelers, this square brick tower almost 26 m in height (pl. 1b)[13] has, in the meantime, also vanished without a trace. Ernst Herzfeld, nevertheless, convincingly attributes its creation to the fourth/tenth century for stylistic reasons.[14] This is corroborated by the minaret's curious position in the courtyard of the mosque complex, which indicates a drastic reduction in usable space after it was erected.

Altogether even these few references attest to the importance of ar-Raqqa at the outset of the Muslim era. It can be assumed that the city continued to prosper as a regional center throughout the Umaiyad period (41/661–132/750), when attention focused on the city of Damascus, which had succeeded the central Mesopotamian city of al-Kūfa as seat of the caliphate.

2. AR-RĀFIQA: THE EARLY ISLAMIC METROPOLIS

With the shift of emphasis back to Mesopotamia in the ʿAbbāsid period, the city of ar-Raqqa gained new far-reaching importance.

Besides its political role, ar-Raqqa also provides extremely valuable evidence for art history. This aspect, so far mostly underestimated, results from the curious absence of monuments from the first quarter century of ʿAbbāsid rule. Yet, in contrast to this, contemporary sources give evidence that the early ʿAbbāsids were fervent builders, probably surpassing even their Umaiyad predecessors.[15] From various chronicles a clear pattern of construction activities emerges.

The first years of the new dynasty were dominated by a constant search for new residences. After the proclamation of the first ʿAbbāsid caliph Abu l-ʿAbbās as-Saffāḥ (meaning "the Shedder of Blood") at Damascus in 132/750, the seat of power was immediately retransferred to the area of al-Kūfa. There, two successive sites were built up, each named Hāshimīya until 136/754, on the death of as-Saffaḥ, his successor al-Manṣūr (136/754–158/775) founded a third Hāshimīya between the neighboring cities of al-Kūfa and al-Ḥīra. Nothing survived from these early residences, presumably constructed in mud bricks, the least durable of all building materials.

Eventually, in 145/762, al-Manṣūr chose a definite site for his permanent residence on the Tigris, about 40 km north of the Sasanian capital of Ctesiphon. It was officially named Madīnat as-Salām, the City of Peace, which later became known as Baghdād.[16] Although here too no traces of the initial foundation survive, Ernst Herzfeld was able to ingeniously reconstruct the original design from detailed literary descriptions.[17] Subsequently his hypothetical scheme was amended first by K. A. C. Creswell[18] and more recently by Jacob Lassner.[19] Forming a perfect circle of 2600 m with four axial gates, its layout obviously follows that of the Sasanian capital of Khusrau I Ctesiphon.[20] But this applies only to the overall concept, as several important differences are in evidence: for topographical reasons the earlier city, for instance, had an elliptical rather than circular shape; and with a diameter of between 2800 and 3300 m it was also considerably larger than the new ʿAbbāsid capital.

For this construction project, according to the historian-geographer al-Yaʿqūbī (d. 284/897), al-Manṣūr ordered every city to send architects and building specialists. Construction started only when a sizeable work force numbering in the thousands was assembled, including experts from Syria and Mosul, from the well-established Mesopotamian cities al-Kūfa, al-Wāsiṭ, and al-Baṣra, and even from western Persia. Several architects implemented the design conceived

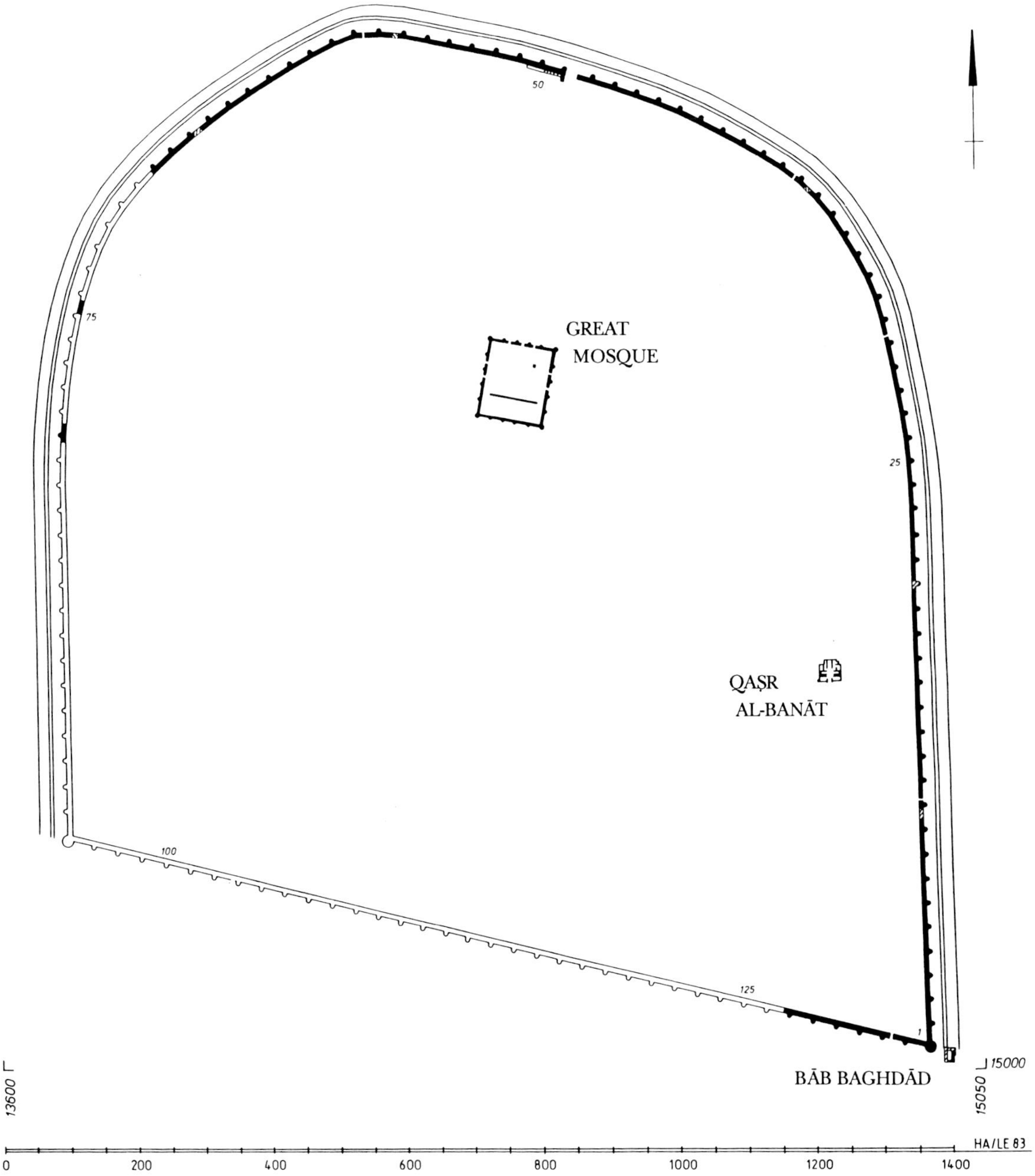

Fig. 2. ar-Raqqa/ar-Rāfiqa: fortification, in scale 1:10,000 (surveyed by Norbert Hagen with Joachim Lesener 1983).

by the caliph personally, of which a certain Rabaḥ was entrusted with the task of constructing the fortified walls, and another, named Ḥajjāj b. Arṭāt, was charged with the marking of the plan layout of the city, as well as with the construction of the Friday mosque, erected at the center of the circle together with the imperial palace. The dominant material is mentioned to have been mud brick; only structural parts were built of burned bricks.

The transfer of the state treasures to the newly founded city already in 146/763–64 indicates the rapid pace of construction; after completion of the imperial city, suburbs with individual markets, palaces, and mosques were built as well, until 154/771. With the termination of this monumental construction project, the impetus shifted to the fortification of the ʿAbbāsid empire. Within this program first in 155/771–72 the Umaiyad cities of Mesopotamia, al-Kūfa, and al-Baṣra, which until that period were obviously not sufficiently fortified, received defensive walls. But the main objective was to create a kind of *limes* on the northwestern border facing Byzantium, which was continuously strengthened and improved over the decades. Among these, the most important construction project and the only one which survives, at least partially, is the foundation of an entire new city named ar-Rāfiqa ("the companion") only several hundred meters west of the Classical Umaiyad city, ar-Raqqa (pl. 1c). The decision to build this sister city already was formulated by al-Manṣūr in 154/770–71, but only the following year was the heir apparent, his son al-Mahdī, charged with its implementation. These building activities continued at least until 158/774–75, when al-Mahdī was sent again to ar-Raqqa to inspect the construction site.[21]

In contrast to Baghdād, the source material for ar-Rāfiqa is tantalizingly scarce. But according to the historian aṭ-Ṭabarī (d. 310/923), the new city was built "with the same gates, *intervallum (fuṣūl)*, squares, and streets as Baghdād." In addition, the chronicle of the so-called Pseudo-Dionysius rather vaguely indicates that workmen were brought from all over Mesopotamia for this construction project.[22] In fact, nothing similar had been achieved throughout the preceding centuries in this area. Its sheer size alone is quite staggering: laid out in the form of an irregular horseshoe, the fortified enclosure (fig. 1, no. 5), methodically surveyed a few years ago, measures 4580 m, of which about 2660 m still survive (fig. 2).[23] Built of mud brick on a stone foundation, the massive walls of 6.20 m on the internal as well as on the external faces were further strengthened by layers of kiln-burned bricks. Altogether 132 towers with a stilted semicircle outline protected the exterior. Nothing remains from the advance defense system, recorded by previous researchers, as the outer wall of 4.5 m forming an *intervallum* of 20.8 m, together with the moat of 15.9 m (pl. 2a), was bulldozed away over a decade ago.

Similarities of ar-Rāfiqa to the city of Baghdād are limited to the general concept. Both ʿAbbāsid cities were fortified by triple lines of defense, and both depended mostly on mud brick as the major building material. But the fortification system at ar-Rāfiqa is markedly stronger. Though the round city of al-Manṣūr had more than double the area of ar-Rāfiqa, there were fewer towers of lesser dimensions. Also most notably the walls of ar-Rāfiqa are definitely more solid in construction, exceeding the earlier model by one meter, exactly the volume of the stabilizing burned-brick facings, not attested for Baghdād. Evidently the location of ar-Rāfiqa near the Byzantine border instigated these improvements, which communicate the impression of a heavily fortified defensive complex.

The layout of the new city, at first glance, only seems to echo faintly the attested model. But this impression results from two conflicting design concepts. The northern part with the rounded outline is oriented according to the *qibla,* as marked by the centrally located Great Mosque (fig. 1, no. 7). Therefore the north half of the city can be interpreted as a half circle with a radius of about 650 m, in general quite similar to Baghdād. Attached to this on the south is a parallelogram resulting from a prolongation of the walls toward the river bank in an almost due north-south direction. The transversal south wall again takes up the *qibla* alignment.

The north gate (fig. 1, no. 6), excavated and partially rebuilt in the ongoing research and restoration program, emphasizes the *qibla* orientation. As is visible on older aerial photographs,[24] a street originally led directly from the gateway to the city center where it linked to the main axis of the Great Mosque. This major gate of ar-Rāfiqa (pl. 2b), probably named the Bāb Ḥarrān (the Ḥarrān Gate), represents the earliest preserved ʿAbbāsid example of its kind: as reconstructed for Baghdād, in this case it is also a tower gate with a rectangular room and a deep entrance niche.[25] On the west the remains of a ramp on vaulted foundations were also detected, leading to the top of the wall of about 18 m in height. The paved gateway is built of stone masonry up to a height of about 2 m; the door opening measures 4 m, almost the maximum size feasible. Two door posts of solid iron were in situ, the last remains of a massive iron door of two wings. Probably this is to be connected with one of the many legendary metal doors mentioned in historic texts in early Islamic cities and palaces. For ar-Raqqa an iron door of Byzantine origin is frequently mentioned, initially transported from the Anatolian city Amorion/ʿAmmūrīya in 223/838 to Sāmarrāʾ by the ʿAbbāsid caliph al-Muʿtaṣim (218/833–227/842), where it was set up at the Bāb al-ʿĀmma, the main entrance to his newly constructed residence. Allegedly sometime in the later third/ninth century this door found its way to ar-Raqqa, only to be again requisitioned about half a century later by the Hamdānid ruler Saif ad-Daula ʿAlī (333/945–356/967) for re-use at the reconstructed Bāb Qinnasrīn at Aleppo. Destroyed during the Mongol conquest of 658/1260, the remaining fragments are said to have then been taken by the Mamluk sultan aẓ-Ẓāhir Baibars (658/1260–676/1277) to the citadels of Damascus and Cairo.[26] Though evidently this information is based on two diverse lines of tradition, it is an indication of the important historic position of the ʿAbbāsid city.

Indeed, with the foundation of ar-Rāfiqa by the caliph al-Manṣūr, the city on the Euphrates became the largest metropolis of Syria and northern Mesopotamia alike. Together with the older sister city of Nikephorion/ar-Raqqa, which continued to flourish, the built-up area and the population should almost have rivaled the seat of ʿAbbāsid power, Baghdād. Certainly the twin cities at that time outclassed the traditional Syrian capital, Damascus. This dominant position is mirrored by the Great Mosque of ar-Rāfiqa (no. 7), founded together with the city and constructed by the same workforce that built the monumental defense system.[27]

With dimensions of 108 × 93 m, the ʿAbbāsid mosque (fig. 3) in space matches that of Baghdād, erected only about a decade earlier. But as in the case of the city walls, this building is evidently also more sophisticated. In contrast to the Baghdād mosque, described as having mud-brick walls and wooden columns, the mosque of ar-Rāfiqa depends decisively on burned bricks. The enclosure walls, like those at Baghdād, feature a series of externally round towers and are stabilized with courses of baked bricks as are ar-Rāfiqa's city walls. As an important innovation, baked bricks were also used exclu-

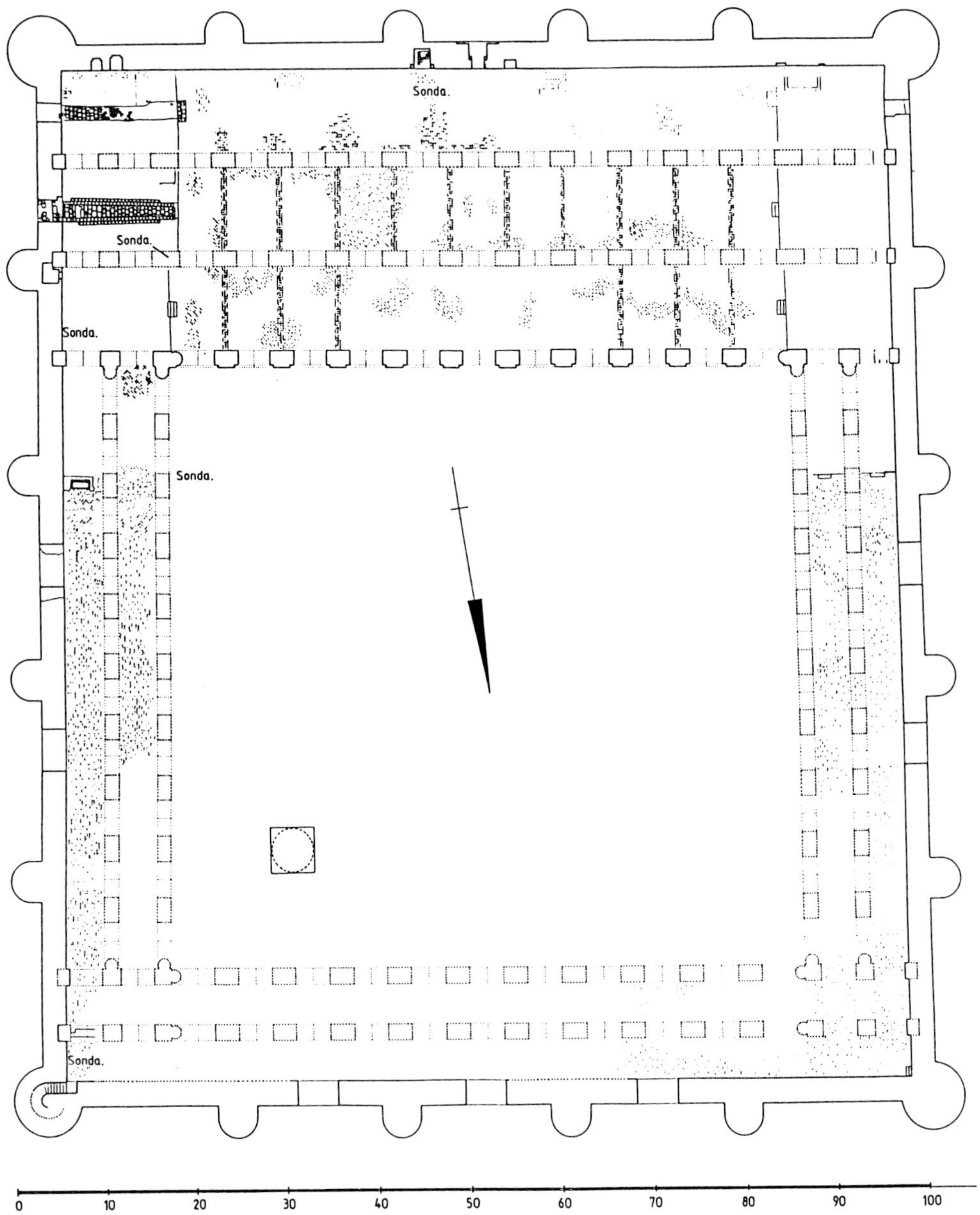

Fig. 3. ar-Raqqa/ar-Rāfiqa, ʿAbbāsid Great Mosque: reconstructed ground plan after recent excavation and clearing, in scale 1:800 (surveyed by Norbert Hagen 1987).

sively for the mosque's interior. According to archaeological investigations carried out during the last decade, rectangular piers were used throughout already in the initial period, permitting a distinctive design, especially for the prayer hall.[28] Instead of uniform sequences of supports for a flat wooden ceiling, as at Baghdād, the rhythm changes at the Rāfiqa mosque between the double arcades of the courtyard and the sanctuary. There the space is divided by only two rows of arcades, set about 9 m apart. This larger span necessitated a gable roof instead of the flat roof of the Baghdād prototype. This in turn indicates an influence from the Umaiyad Great Mosque of Damascus[29] or other earlier mosques of Umaiyad origin in the nearby regions of Syria.[30]

Nevertheless, as a reconstruction was carried out in 561/1165–66 by the Zengid ruler Nūr ad-Dīn Maḥmūd, attested by the still standing arcades of the prayer hall façade and the circular minaret in the courtyard (pl. 3a), this might have caused changes in the original plan.[31] Therefore, intentionally we conducted a series of soundings in search for a primitive plan layout following the Baghdād arrangement. But no traces of any changes were in evidence, and consequently the Rāfiqa mosque is, in fact, to be considered the starting point of a new chapter of mosque architecture, and the first of a long series of similar constructions.

In contrast to the previous stage, when mosques either depended on re-used building material from the Classical periods, as in the case of the venerated Umaiyad mosque of Damascus and at the earlier Friday mosque of the sister city Nikephorion/ar-Raqqa, or wooden supports were substituted for antique columns, the Rāfiqa mosque is the first to be based on a coherent, integrated plan. Tellingly the first mosque to follow its lead was that of Baghdād rebuilt in 192/808 with kiln-baked bricks on order of the caliph Hārūn ar-Rashīd (170/786–193/809), who must have had an especially intimate knowledge of the Rāfiqa mosque, as will be outlined later on.[32] This feature was later taken up by the mosques of Sāmarrā'[33] and passed from there to the mosque of Aḥmad Ibn Ṭūlūn at Cairo,[34] completed in 265/879, and later on it decisively influenced the local Egyptian development.

Nothing is known about the interior layout of the ʿAbbāsid city of ar-Rāfiqa, which in the last decades has been completely built over by modern housing construction. Two monuments, often attributed to early Islamic times, after detailed investigation have proved to originate from the medieval revival of the city. This is the case with the Baghdād Gate (fig. 1, no. 8), marking the northeastern corner of the exterior wall of ar-Rāfiqa,[35] and with the Qaṣr al-Banāt (no. 9), the so-called "Girls' Palace," erroneously attributed to the ʿAbbāsid caliph Hārūn ar-Rashīd.[36]

Nevertheless, the ʿAbbāsid city of ar-Rāfiqa, even according to the regrettably few remains, reflects a remarkable architectural achievement. As similar large-scale construction work previously was nowhere implemented in Upper Mesopotamia or Northern Syria, it must be assumed that architects and construction specialists alike were sent directly from the ʿAbbāsid capital Baghdād, almost 580 km farther southeast. The imperial patron al-Manṣūr must be credited as the motivating force for this huge building program; he commissioned its implementation by his heir, the future caliph al-Mahdī (158/775–169/785). The artists designing and actually building the new city were not merely repeating previous schemes, but achieved technical improvements and even introduced new inventions inspired by regional traditions and architectural masterpieces.

3. HĀRŪN AR-RASHĪD AT AR-RAQQA: THE NEW CENTER OF THE ISLAMIC WORLD

The tremendous improvement of ar-Raqqa by the caliph al-Manṣūr set the stage for its even greater prominence in the days of his grandson Hārūn ar-Rashīd. But for over two decades the city on the Euphrates, where a garrison of soldiers from Khurāsān was stationed to protect and pacify the area, remained virtually unmentioned in contemporary chronicles. The caliph al-Mahdī obviously followed the advice of his father, who urged him to take up residence in the city of Baghdād, and who is recorded by aṭ-Ṭabarī to have told his son "not to exchange it for another [city], for it is your house and your glory."[37] al-Mahdī's son al-Hādī (169/785–170/786) also remained at Baghdād, but not his second succeeding son, Hārūn ar-Rashīd, the most famous of all ʿAbbāsid caliphs. Hārūn ar-Rashīd, who became caliph in 170/786 at the age of twenty-two, also resided at Baghdād for the first decade of his rule, before deciding in 180/796 to transfer his residence to ar-Raqqa, the metropolis on the Middle Euphrates, which had been tremendously enlarged by his grandfather, al-Manṣūr. But even before that date the caliph was preparing to shift to another site, as recorded by the historian aṭ-Ṭabarī, who quotes the following remark by one of the court officials of the caliph al-Muʿtaṣim (218/833–227/842), the youngest of the three reigning sons of Hārūn ar-Rashīd: "al-Muʿtaṣim asked me where ar-Rashīd had diverted himself when he was disgusted with staying in Baghdād and I said to him, 'In al-Qāṭūl'. He had built there a city whose traces and walls still remained, for he feared from the army *(al-jund)* what al-Muʿtaṣim feared. But when the people in Damascus in Syria rose up and rebelled, ar-Rashīd went to ar-Raqqa and stayed there and the city of al-Qāṭūl remained and was not completed."[38]

Only recently has the site of al-Qāṭūl been convincingly identified by Alastair Northedge with a large structure traditionally named Ḥiṣn al-Qādisīya on the southern extension of the monumental ruin area of Sāmarrāʾ, about 90 km northwest of Baghdād, higher up on the Tigris.[39] The ruin evidently has to be interpreted as another variation of the centralized town design, implemented a generation earlier at the round city of Baghdād by the caliph al-Manṣūr. In contrast to the circular outline of Baghdād, al-Qāṭūl is characterized by a huge fortified octagonal enclosure of about 1500 m from side to side, entirely built of mud brick. Access is provided by altogether eight gateways, positioned on the axis of each side of the octagon. The layout of these gates, set into half-round towers, closely resembles the excavated north gate of ar-Rāfiqa, where the ramps leading to the top of the wall also find an exact parallel. Only the fortification walls have obviously been completely built. The interior plan of the city, including two adjacent plots in the center of the ruin, probably reserved for the mosque and the palace, seems never to have been finished.

Once at ar-Raqqa, Hārūn ar-Rashīd was to engage fully in the pleasures of patronizing large-scale construction projects. During the twelve years of his residence at ar-Raqqa, which remained the seat of the caliphate until 192/808, a huge imperial city was built to the north of the older twin cities, eventually extending over nearly fifteen square kilometers.[40] This again could not have been implemented by the local labor force alone, but only with the participation of imported workers. In view of the unfinished state of al-Qāṭūl, it can be assumed that once Hārūn ar-Rashīd had firmly decided to move to the Middle Euphrates, he ordered the interruption of building activities in central Mesopotamia and sent the whole construction workshop to ar-Raqqa instead, to start to improve his new residence prior to his arrival. From then on construction evidently continued for the whole period. Not only was a continuous series of palaces built, but the area also had to be irrigated, for which a sophisticated system of canals and subterranean water conduits was laid out, ensuring a permanent water supply.[41]

This remarkable palace city, an agglomerate of seemingly loosely interrelated large buildings, often positioned in huge garden enclosures, with large avenues and race courses as well as various infrastructural installations, can now only fully be appreciated with the aid of older aerial photographs (pls. 1c, 4a, 6a).[42] Of the entire palace belt, only tantalizingly few parts remain visible due to the rapid development of the modern town of ar-Raqqa, which in the course of only three decades grew from a small village into an urban metropolis with over 100,000 inhabitants. Consequently, most of the archaeological area was sacrificed to modern housing construction. Motivated by this development, the German Archaeological Institute in Damascus has for a decade been joining the long-lasting and continuous efforts of the Syrian Antiquities Authorities to research and preserve the historic heritage of this important Islamic site. Prior to destruction, five of the palaces outside the ʿAbbāsid city of ar-Rāfiqa had at least partially been excavated by the Antiquities Authorities; and recently five additional complexes were archaeologically investigated during ten seasons of rescue excavations. From the results of these excavations the pattern of the site, as well as a mosaic pointing to the architectural style and decoration of the period, has sketchily been emerging.

Two structures stand out among the many ruins: a rectangular building (fig. 1, no. 10) of c.160 × 130 m near the north gate of ar-Rāfiqa,[43] and a second of decidedly more monumental dimensions over one kilometer farther northeast (no. 11), both distinguished by double enclosures. Though the first, in the immediate vicinity of the city, might in fact be the oldest building of the caliphal residence, the latter obviously has to be regarded as the central palace. Probably this large complex of c. 340 × 270 m (pl. 4a) can be identified with the Qaṣr as-Salām, the Palace of Peace, testified by chronicles to have been built by Hārūn ar-Rashīd at ar-Raqqa. The original plan layout now unfortunately is obscured by later constructions, but an especially sumptuous decoration, including floor frescoes and high-relief stucco ornaments, has been attested through excavated fragments, pointing to the central importance of the building within the caliph's residence.[44]

On the east follow three palaces (fig. 1, nos. 12–14) in a graduated sequence, each decidedly smaller than the central palace, though with dimensions of about 170 × 75 m, 140 × 110 m, and 100 × 100 m, each of considerable size, combining courtyards for housing, the customary triple audience halls, and small mosques; they were probably the residences of family members or the closest court associates of Hārūn ar-Rashīd (compare pl. 4a with fig. 4).[45] At the closest of these palaces to the central complex, a fresco inscription has been found, naming the caliph al-Muʿtaṣim billāh (278/833–227/842), the last of the succeeding sons of Hārūn ar-Rashīd; it could belong to a later period of reuse or redecoration.[46]

The group of buildings on the southeastern corner of the palace belt (fig. 1, nos. 15–17; fig. 4), bordering on a public square, conspicuously lacks the external series of buttresses characterizing the imperial residences, and therefore obviously was not used by the inner circle of the caliph's court.[47] The square structure, 150 m on a side, situated immediately south of the princely residence where the inscription of al-Muʿtaṣim was discovered, can be identified as a barracks for the palace guard because of its series of identical chambers. Centrally placed living quarters with three contiguous courtyards were probably reserved for the commander of the palace. Its excavation yielded a group of particularly luxurious glass vessels, including a truly exceptional drinking horn, which attest to the remarkable living standards of lesser court ranks as well.[48]

The buildings farther south, flanking the public square, are functionally dependent on the barracks. The installations for social entertainment, missing at the barracks, are provided on the eastern side of the public square, first by a building of c. 65 × 45 m with a rather complicated layout, curiously shifted out of the general north-south alignment (fig. 5),[49] and then by a relatively small reception structure of c. 70 × 40 m (fig. 1, no. 17; pl. 4b), devoid of living quarters and solely devoted to festive assemblies.[50] In the building measuring about 120 by 95 m located on the western side of the square (fig. 1, no. 16; pl. 5a) private and official quarters are again close together,

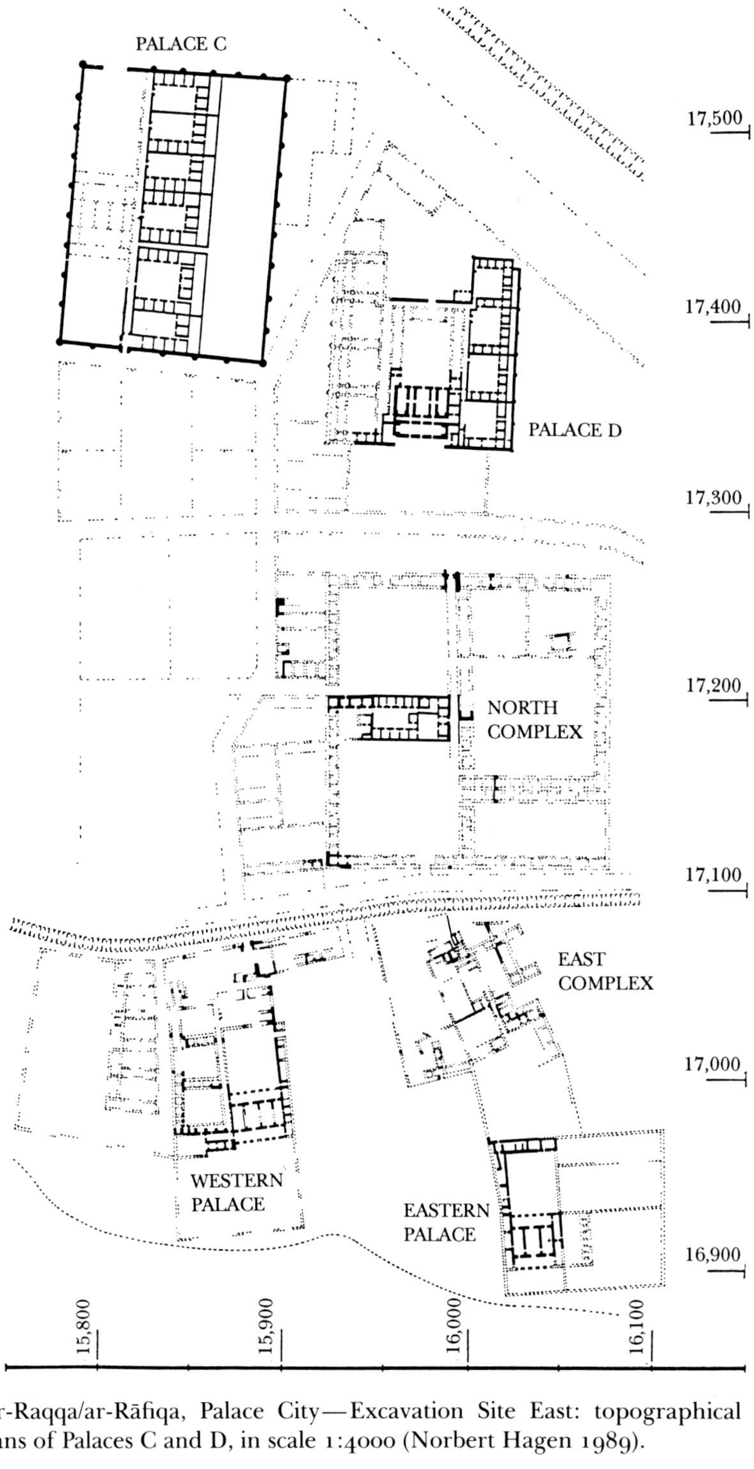

Fig. 4. ar-Raqqa/ar-Rāfiqa, Palace City—Excavation Site East: topographical map with sketch plans of Palaces C and D, in scale 1:4000 (Norbert Hagen 1989).

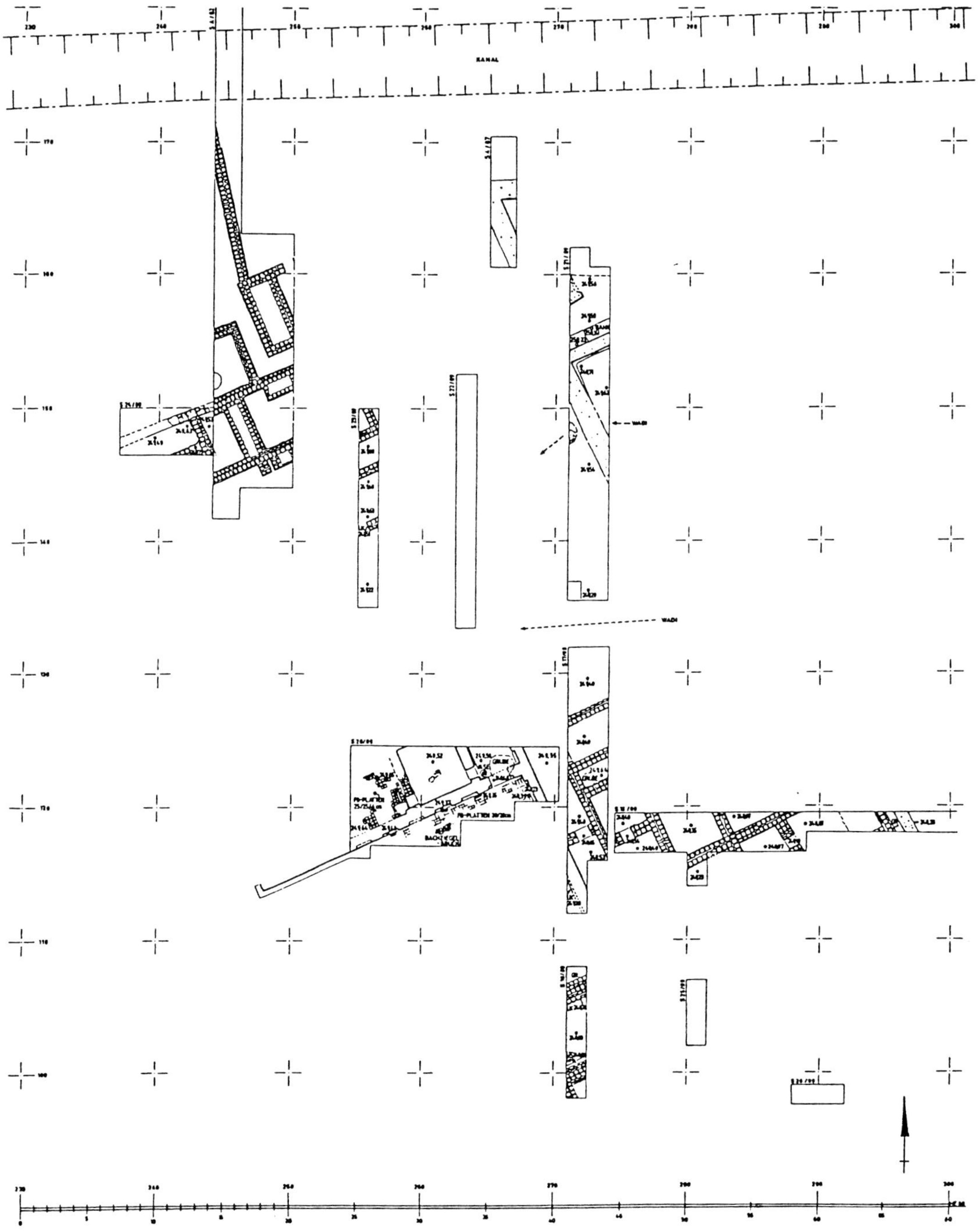

Fig. 5. ar-Raqqa/ar-Rāfiqa, Palace City—Excavation Site East: East Complex, plan of trenches, in scale 1:500 (Jan-Christoph Heusch 1989).

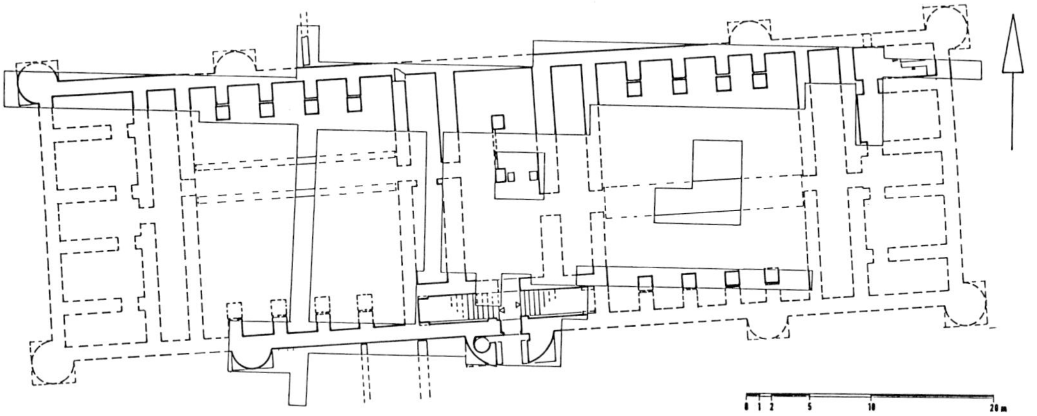

Fig. 6. ar-Raqqa/ar-Rāfiqa, Palace City—Excavation Site Northeast: Northeast Complex, reconstructed plan of main building, in scale 1:600 (Hans Mismahl 1989).

but this building also served a religious purpose. It contains a number of individual praying places as well as a small mosque which has a monumental entrance facing the barracks. At this structure the cycle of stucco friezes, framing the prayer niches and the doors of the semipublic reception rooms, was especially well preserved (pls. 5b–c, 7a).[51] As attested by numerous examples from all investigated architectural complexes, these stucco friezes also feature countless variations of vine scrolls, alluding to pre-Islamic decorative patterns.[52] In contrast to the practice in Mesopotamia and further east where large areas of wall surface had stucco decoration in this building it was limited to door-jambs and *miḥrābs*. This use of decoration to emphasize key architectural features reflects the practice of pre-Islamic, Classical Syria as does that decoration's ornamental repertoire of vine-scrolls. Therefore, in a process similar to the inventive design of the Great Mosque at ar-Rāfiqa, influenced by older Syrian models, the peripatetic stucco specialists obviously also appreciated and exploited ornamental features previously characteristic of Syria. This post-Classical style constituted the starting point for the later development recorded especially at Sāmarrāʾ, after 221/836 the new seat of the ʿAbbāsid caliphate.[53]

In the later years of Hārūn ar-Rashīd's reign, the palace area evidently was extended to the north. One of the last complexes to have been erected, on the northeastern border of the palace belt (fig. 1, no. 18; pl. 6a), was also investigated recently.[54] Though most of the built-up area was sacrificed to modern development, the main building of 22 × 75 m, positioned at the northwestern corner of the complex, again is characterized by a stately design (fig. 6). Surrounded by round towers, only a single portal on the central axis (pl. 6b) provides access to a double courtyard structure, of which over 2 m are still preserved. Remarkably, the adjacent installations surrounding a sequence of larger courtyards revealed almost no trace of intensive use, and therefore it can be assumed that the complex was left unfinished when Hārūn ar-Rashīd in 192/808 decided to move back to Baghdād, the original center of the ᶜAbbāsid caliphate.

The same is the case with another highly important monument of Hārūn ar-Rashīd, about 10 km west of ar-Raqqa, locally named Hiraqla (pl. 7b). Ernst Herzfeld has already attributed this building to Hārūn ar-Rashīd,[55] which was corroborated by recent research based on archaeological investigation.[56] Evidently it was conceived as a victory monument, to memorialize the conquest of the Byzantine city of Heraclea, today's Ereğli in Anatolia, directed personally by Hārūn ar-Rashīd in 190/806. With a fortified circular enclosure of 500 m and four gates on the cardinal axes, this monument uses the design of the round city of Baghdād on a diminutive scale. The square structure of 100 m each side marking the center, is characterized by a curious layout. Only four large vaulted rooms oriented toward the cardinal entrances are accessible; all other parts were built as hollow shafts, systematically filled up with pebbles. Therefore the preserved block of masonry obviously only represents the foundation for an intended higher structure, which was never built. Most remarkably the building technique—rubble masonry originally with a facing of refined stone masonry—decidedly contrasts the mudbrick and occasionally burned-brick structures of Hārūn ar-Rashīd's residence. Evidently the building of this monument was not commissioned to the available construction atelier, but to foreign specialists, probably of Byzantine background, forcibly ordered to create this monument of imperial might. The architectural decoration points to the same connection, determined by typical Classical features, including dentil patterns, egg and dart, and bead molding.[57] Iconographically this monument was meant to express the superiority of the Muslim world over the Byzantine empire. The centralizing arrangement of the complex furthermore symbolizes the imperial intent: in the presence of the caliph, this very place constituted the center of the world, an interpretation valid also for the round city of Baghdād and the octagonal city of al-Qāṭūl.

History interfered before the completion of his victory monument: Hārūn ar-Rashīd, after a period of twelve years at ar-Raqqa, was distracted by revolts in the eastern parts of his empire, which led to the decision to move his residence back to Baghdād; he died soon afterwards in 193/809 on a campaign to Khurāsān in eastern Persia. Together with Hārūn ar-Rashīd, most of the sizable construction force seems to have disappeared from the area. Later on, the expertise gained at ar-Raqqa, for instance, in the following generations, instigated the transformation of Classical patterns into the seemingly abstract beveled style (pl. 3b), especially dominant in the Sāmarrā' monuments.[58]

For a short moment in history, ar-Raqqa on the Euphrates indeed was the center of the world because of the presence of Hārūn ar-Rashīd. Occasionally also later caliphs for a limited period of time took up residence at the city, also renovating parts of the palace area. But gradually the size of the population diminished, until the initial city of Nikephorion/ar-Raqqa was completely deserted. Furthermore, the modest revival of the settlement in the period of increasing prosperity under the Zengid and Aiyūbid dynasties certainly could not match the glorious past. At a time when the rival urban centers of Aleppo in northern Syria and Mosul in northern Mesopotamia gained new political importance, ar-Raqqa seems to have survived mainly on the mono-industry of luxury pottery, widely appreciated in the Islamic world.[59] During the decades before the Mongol invasion, not even half of the ʿAbbāsid city was still inhabited, and eventually the previous power center of the Islamic world altogether ceased to play a noticeable role in later history.

4. FORCED LABOR VERSUS LOCAL SCHOOLS OF ARCHITECTURE

Despite its exceptional historic importance, the city of ar-Raqqa does not seem to have been equipped with a sizable school of architecture during any period of its development. Presumedly there were craftsmen of the building trade who met the local demand. But judging from the absence of any of these works, their products hardly exceeded a functional standard in technique or artistic ambition, and consequently were not maintained and preserved. Furthermore, the local expertise obviously was not self-dependent enough to manage the occasional acceleration of building activities, and therefore, at least for both early ʿAbbāsid construction programs, outside labor forces had to be imported. As speedy completion of construction projects was one of the conditions demanded by the imperial patrons, speed can be indicated as a major formative factor. First, this necessitated large labor forces, which could not be mustered in the region alone but had to be managed centrally by the government administration. Second, this affected also the choice of building material, and as the fabrication of mud bricks required only low costs and low time investment, the ʿAbbāsid monuments of ar-Raqqa predominantly were built with mud bricks. Their protective layer of plaster, furthermore, dictated a preference of stucco carvings for the decoration of the newly erected mud-brick buildings. Once the commissioned structures were completed, the labor force was transferred to perform other tasks in different areas of the Islamic world. This pattern, in evidence since the last decades of the Umaiyad empire, though to a much lesser degree, explains the absence of regional or urban schools of architecture.

On the other hand, this larger organizational proportion did not necessarily exclude an innovative stylistic synthesis. This is also in evidence at ar-Raqqa, where Syrian features were combined with Mesopotamian experiences. The multitude of building projects in the early Islamic empires, and the determining urgency must have provided a constant fluctuation of the labor force. On demand, the construction ateliers were enlarged by locally available workmen and artisans, or even with more specialists from other parts of the Islamic world. The resulting mixture of experience enabled different artistic solutions. But in general, the architecture of the early ʿAbbāsid period has to be regarded as an imperial architecture rooted in the cultural and political capital, Baghdād. In contrast, regional schools of architecture are a later phenomenon, as will be outlined in the following chapter.

Notes

1. Ernst Herzfeld *apud* Friedrich Sarre and E. Herzfeld, *Archäologische Reise im Euphrat- und Tigris-Gebiet* I (Berlin, 1911), pp. 156–161, figs. 69–70; II (1920), pp. 349–364, figs. 318–344; III (1911), pls. 63–70.
2. For short summaries on the history of ar-Raqqa including bibliographies, see Meinecke in: Kay Kohlmeyer and Eva Strommenger, eds., *Land des Baal. Syrien—Forum der Völker und Kulturen* (Mainz, 1982), pp. 261–263, and in Harvey Weiss, ed., *Ebla to Damascus: Art and Archaeology of Ancient Syria* (Washington, D.C., 1985), pp. 493–496; and the updated and extended version in *The Encyclopaedia of Islam,* new edition VIII/137–138 (Leiden, 1994), pp. 410–414; cf. the outline of the Raqqa project: "Raqqa on the Euphrates: recent excavations at the residence of Harun ar-Rashid," in Susanne Kerner, ed., *The Near East in Antiquity* II (Amman, 1991), pp. 17–32.
3. By coincidence the basic reference work of K. A. C. Creswell, summarizing the information on Islamic ar-Raqqa, was published already shortly before the excavations started: *EMA* II (1940), pp. 39–48, figs. 27–34, pls. 1f–g, 2–4; see also the condensed version: *A Short Account of Early Muslim Architecture* (Harmondsworth, U.K., 1958), pp. 183–190, figs. 35–36, pls. 32–33. The latter was lately revised and supplemented by James W. Allen; the new edition now also includes some indications concerning more recent research: *op.cit.* (Aldershot, 1989), pp. 242–248, 270–278, figs. 142–145, 168–172.
4. On the sources concerning the Classical and Muslim city: Alois Musil, *The Middle Euphrates: A Topographical Itinerary* (New York, 1927), pp. 325–331; see also Dieter Sturm, "Zur Bedeutung der syrischen Stadt ar-Raqqa von der arabischen Eroberung bis zur Gegenwart," *Hallesche Beiträge zur Orientwissenschaft* 1, 1979, pp. 35–72.
5. Murhaf al-Khalaf and Kay Kohlmeyer, "Untersuchungen zu ar-Raqqa—Nikephorion/Callinicum," *Damaszener Mitteilungen* 2, 1985, pp. 133–162.
6. On Damascus more recently, see Dorothée Sack, *Damaskus: Entwicklung und Struktur einer orientalisch-islamischen Stadt,* (Mainz, 1989) *Damaszener Forschungen* 1.
7. Ahmad al-Balādhurī (d. 279/892), *Kītāb futūḥ al-buldān,* ed. Michel Johan De Goeje (Leiden, 1866), p. 173; trans. Philip Khūri Hitti (New York, 1916), pp. 271–272.
8. Herzfeld, *op.cit.,* note 1, II (1920), pp. 353–355, figs. 324–329.
9. An especially well researched parallel constitutes the Mosque of ʿAmr Ibn al-ʿĀṣ in al-Fusṭāṭ/Cairo, founded in 21/640–41 and several times enlarged until the final design in 212/827; Creswell, *EMA* II (1940), pp. 171–196, figs. 157–170, pls. 37–43.
10. ʿAlī al-Harawī (d. 611/1215), *Kitāb az-ziyārāt,* ed./trans. Janine Sourdel-Thomine (Damascus, 1953/1957), pp. 63, 141–142.
11. Herzfeld, *op.cit.,* note 1, II (1920), pp. 349–350; also Eduard Sachau, *Reise in Syrien und Mesopotamien* (Leipzig, 1883), pp. 243–244.

12. Nikita Elisséeff, *Nūr ad-Dīn: Un grand prince musulman de Syrie au temps des Croisades (511–569 H./1118–1174)* (Damascus, 1967), p. 153.
13. Gertrude L. Bell, *Amurath to Amurath* (London, 1911), pp. 55–56, fig. 35; with photograph of 1909 (republished here on pl. 1b), when the tower was already heavily leaning and apparently collapsed soon after.
14. Herzfeld, *op.cit.*, note 1, II (1920), pp. 354–355, figs. 327–329.
15. The early ʿAbbāsid construction projects listed by Creswell, *EMA* II (1940), pp. 379–384, should be further supplemented and extended.
16. The sources on this dominant political and cultural center of the Islamic world were first collected by Guy Le Strange, *Baghdad during the Abbasid Caliphate from Contemporary Arabic and Persian Sources* (Oxford, 1900).
17. Herzfeld, *op.cit.*, note 1, II (1920), pp. 106–139, figs. 180–184.
18. *EMA* II (1940), pp. 4–38, figs. 2–5, 24–26, pl. 1/a–e.
19. Jacob Lassner, *The Topography of Baghdad in the Early Middle Ages: Text and Studies* (Detroit, 1970).
20. Oscar Reuther, *Die Ausgrabung der deutschen Ktesiphon-Expedition im Winter 1928/29* (Berlin, [1930]), pp. 6–9, fig. 1.
21. Muḥammad aṭ-Ṭabarī, *Tārīkh ar-rusul wa l-mulūk*, ed. Michel Johann De Goeje III (Leiden, 1880), pp. 372, 373, 381, 383–384, 385; vol. 29 trans. by Hugh Kennedy (New York, 1990), pp. 67–68, 69, 81, 84, 85–86; see also al-Balādhurī, *op.cit.*, note 7, ed. De Goeje p. 179; trans. Hitti, p. 280.
22. Quoted by Creswell, *EMA* II (1940), p. 39.
23. Murhaf al-Khalaf, "Die ʿabbāsidische Stadtmauer von ar-Raqqa/ar-Rāfiqa," including an appendix by Norbert Hagen, *Damaszener Mitteilungen* 2, 1985, pp. 123–131, plan on p. 126, pls. 40–43.
24. First an aerial photograph of 1924 was published by Jean Sauvaget, "Tessons de Rakka," *Ars Islamica* 13–14, 1948, fig. 5; republished in *Damaszener Mitteilungen* 2, 1985, pls. 34, 45.
25. To be published in the forthcoming volumes of final reports.
26. On this compare Ernst Herzfeld, *Geschichte der Stadt Samarra* (Hamburg, 1948), pp. 143–144, with Marius Canard, *Histoire de la dynastie des H'amdanides* I (Algier, 1951), p. 632.
27. Herzfeld, *op.cit.*, note 1, II (1920), pp. 359–363, figs. 333–341, pls. 66–69a; Creswell, *EMA* II (1940), pp. 45–48, figs. 33–34, pl. 4; al-Khalaf, *op.cit.*, note 23, pp. 129–130, pl. 44.
28. The recent research and restoration work, carried out by the Antiquities Authorities, and assisted by the German Archaeological Institute, will be documented in the forthcoming project publications (together with the report mentioned in note 25).
29. Creswell, *EMA* I.1 (1969), pp. 151–210, figs. 79–94, 96, 99–100, 118, 127, pls. 40–62A.
30. In addition to Creswell's reference works, Jean Sauvaget's study, *La mosquée omeyyade de Médine* (Paris, 1947), also provides suggestive information. On the Umaiyad mosque at ar-Ruṣāfā, only 40 km southwest of ar-Raqqa and recently

investigated archaeologically, a monograph by Dorothée Sack is currently in preparation.

31. Recently discussed by Robert Hillenbrand, "Eastern Islamic influences in Syria: Raqqa and Qalʿat Jaʿbar in the later 12th century," in Julian Raby, ed., *The Art of Syria and the Jazīra 1100–1250. Oxford Studies in Islamic Art* I (Oxford, 1985), pp. 21–48, figs. 1, 5, 12–13; on the building inscriptions: *RCEA* nos. 3269–70.
32. Creswell, *EMA* II (1940), pp. 31–32.
33. Especially at the Mosque of Abū Dulaf, completed in 247/861: Creswell, *EMA* II (1940), pp. 278–282, fig. 223, pls. 70–72a.
34. Creswell, *EMA* II (1940), pp. 332–359, figs. 245–257, pls. 96–114, 122, 123a–b.
35. Attributed to the foundation period of ar-Rāfiqa by Creswell, *EMA* II (1940), pp. 42–45, figs. 28–32, pls. 2d–e, 3a–b, d–e; but recently redated first by John Warren, "The date of the Baghdad Gate at Raqqa," *Art and Archaeology Research Papers* 13, 1978, pp. 22–23; and finally by Hillenbrand, *op.cit.*, note 31.
36. Initially dated to the period of Hārūn ar-Rashīd by Henry Viollet, "Description du palais de al-Moutasim fils d'Haroun -al-Raschid à Samarra et de quelques monuments arabes peu connus de la Mésopotamie," *Mémoires présentés par divers savants à l' Académie des Inscriptions et Belles-Lettres* 12, 1909, pp. 568–569, fig. 1, pl. 2.1; this wrong attribution was frequently repeated, despite the opinion of Herzfeld, *op.cit.*, note 1, II (1920), pp. 363–364, figs. 342–344; III (1911), pls. 69–70, who advanced a medieval date. This has been attested by recent arachaeological investigation: Kassem Toueir, "Der Qaṣr al-Banāt in ar-Raqqa. Ausgrabung, Rekonstruktion und Wiederaufbau (1977–1982)," *Damaszener Mitteilungen* 2, 1985, pp. 297–319, figs. 1–12, pls. 72–82; cf. also Hillenbrand, *op.cit.*, note 31.
37. aṭ-Ṭabarī, *op.cit.*, note 21, ed. De Goeje III (1901), p. 444; trans. Kennedy (1990), p. 150.
38. aṭ-Ṭabarī, *op.cit.*, note 21, ed. De Goeje III (1901), p. 1180; trans. Elma Marin, *The Reign of al-Muʿtaṣim (833–842)* (New Haven, 1951), p. 16.
39. Alastair Northedge and Robin Falkner, "The 1986 survey season at Sāmarrāʾ," *Iraq* 49, 1987, pp. 151–155, figs. 4–6, pls. 26–28; Alastair Northedge, *Samarra: Residenz der ʿAbbāsidenkalifen 836–892 n. Chr. (221–279 Hiğrī)* (Tübingen, 1990), p. 9, fig. 8.
40. Unrecorded by the initial researchers; first observed with the aid of aerial photographs by Jean Sauvaget, *op.cit.*, note 24. One of the reasons for moving the residence to ar-Raqqa was the attachment of Hārūn ar-Rashīd to the border province of the empire; on this see Michael Bonner, "al-Khalīfa al-Mardī: The accession of Hārūn al-Rashīd," *Journal of the American Oriental Society* 108, 1988, pp. 79–91.
41. One of the major canals described by Kassem Toueir, "Le Nahr el-Nil entre Raqqa et Heraqleh," in Bernard Geyer, ed., *Techniques et pratiques hydro-agricoles traditionelles en domaine irrigué* I (Paris, 1990), pp. 217–227, figs. 1–6.
42. Maurice Dunand, *De l'Amanus au Sinai: Sites et monuments* (Beyrouth, 1953),

fig. on pp. 96–97; see also note 24, and the article by Toueir, *op.cit.*, note 41, figs. 5–6.

43. The rescue excavations of 1969/1970 briefly mentioned by P. H. E. Voûte, *Anatolica* 4, 1971–1972, pp. 122–123; a report by Kassem Toueir is being prepared for the Raqqa project publications.

44. On the stucco decoration retrieved in 1987: Michael Meinecke, "Early ʿAbbāsid stucco decoration in the Bilād al-Shām," in Muhammad Adnan al-Bakhit and Robert Schick, eds., *Bilād al-Shām during the ʿAbbāsid Period. Proceedings of the Fifth International Conference on the History of Bilād al-Shām 1990* (Amman, 1991), p. 228, fig. 1.

45. Published in a series of excavation reports: Selim Abd al-Haqq, "Les fouilles de la Direction Générale des Antiquités à Rakka," *Les Annales archéologiques de Syrie* 1, 1951, pp. 111–121; Nassib Saliby/Nassīb Ṣalībī, "Rapport préliminaire sur la deuxième campagne de fouilles à Raqqa (automne 1952)," *loc.cit.* 4–5, 1954–1955, pp. 205–212, Arabic section, pp. 69–76; *idem*, "Ḥafrīyāt ar-Raqqa: taqrīr auwalī ʿan al-mausim ath-thālith, kharīf 1953, iktishāf al-qaṣr," *loc.cit.* 6, 1956, Arabic section, pp. 25–40; *idem*, "Les fouilles du palais D à al-Raqqa (1954 et 1958)," (in preparation for the coming volumes of final reports on the Raqqa project).

46. Now exhibited in the National Museum, Damascus: M. Abû-l-Faraj al-ʿUsh, ed., *Catalogue du Musée National de Damas* (Damascus, 1969), p. 169, fig. 67.

47. On this group of buildings: Jan-Christoph Heusch and Michael Meinecke, "Grabungen im ʿabbāsidischen Palastareal von ar-Raqqa/ar-Rāfiqa: 1982–1983," *Damaszener Mitteilungen* 2, 1985, pp. 85–105, pls. 29–34; *idem*, "ar-Raqqa/ar-Rafiqa: The ʿAbbasid palace area," *Les Annales Archaéologiques Arabes Syriennes* 33.2, 1983 (1986), pp. 18–20, 42–43, figs. 7–10; see also note 50.

48. Now on display in the museum of ar-Raqqa.

49. This eventually could have been a tavern, as attested elsewhere in the ʿAbbāsid empire; see David Storm Rice, "Deacon or drink: Some paintings from Samarra re-examined," *Arabica* 5, 1958, pp. 15–33.

50. The excavated structure has been preserved by partial rebuilding: Jan-Christoph Heusch and Michael Meinecke, *Die Residenz des Harun al-Raschid in Raqqa* (Damascus, 1989).

51. Exhibited together with many other examples of ʿAbbāsid stucco in the museum of ar-Raqqa.

52. On the style of these stuccos and the variations in their patterns, see the study quoted in note 44, and the following articles: Michael Meinecke and Andreas Schmidt-Colinet, "Palmyra und die frühislamische Architekturdekoration von Raqqa," in Erwin M. Ruprechtsberger, ed., *Syrien. Von den Aposteln zu den Kalifen* (exhibition catalog: Linz, 1993), pp. 352–359; Michael Meinecke, "ʿAbbāsidische Stuckdekorationen aus ar-Raqqa," in Barbara Finster, ed., *Rezeption in der islamischen Kunst* (in preparation); *idem*, "From Mshattā to Sāmarrāʾ: The Architecture of ar-Raqqa and Its Decoration," in Roland-Pierre Gayraud, ed., *Colloque International d'Archéologie Islamique, Le Caire 1993* (in preparation).

53. As described by Ernst Herzfeld, *Der Wandschmuck der Bauten von Samarra und seine Ornamentik* (Berlin, 1923).

54. For a documentation of the whole complex: Michael Meinecke, "Photographie und Archäologie: Photographische Dokumente verlorener islamischer Baudenkmäler," *Museumsjournal. Berliner Museen,* 5th series 3.2, 1989, pp. 13–15, esp. p. 15, figs. 6–7.

55. Herzfeld, *op.cit.,* note 1, I (1911), pp. 161–163, fig. 71; III (1911), pl. 25; followed by Creswell, *EMA* II (1940), pp. 165–166, fig. 154.

56. Kassem Toueir, "Heraqlah: A unique victory monument of Harun ar-Rashid," *World Archaeology* 14.3, 1983, pp. 296–304, fig. 1, pls. 10–13; *idem,* "Il sogno di Harùn ar-Rascìd," *Archeologia Viva* 10: new series, February 1991, pp. 24–35; *idem,* "L'Hiraqla de Hārūn al-Rašīd à Raqqa: réminiscences byzantines," in Pierre Canivet and Jean-Paul Rey-Coquais, eds., *La Syrie de Byzance a l'Islam VII*[e]*-VIII*[e] *siècles. Actes du Colloque international, Lyon-Paris, 1990* (Damascus, 1992), pp. 179–185, figs. 1–8.

57. Some of the stone fragments are published in the article *op.cit.,* note 44 (1991), p. 233, figs. 21–22.

58. Creswell, *EMA* II (1940), pp. 286–288: "The ornament of Sāmarrā"; and Herzfeld, *op.cit.,* note 53.

59. Studied recently by Venetia Porter, *Medieval Syrian Pottery (Raqqa ware)* (Oxford, 1981); see also Helen Philon, "Stems, leaves and water-weeds: Underglaze-painted pottery in Syria and Egypt," in Julian Raby, ed., *The Art of the Jazīra 1100–1250. Oxford Studies in Islamic Art* I (Oxford, 1985), pp. 113–126, figs. 1–20. Recent investigation even points to ar-Raqqa as the place of production for the type of luxurious luster pottery usually associated with Tall Minis: Venetia Porter and Oliver Watson, " 'Tell Minis' wares," in James Allan and Caroline Roberts, eds., *Syria and Iran: Three Studies in Medieval Ceramics. Oxford Studies in Islamic Art* IV (Oxford, 1987), pp. 175–248. See also the extensive and analytical bibliography by Christina Tonghini and Ernst J. Grube, "Towards a history of Syrian Islamic ceramics before 1500," *Islamic Art* 3, 1988–1989, pp. 59–93.

CHAPTER 2

Buṣrā: From the Provincia Arabia to the Darb al-Ḥajj

This chapter deals with the Islamic fabric of a famous classical site, Buṣrā, in Syria about 115 km south of Damascus (fig. 8), important in the first centuries of the Christian Era as capital of the Roman Provincia Arabia.[1] Today a rather remote, underdeveloped provincial town, Buṣrā is famous for its numerous Nabatean, Roman, and Early Christian monuments, many of which have stately grandeur (fig. 8, nos. 1–24).[2] Often overlooked, an impressive corpus of Islamic buildings survives in the shadow of these earlier monuments (nos. 25–33). Comprising about ten historic structures, they are testimony to the Islamization of the Classical metropolis.[3] In Islamic times the city served as the southernmost outpost of Damascus, which was the political center of several Islamic dynasties beginning in the early Islamic period with the Umaiyads. In the Middle Ages it regained international stature as the residence of first the Saljūq rulers and then of their successors the Atābeks, Zengids, and Aiyūbids. Subsequently it housed the Mamluk viceroy, or governor, of Syria. Buṣrā benefited from its proximity to Damascus, although its status was also boosted by a role as a gathering place for the yearly pilgrim caravan heading for the holy cities of Mecca and Medina in

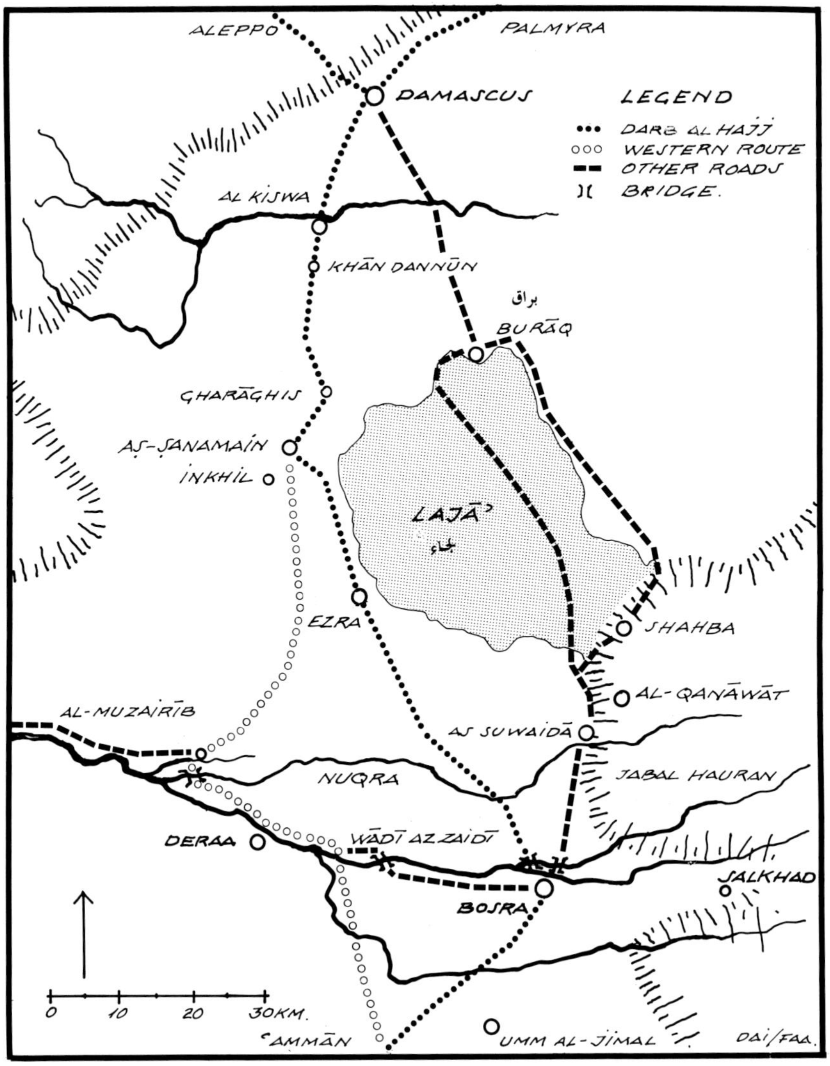

Fig. 7. Darb al-Ḥajj: alternative routes in South Syria, in scale 1:100,000 (Flemming Aalund 1990).

the Ḥijāz (fig. 7). Although Buṣrā's location on the Darb al-Ḥajj ensured its prosperity, nevertheless, its status mirrors fluctuations in the fate of Damascus.

In Islamic as well as Classical periods Buṣrā was administrative center of the south Syrian province of the Ḥaurān, a volcanic and extremely fertile region now divided by the Syro-Jordanian border.

The region's architectural character has been determined by its abundant supplies of black basalt, the dominant building material in all historical periods, which created a distinctive regional style of architecture. The scarcity of timber, for instance, induced the substitution of wood by basalt, which was consequently also used for roofing and for doors or window screens. The use of basalt for the ceilings, cut into long, narrow beams, resulted in binding construction standards due to statical preconditions. The limitation in the size of the stone beams motivated a special architectural system with successive transverse arches carrying the stone roof (as on pls. 8a, 11a). In order to enlarge the intervals between the supporting arches and walls, corbels were introduced (as for instance on pls. 8b, 11b), though in general not exceeding a maximum span of about 4 m.

In contrast to other regions of the Islamic world, which relied on less durable building materials such as mud brick, baked brick, or timber, the basalt masonry of the Ḥaurān ensured the preservation of many medieval monuments. In addition, the survival of numerous Classical monuments encouraged the re-use of older building material, which also facilitated the construction of Islamic monuments at Buṣrā.

Formulated already in pre-Islamic times, the local Ḥaurān type of architecture constitutes the basis for the built fabric of all historic periods until the recent past. But in order to avoid repetitive designs, the patrons of ambitious construction projects consequently had to search for outside expertise, eventually implementing the stately monuments that still grace the townscape of Buṣrā. This search for alternatives surpassing the limitations of the traditional Ḥaurān architecture is also reflected by the Islamic fabric of Buṣrā. Most important in this respect, as will be outlined later on, are the interrelations with the nearby metropolis of Damascus, which account for a surprising stylistic synthesis.[4]

The Islamic fabric of Buṣrā, researched for a decade within the framework of a cooperative survey and restoration project of the Buṣrā Directorate of Antiquities and the German Archaeological Institute Damascus, originates from three medieval periods:[5] (1) the Saljūq and subsequent Atābek period of the early sixth/twelfth century, (2) the Aiyūbid period of the first half of the seventh/thirteenth century, and (3) the Mamlūk period of the eighth/fourteenth century.

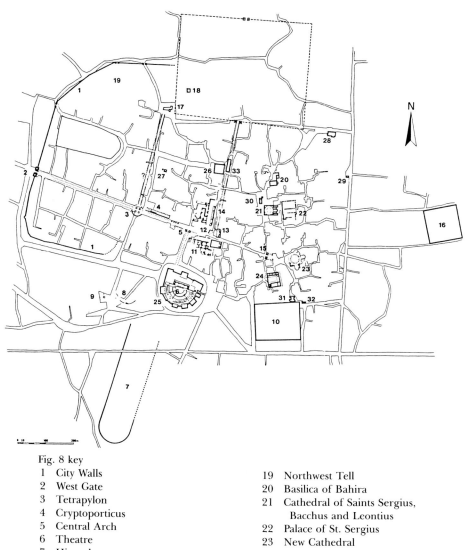

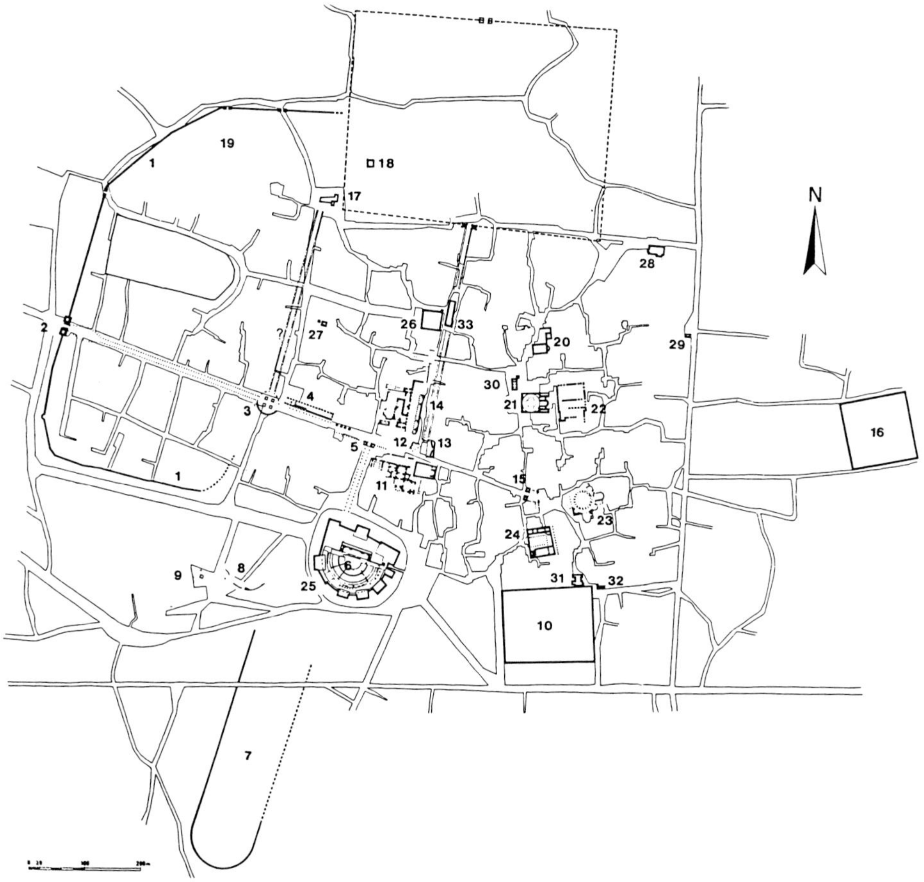

Fig. 8 key

1 City Walls
2 West Gate
3 Tetrapylon
4 Cryptoporticus
5 Central Arch
6 Theatre
7 Hippodrome
8 Elliptical Building
9 Mausoleums (Tell Aswad)
10 South Reservoir/Birkat al-Ḥajj
11 South Baths
12 Nymphaeum
13 Kalybe
14 Central Baths
15 Nabatean Arch
16 East Reservoir
17 Spring of al-Jahir
18 North Baths
19 Northwest Tell
20 Basilica of Bahira
21 Cathedral of Saints Sergius, Bacchus and Leontius
22 Palace of St. Sergius
23 New Cathedral
24 Palace
25 Citadel
26 al-ᶜUmarī Mosque
27 al-Khiḍr Mosque
28 al-Mabrak Mosque
29 Dār al-Qur' ān of ᶜAbd al-Wāhid ash-Shafiᶜi
30 al-Fāṭima Mosque
31 ad-Dabbangan Mosque Madrasa of Sunqur al-Hakīmī
32 Masjid Yāqūt
33 Ḥammām Manjak

Fig. 8. Buṣrā: location map of monuments, in scale 1:13,000 (Directorate General of Antiquities and Museums, Damascus; with additions by Jean-Marie Dentzer and Flemming Aalund).

1. REDEVELOPMENT BY AMĪN AD-DAULA KUMUSHTAKĪN (EARLY SIXTH/TWELFTH CENTURY)

As was true in the city of Damascus, at Buṣrā the topography was also not altered substantially in the days of early Islam. Conquered by the Muslim forces already in 13/634, the population only gradually adopted the new faith and continued to utilize the available structures of the past.[6] Only two isolated building inscriptions, previously incorporated as spolia into later masonry of the Great Mosque (fig. 8, no. 26), attest to construction activities in 102/720–21 and 128/745–46, in the decades prior to the fall of the Umaiyad empire.[7] After a hiatus of over three centuries, another inscription, again originating from the Great Mosque, points to undetermined constructions in the year 460/1067–68, shortly before the expulsion of the Fāṭimids from Syria.[8] Nevertheless, first signs of systematic improvement point to the period following the arrival of the Saljūqs in Syria in 468/1076. At first the Roman theater of Buṣrā (no. 6), the major monument of the Classical city, was adapted as fortification (no. 25). In 481/1088 the external staircase towers flanking the skene received an additional story for defensive purposes, internally divided by two transverse arches (pl. 8a) and thus characterized by the traditional Ḥaurān pattern of architecture. Though these building measures remained rather limited, the theater consequently regained a new function as stronghold and focal point of the Muslim settlement. About sixty years later, due to the advancing Crusaders, another fortified tower was attached to the southwestern side of the cavea in 542/1147–48.

The pace of redevelopment accelerated in the early sixth/twelfth century, when the Turkish general Amīn ad-Daula Abū Manṣūr Kumushtakīn (d. 541/1146)[9] received the entire Ḥaurān as a personal fief from the Būrid ruler of Damascus, the Atābek Ṭughtakīn. The new governor of the Ḥaurān province improved the Islamic profile of Buṣrā with the construction of an impressive series of religious monuments. First in 506/1112–13 a Friday mosque was built or rebuilt, the nucleus of the venerated al-ʿUmarī Mosque (fig. 8, no. 26; fig. 9), which until today is the Muslim center of the settlement.[10] Though constructed in rather modest proportions of about 28 × 36 m, mirroring in volume the still rather limited size of the Muslim community, this initial mosque transmits a remarkable aesthetic standard. At the prayer hall of two perpendicular aisles on

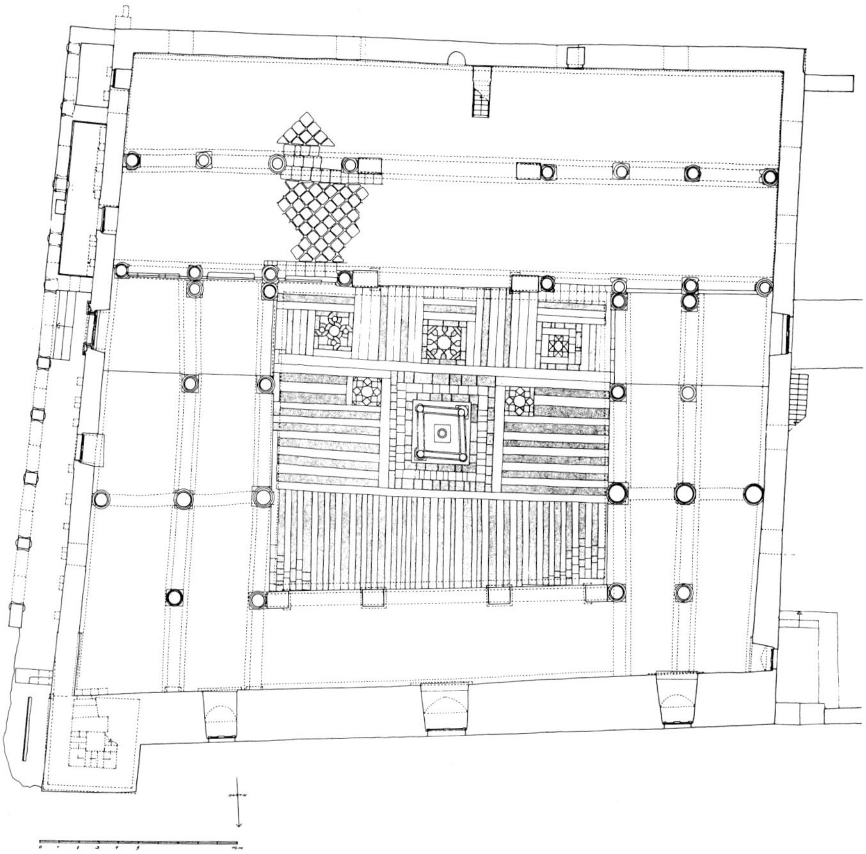

Fig. 9. Buṣrā, al-ʿUmarī Mosque: ground plan, in scale 1:500 (surveyed in 1986 by Flemming Aalund with Thomas Kampmann).

white columns (pl. 10a), the middle axis is emphasized by markedly wider-spaced central arcades on rectangular pillars, echoing the transept of the venerated Umaiyad Friday mosque of Damascus. The dependence on the Damascus model also argues for wooden gable roofs on both aisles of the prayer hall, as the distance of nearly 5 m could not be bridged with the customary basalt slabs of the Ḥaurān tradition. Most remarkably, in the sanctuary the black basalt was hidden by a masking layer of white plaster, decorated with multicolored fresco ornaments on the central pillars and by exceptional stucco carvings on the *qibla* wall. The stucco decoration of horizontal inscription bands traversing the entire south wall (pl. 10c), and the wide frame of the prayer niche featuring richly variegated vegetal and geometric patterns (pl. 10b), finds parallels only outside Syria, in the homelands of the Saljūqs.[11] Therefore this medieval masterpiece evidently could not have been implemented by local specialists alone, but only with the aid of outside experts. The close relation with the Great Mosque of Damascus clearly indicates that these building and decoration specialists were originally based at Damascus and employed only temporarily at Buṣrā for the mosque's construction.

This pattern finds indirect confirmation by two later constructions of the governor Kumushtakīn. The al-Khiḍr mosque (fig. 8, no. 27) of 528/1134 marking the northwestern extension of the Muslim settlement, completely depends on the local Ḥaurān architecture. The small building, erected on a slightly rectangular plot of c. 10 × 9 m, is divided in the interior by two transverse arches, carrying the flat ceiling of basalt slabs. As is especially characteristic for the Ḥaurān, all windows are closed by pierced-stone screens, and the single entrance is protected by a movable stone slab. Similar features also characterize the massive minaret tower 12 m tall, set slightly apart, obviously a somewhat later addition.

In contrast, the last of Kumushtakīn's constructions, the madrasa attached to the ancient Muslim shrine (fig. 8, no. 28) that houses the imprints of the camel's knees *(mabrak an-nāqa)* which are associated with the Prophet Muḥammad and the Holy Koran of the caliph ʿUmar and begun only two years after the al-Khiḍr mosque in 530/1136, features a decidedly more sophisticated layout. The center of the building of about 20 × 17 m is marked by a square courtyard c. 6 m each side, probably originally covered by a wooden or brick dome, to which four axial *īwāns* are oriented. Of these the south *īwān,* containing the prayer niche, is considerably more spacious to gain additional room for prayer. Consequently, to permit its roofing by basalt slabs, the *īwān* is bisected by a transverse arch (pl. 8b) and also closed on the interior courtyard façade by a screen wall with triple doors in a triangular arrangement (pl. 9a). Also all the other rooms of the structure, partly built up in two stories to provide chambers for housing, feature identical stone ceilings customary for the Ḥaurān. In contrast to the elevation, the axial plan reflects a new design concept, linked with the function as madrasa for the theological school of Abū Hanīfa an-Nuʿmān, attested by the building inscription. This monument at Buṣrā therefore has to be considered the oldest surviving example of a new class of religious buildings, invented in Saljūq Iran in the middle of the fifth/eleventh century.[12] This type of building was certainly introduced to Damascus earlier, following the Saljūq conquest. According to contemporary chronicles, the first madrasa at the Syrian capital was already founded in 491/1098; the second in date, the Madrasa al-Amīnīya, was built at Damascus in 514/1120 by the same Amīn ad-Daula Kumushtakīn, who also commissioned the Buṣrā madrasa.[13] Therefore it can be assumed that the axial plan layout was already well established at Damascus before being transferred to the provincial town of Buṣrā, where the design was altered according to local Ḥaurān architectural tradition.

2. GOLDEN AGE OF AṢ-ṢĀLIḤ ISMĀᶜĪL (FIRST HALF OF SEVENTH/THIRTEENTH CENTURY)

The building projects of the Turkish governor Amīn ad-Daula Kumushtakīn, although strongly enhancing the Islamic aspect of Buṣrā, altogether resulted in only a rather limited improvement of the city. In the following generations remarkably few and modest constructions have been attested, mostly by isolated building inscriptions. The situation drastically changed in the time of the Aiyūbid ruler al-ᶜĀdil Abū Bakr (592/1196–615/1218), who implemented an enormous program of fortification projects in Syria and Egypt as a protective measure against the Crusaders. At the same time the citadels of most of the major cities of the Aiyūbid state were strengthened by additional series of huge towers, for instance at Cairo, Damascus, and Aleppo, in addition to several other places of regional importance, such as Baalbek, Mount Tabor, Qalᶜat Najm on the Euphrates, and also Buṣrā.[14] The tremendous acceleration of large-scale building enterprises could be achieved only by a centrally organized labor force, similar to the pattern described for the early ᶜAbbāsid period. It still remains a challenging task to research in detail the sequence of fortification work, its technical refinement, and its impact on the style of Aiyūbid architecture in general.[15] At Buṣrā the Roman theater, already previously fortified as the citadel of the city (fig. 8, nos. 6, 25), received an exterior chain of eight towers of stately proportions.[16]

At Buṣrā work started in 599/1202–3, at the same time as in

Damascus, with the northwestern corner tower, a massive block of 31 × 22 m in three stories, designed as *donjon* with an individual entrance. The parallel tower on the northeastern corner, commissioned in 608/1211–12, was built in even larger dimensions of 25 × 37 m including the main gate that features the characteristic bent entrance of Muslim fortifications. The staggering size of these first Aiyūbid fortifications in comparison with earlier Islamic monuments of Buṣrā is quite striking. All the earlier buildings together occupy less space than those two Aiyūbid corner towers. Construction of the defenses continued with several intervals until 649/1251–52, when the southeastern tower of the external ring was enlarged. All parts of the Buṣrā citadel share the same characteristic: though built in basalt masonry, the typical flat roofing of the Ḥaurān architecture is almost completely replaced by an intricate vaulting system, including barrel vaults, cross vaults, and hanging domes. This tendency reflects the contemporary development of Aiyūbid imperial architecture at the nearby Syrian capital, Damascus.

The central northern tower of 20 × 25 m, completed in 612/1215–16, obviously was designed also for ceremonial functions. The second story is reserved for a stately hall of axial layout, closely resembling in scheme and proportion the madrasa of Kumushtakīn from 530/1136. The same plan reappears at the Buṣrā Citadel in two slightly later towers (pl. 9b), all featuring the characteristic bearing walls with triple openings in a triangular arrangement on two sides of the central square, similar to the older madrasa (pl. 9a). A variation was also adopted at the Damascus Citadel,[17] terminated in 617/1216. Most probably the fortification experts from Damascus working at Buṣrā were attracted by this special feature, which consequently not only was incorporated in their designs at Buṣrā, but eventually also was further developed in parallel constructions in Damascus. Once heavily fortified, the citadel of Buṣrā remained under direct administration of the ruling Aiyūbid family. At the death of al-ʿĀdil Abū Bakr in 615/1218, the fief of Buṣrā passed to his younger son aṣ-Ṣāliḥ Ismāʿīl, who took up residence in the newly enlarged citadel. That Buṣrā at that time no longer should be regarded as a remote location can be deduced from the fate of this Aiyūbid prince, who twice occupied the sultanate of Damascus, first from 634/1237 till 635/1238, and again from 637/1239 till 643/1245.[18] After his first term of office at Damascus he also held the

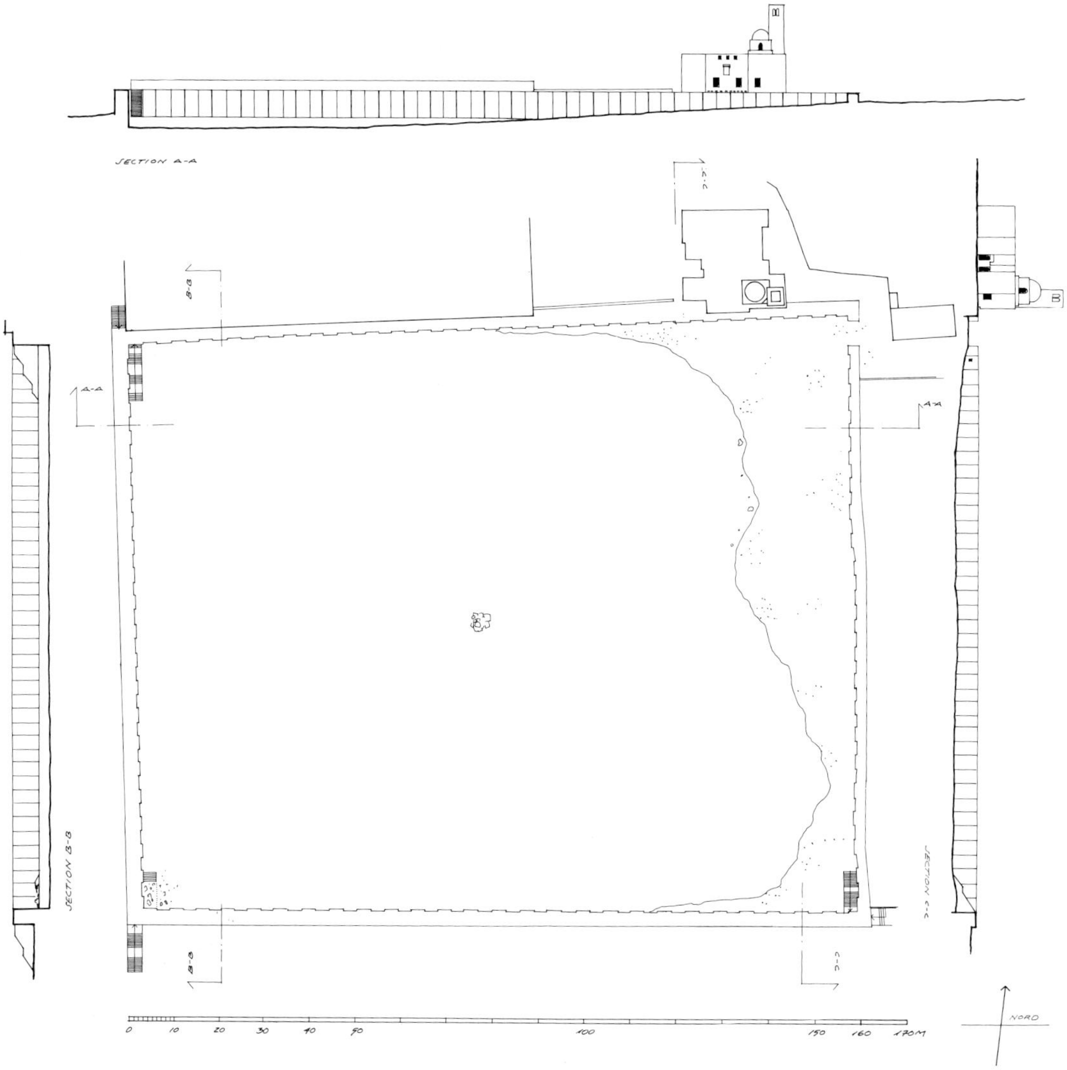

Fig. 10. Buṣrā, Birkat al-Ḥajj: plan and sections, in scale 1:1600 (surveyed in 1985 by Flemming Aalund with Vera Hellborg).

important fief of Baalbek, which became his preferred residence until his death in 644/1246.[19]

One of the first measures implemented in the time of aṣ-Ṣāliḥ Ismāʿīl was the enlargement of the Friday mosque in 618/1221–22 (fig. 9), commissioned apparently by a member of the city community. The north wall of the initial building of 506/1112–13 was completely taken down and reset about 4 m farther north to enlarge the interior space of the mosque. In connection with this operation, the square minaret on the southwestern corner was also erected and is still a landmark of the city today.[20] The exceptional thickness of the newly erected north façade, measuring over 2.0 m, is caused by the incorporation of column drums, a feature first occurring at the Buṣrā citadel, and rather awkwardly repeated there by masons rooted in the local architectural tradition.[21]

At about the same time, as an important measure to improve the infrastructure of the city, the huge pre-Islamic water reservoir east of the citadel (fig. 8, no. 10; fig. 10) was reactivated. Though the topographer-historian ʿIzz ad-Dīn Ibn Shaddād (d. 684/1285) credited the Aiyūbid ruler of Damascus al-Muʿaẓẓam ʿĪsā (615/1218–624/1227) with this decisive improvement,[22] the work including also the restoration of the water conduits of the city evidently was implemented under the supervision of the governor in residence, aṣ-Ṣāliḥ Ismāʿīl. The water channel from the aqueduct leading to the citadel is marked by an impressive religious building (fig. 8, no. 31), commissioned in the name of that Aiyūbid prince by the military commander Shams ad-Dīn Sunqur al-Hakīmī.[23] Built in 622/1225–26, the building later was enlarged by the mausoleum of the founder in 630/1232–33, and eventually also surmounted by a square tower. Originally conceived as a madrasa, the building again follows an axial design, similar to the first madrasa of Buṣrā built in the preceding century.[24] Though its layout is determined by Ḥaurān features, especially in evidence at the main *īwān* with the prayer niche, divided by a pair of transverse arches, smaller parts of the structure are covered by barrel vaults, reflecting the expertise of the local architects gained from the ongoing citadel construction project.

The restoration of the open cistern, until today named the Birkat al-Ḥajj, proved to be beneficial to the pilgrim caravans on the way to the holy cities of the Ḥijāz. But even more important in local perspective was the supplying of water to the citadel, which served as the princely residence. The Aiyūbid prince aṣ-Ṣāliḥ Ismāʿīl devoted much of his resources to the internal improvement of the fortified theater. Starting with the erection of a small Friday mosque on the skene in 620/1223–24, construction continued with a vaulted cistern on the cavea, probably concurrent with the erection of the madrasa on the Birkat al-Ḥajj. Soon afterwards, in 625/1227–28 and 629/

1231–32, two additional stories of vaulted halls were built over the cistern to serve as storage space and arsenal. The water supply was even sufficient to operate a spacious bath of 16 × 20 m inserted into the theater's eastern portico.[25] As these interior structures were recently removed to facilitate the theater's use in annual festival performances, only the central basin of the bath, reset in one of the towers (pl. 9b), still testifies to the quite agreeable environment of the prince's residence. The overflow channel surrounding the square marble basin shows a quite remarkable decoration in colored mosaic, depicting animals, birds, and fishes.[26] Evidently the standard of luxury in Buṣrā easily matched that in other contemporary residences, as for instance the palace of the Artuqid ruler Nāṣir ad-Dīn Maḥmūd (597/1201–619/1222) at Āmid/Diyarbakır on the Tigris, about 700 km away, where a similar mosaic decoration was recently excavated.[27]

Despite the attention lavished on this fortified residence, the population seems to have benefited only marginally from the imperial presence. New religious foundations remained quite restricted in number and size. A small building in the city center, for example, the al-Fāṭima mosque (fig. 8, no. 30), can be attributed to the Aiyūbid period. Originally constructed on a plot of about 13.50 × 11 m, the mosque consisted of a single room with three transverse arches following the traditional pattern of Ḥaurān architecture (pl. 11a).[28] The same can be observed at a small structure near the al-Mabrak mosque at the northeastern corner of the Islamic settlement (fig. 8, no. 29), identified by an inscription as the Dār al-Qurʾān, a madrasa for the teaching of the Koran, endowed in 652/1254 by a local dignitary, ʿAbd al-Wāhid ash-Shāfiʿī.[29] The tiny building, characterized by an attractive frontal arch opening, contains only a small rectangular room of 3.50 × 7 m (pl. 11b). Built almost exclusively of recycled ancient masonry, this structure represents the reduction of the local architectural scheme to the smallest possible unit.

In contrast, the small burial mosque on the northeastern corner of the Birkat al-Ḥajj, the Masjid Yāqūt (fig. 8, no. 32), squeezed into a plot of 7 × 14 m and erected only a few years later in 655/1257–58, follows more sophisticated architectural patterns. Both rooms, used for prayer and for burial respectively, are covered by cross vaults. Its founder is identified by inscriptions as commander of the nearby citadel, who had previously supervised the enlargement of one of the southeastern towers of that fortification in 649/1251–52, the last attested construction phase on the citadel. This funerary mosque, modest in scale by comparison with the citadel towers, was evidently erected by masons who belonged to the local building force, formerly employed on that military project, who had finally adopted some of the basic elements used by contemporary Aiyūbid imperial construction ateliers.

3. BUṢRĀ IN ECLIPSE: THE MAMLUK PERIOD (EIGHTH/FOURTEENTH CENTURY)

Despite its heavily fortified citadel, an outstanding masterpiece of military architecture, the city of Buṣrā was an easy prey to the victorious Mongol army, which swept away the Aiyūbid dynasty in 658/1260. Though recaptured the same year and subsequently again restored by the Mamluk sultan aẓ-Ẓāhir Baibars (658/1260–676/1277),[30] the citadel never regained its previous splendor, but was used only by a small garrison protecting the region. Throughout the Mamluk period the city of Buṣrā depended on the earlier achievements. The population, obviously reduced in size due to the devastating Mongol occupation, continued to use buildings from earlier periods of prosperity without any substantial improvement. Altogether only two construction projects are attested at Buṣrā for the later Middle Ages.

Only about half a century after the Mongol invasion, in the time of the Mamluk sultan an-Nāṣir Muḥammad (with interruptions 698/1299–741/1341), a minaret was erected for the al-Fāṭima mosque (fig. 8, no. 30) in the city center. Tellingly, this tower was commissioned in 705/1306 not by any known personality, but by a certain Aiyūb b. Majd ad-Dīn ᶜĪsā an-Najrānī, probably a wealthy member of the local community.[31] Architecturally the impressive tower of nearly 19 m closely imitates the minaret of 618/1221–22 of the Great Mosque nearby. With the exception of an inscription band of white limestone, nothing indicates any stylistic alteration or formal improvement. Consequently it can be assumed that the minaret was built by masons from the Ḥaurān without involvement of outside experts. Nevertheless, in the absence of literary sources, this modest construction testifies to a limited revitalization of the city of Buṣrā during the early eighth/fourteenth century, when the Syrian part of the Mamluk empire in general witnessed a new period of tranquility and prosperity.

Only after a hiatus of over two generations were further construction activities attested in the city center. Opposite the main entrance of the Great Mosque, the Mamluk governor of Damascus, Manjak al-Yūsufī, ordered the erection of a sizable bath complex (fig. 8, no. 33; figs. 11.1, 12) which was inaugurated in 773/1372.[32] Built on a plot of about 45 × 14 m, this monument is one of the biggest Islamic structures in the town, and certainly the most refined. Excavated, restored, and partially rebuilt in the past decade,[33] the bath structure evidently equals the most luxurious examples of this building type at the Syrian capital of Damascus (fig. 11.2).[34] Access is provided by a niched portal in the south façade, featuring alternating black and white layers of masonry, especially characteristic for Damascus.[35] From there a vaulted corridor leads into the reception room determined by an axial plan layout originally covered by a dome on *muqarnaṣ* pendentives (fig. 12; pl. 12a). This special type of dome transition, providing a high rising tambour, is known only from a few similar examples of the eighth/fourteenth and ninth/fifteenth centuries, as for instance at the mausoleum of 823/1420 in the mosque of Khalīl at-Taurīzī in Damascus (pl. 12b).[36] The bath proper, reached through a small door in the northwestern corner of the domed reception hall, centers on two larger rooms of polygonal and rectangular form, to which individual bath chambers are attached (pl. 13b). The geometry of the first polygonal room—remarkably neither a hexagon nor an octagon, as in most bath complexes, but a decagon—again points to Damascus. So far, this particular feature only is known from three Damascene baths of the Mamluk period, of which the somewhat later Ḥammām at-Taurīzī (fig. 11.2), especially well preserved, can serve as example also for the original type of vaulting (pls. 13b, 14b), almost completely lost at the Buṣrā complex (pl. 14a).[37] The sumptuous marble floor, including multicolored opus sectile, as well as the intricate technical installations testify to the highest standard of architecture and decoration. This masterpiece of engineering architecture was certainly not achieved by locally available specialists, but by an experienced building atelier from Damascus.

Due to its singular position within the historic fabric of this south-Syrian town, the bath complex transcends its local setting. Neverthe-

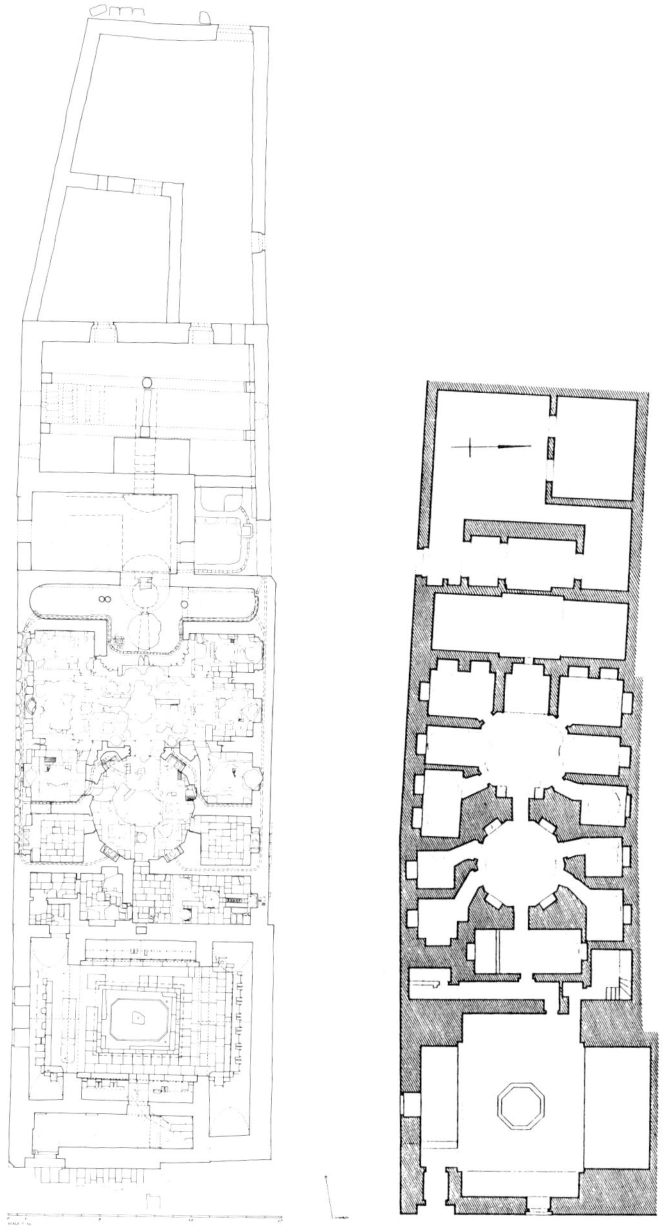

Fig. 11. (1) Buṣrā, Ḥammām Manjak: ground plan after excavation, in scale 1:400 (Flemming Aalund, Michael Meinecke, and Philipp Speiser 1982–1989). (2) Damascus, Ḥammām at-Taurīzī, ground plan, in scale 1:400 (redrawn after Michel Écochard and Claude Le Coeur, *Les bains de Damas* II [1943], fig. 72).

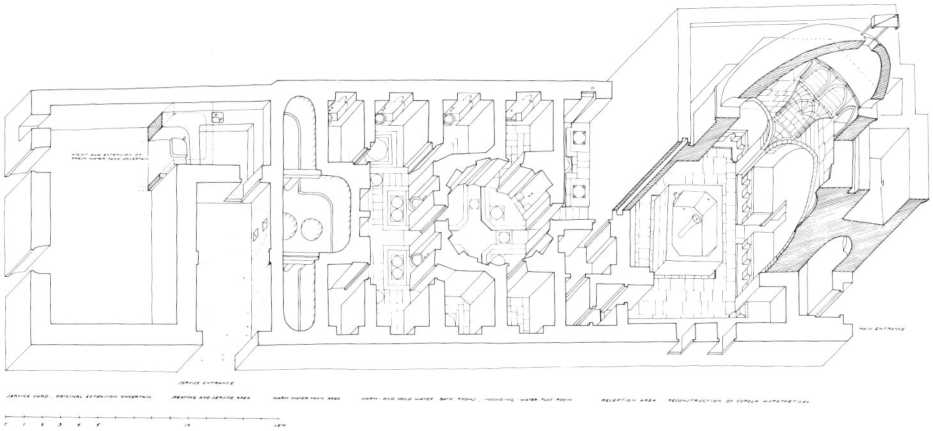

Fig. 12. Buṣrā, Ḥammām Manjak: axonometric reconstruction, in scale 1:400 (Flemming Aalund 1990).

less, this Mamluk building also demonstrates the potential of Buṣrā's water-system, which had been simultaneously renovated by the same Damascus governor, Manjak al-Yūsufī. However, the bath building was probably not intended to serve the population of Buṣrā alone. Undertaken by the highest-ranking representative of the Mamluk empire in Syria, almost certainly its major objective was the improvement of the Pilgrim Route, the Darb al-Ḥajj. That same governor is credited with yet another component within this larger project, the erection of a religious complex at al-Kiswa (pl. 15a),[38] a stopping place for pilgrim caravans between Damascus and Buṣrā. In connection with this program the Khān Dannūn, a large caravanserai completed in 778/1376, was built nearby.[39] Though erected in the characteristic basalt masonry of the Ḥaurān, both monuments are characterized by the use of vaults quite similar to those in the Buṣrā bath, again opposing the specific architectural tradition of the region.

The choice of location of the Ḥammām Manjak in the immediate vicinity of the Great Mosque of Buṣrā is an indication of the continued maintenance of the religious center of the town throughout the eighth/fourteenth century; but its final construction phase of undetermined date, though most probably in the Mamluk period, also reflects the limited resources of the Muslim city. Eventually the timber gable roofs of the al-ʿUmarī Mosque, covering the prayer hall

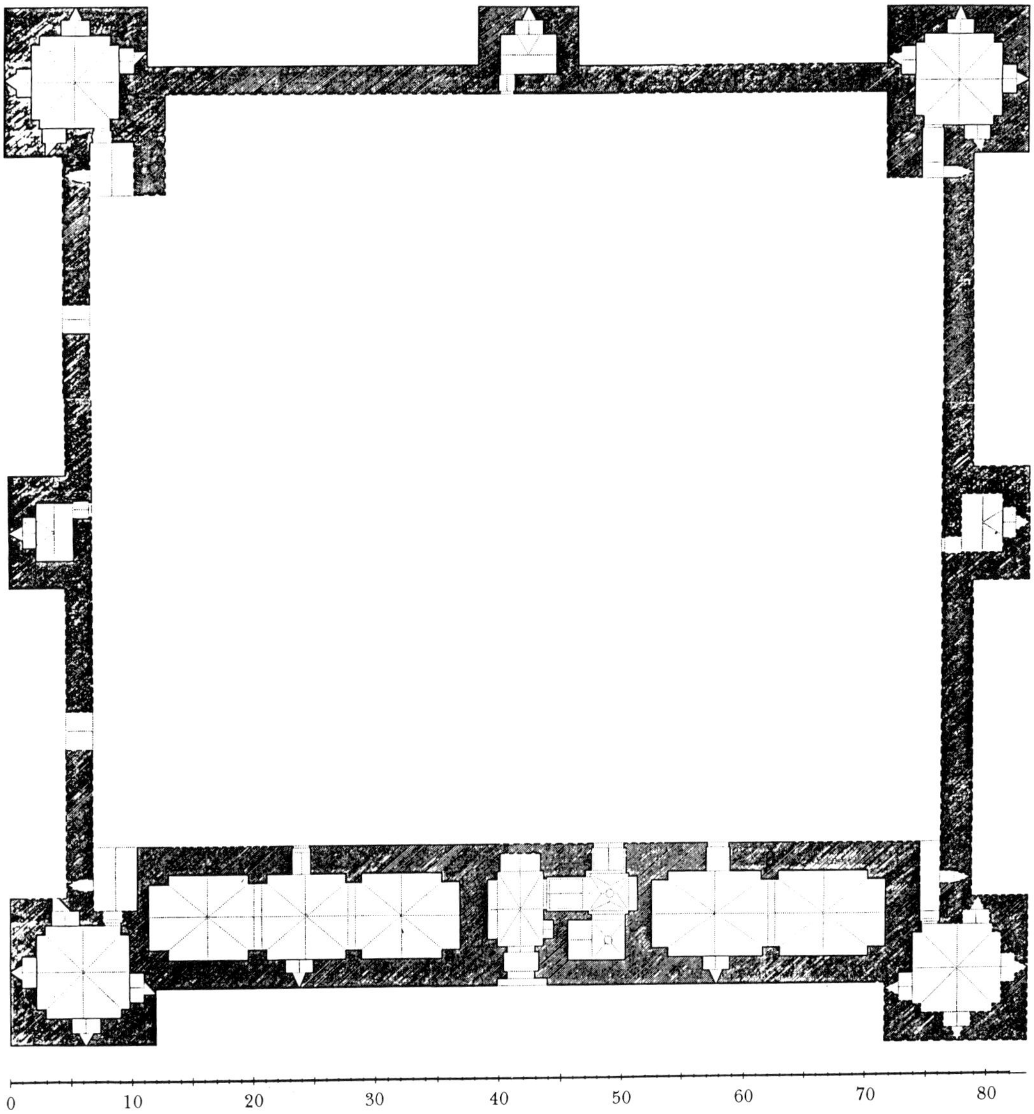

Fig. 13. al-Muzairīb, Khān: reconstructed ground plan, in scale 1:600 (surveyed in 1987/1988 by Norbert Hagen and Emad Terkawi).

of 506/1112–13 and the northernmost aisle, constructed in 618/1221–22, could no longer be maintained. Instead of a costly repair to the wooden roof construction, a new series of supports were erected, reducing the intervals of the arcades, which then could be bridged easily by the locally available basalt slabs.[40] The Ḥaurānization of the Great Mosque symbolizes the final stage in the long-lasting history of the traditional city of Buṣrā.

Though the chronicles cease to take notice, it can be assumed that the Tīmūrid conquest of Damascus in 802/1400 also seriously affected the dependent regions.[41] Damascus, nevertheless, recovered within a few decades and lived through another long period of prosperity until the final integration of Syria into the Ottoman empire in 922/1516,[42] but Buṣrā never again regained its former position. The pilgrim caravans ceased to pass through Buṣrā and preferred an alternative route about 60 km farther west (fig. 7), where at latest in the early days of Ottoman rule a new pilgrim center was erected near the lake of al-Muzairīb (fig. 13; pl. 15b).[43] Thus deprived of its economic base, the population of Buṣrā eventually dwindled away, till the site was almost completely deserted in the Ottoman period.

Only since the mid-nineteenth century has southern Syria gained new attraction as agriculture was reactivated, especially for grain export to the European market.[44] Deserted Classical sites in the Ḥaurān subsequently were repopulated, and also old monuments were readapted as housing. During this most recent development the traditions of Ḥaurān architecture were again revived. The medieval al-Fāṭima Mosque at Buṣrā, for instance, the only active religious monument of the settlement at the turn of the century, soon was almost doubled in size, when the prayer room was extended by three additional transverse arches (pl. 11a), repeating the traditional pattern of basalt architecture.[45]

4. LIMITATIONS OF LOCAL STYLES OF ARCHITECTURE

This final example is also a case in point, illustrating the interdependence of building material and architectural form. The brittle basalt, especially hard and durable, determined the use of certain patterns of masonry. Once invented, or better, developed, the same features were faithfully repeated without much notable alteration or improvement. This conservative tendency accounts for the uniformity of traditional Ḥaurān architecture throughout all historic periods. In the Ḥaurān, differences in the aesthetic quality of architecture consequently could not result from innovations in the plan, as is the case in other regions of the Islamic world, but only from higher degrees of technical perfection of masonry, or the inclusion of new ornamental variations in the decorative repertoire. Many monuments in the Ḥaurān, in fact, reveal the remarkable potentials of this traditional architectural school.

On the other hand, more ambitious construction projects often surpassed the locally available expertise. Due to the inherent limitations of Ḥaurān architecture, most divergences from traditional patterns reflect influences from different architectural schools. In minor regional centers usually only isolated indications pointing to outside contacts are in evidence, but at places of greater importance, as at Buṣrā, the interrelations with exterior lines of architectural traditions constitute the basic pattern of development. In the case of Buṣrā, its administrative dependence on the Syrian metropolis Damascus is faithfully reflected by the historic fabric. Monuments transcending the limitations posed by the Ḥaurān architectural tradition are in all cases interrelated with contemporary developments at Damascus. It can be assumed that construction specialists from the capital did not migrate to Buṣrā on their own, but were employed for special tasks. Therefore, in general the patrons are to be identified as the motivating force for more sophisticated architectural designs. Consequently the construction specialists from Damascus returned to their place of origin soon after they accomplished their tasks. Though local labor surely participated in these greater construction projects, only few of the outside features were assimilated to the local repertoire. But even modest improvements of the traditional skills at the end of the Aiyūbid period proved short-lived due to political circumstances. No subsequent evidence points to any change in the local tradition of Ḥaurān architecture.

Notes

1. Buṣrā was surveyed twice at the turn of the last century, first in 1898 by Rudolf Ernst Brünnow and Alfred von Domaszewski, *Die Provincia Arabia* III (Strasbourg, 1909), pp. 1–84, figs. 865–892, pls. 50–51, and then in 1904 by Howard Crosby Butler, *Ancient Architecture in Syria. Publications of the Princeton University Archaeological Expedition to Syria* II.A.4 (Leiden, 1914), pp. 215–295. Both records also include Muslim monuments.
2. Several recent publications have centered on the Classical city of Buṣrā, resulting from long-lasting research projects of French and Italian archaeolo-

gists: Maurice Sartre, *Bostra: Des origines à l'Islam* (Paris, 1985); Jean-Marie Dentzer, ed., *Hauran I: Recherches archéologiques sur la Syrie du Sud à l'époque hellénistique et romain* (Paris, 1985); Raffaella Farioli Campanati, ed., *XXXV Corso di cultura sull'arte ravennale et bizantina, Ravenna, 1988* (Ravenna, 1988); see also two of the last issues of *Berytus* 32, 1984 (1986); and 33, 1985 (1987).

3. Fully described by Flemming Aalund, Michael Meinecke, and Riyadh Sulaiman al-Muqdad, *Islamic Bosra: A Brief Guide* (Amman,, 1990); see also Sliman Mougdad and Solange Ory, "Bosra, cité islamique," *Archéologia,* no. 148, November 1980, pp. 22–32, with 22 illus.
4. On these interrelations see also Michael Meinecke, "Der Ḥammām Manǧak und die islamische Architektur von Buṣrā," *Berytus* 32, 1984 (1986), pp. 181–190; *idem,* "Islamic architecture of the Hauran and the Hammam Manjak at Bosra," in Susanne Kerner, ed., *The Near East in Antiquity* II (Amman, 1991), pp. 33–46.
5. The project initially centered on the excavation and restoration of a Mamluk bath complex, the Ḥammām Manjak (see below); subsequently, comparative studies were carried out, resulting in the survey of all historic monuments from the Islamic periods in the Ḥaurān. For project publications and preliminary reports, see notes 3, 4, and 32–33. Previously the Arabic epigraphy, including also about sixty tomb stones, and the Islamic history of Buṣrā were researched in detail by Solange Ory, Les monuments et les inscriptions de la ville de Buṣrā aux époques umayyade et salǧūqids (unpublished Ph.D. thesis, Paris, 1969); a related survey of the region has recently been published: Solange Ory, *Cimetières et inscriptions du Ḥawrān et du Ǧabal al-Durūz* (Paris, 1989).
6. On the city of Damascus most recently and exhaustively, see Dorothée Sack, "Damaskus, die Stadt *intra muros,*" *Damaszener Mitteilungen* 2, 1985, pp. 207–290; idem, *Damaskus. Entwicklung und Struktur einer orientalisch-islamischen Stadt* (Mainz, 1989). *Damaszener Forschungen* 1.
7. Both inscriptions, now in the lapidarium of the Islamic Museum (Ḥammām Manjak), were detected during a modern restoration by Michel Écochard and subsequently published by Jean Sauvaget, "Les inscriptions arabes de la mosquée de Bosra," *Syria* 22, 1941, pp. 54–57 nos. 1–2, pl. 7; compare also the epigraphical indications based on the 1904 survey by Enno Littmann, *Arabic Inscriptions. Publications of the Princeton University Archaeological Expedition to Syria* IV.D (Leiden, 1949), pp. 24–25 no. 30. The lack of Umaiyad remains probably is the result of the earthquake of 129/747, which caused the destruction, for instance, of a larger farmhouse from the Umaiyad period; Muhamed Kadour and Helga Seeden, "Busra 1980: Reports of an archaeological and ethnographic campaign," *Damaszener Mitteilungen* 1, 1983, pp. 77–101; Helga Seeden, "Busra 1983–84: Second archaeological report," *Damaszener Mitteilungen* 3, 1988, pp. 387–411; Gernot Rotter, "Die Münzen des umayyadischen Hauses in Buṣrā," *Berytus* 33, 1985 (1987), pp. 47–50. About the same time also some of the Roman buildings collapsed, as indicated by Sophie Berthier, "Sondage dans le secteur des thermes sud à Buṣrā (Syrie) 1985," *Berytus* 33, 1985 (1987), pp. 5–45.

8. Also published by Sauvaget, *Syria* 22, 1941, p. 58 no. 3, pl. 7. Another medieval inscription from the same location, eventually to be dated about (4)4(0)/1048–49, was recorded by Littmann (1949), pp. 22–23 no. 28; cf. *RCEA* no. 2559.
9. On this personality, see Solange Ory, "De quelques personnages portant le nom de Kumuštakīn a l'époque salğūqide," *Revue des Études Islamiques* 35, 1967 (1968), pp. 119–134, esp. pp. 126–129.
10. On the basis of the two early inscriptions (see note 7) an Umaiyad origin of the mosque was suggested by Jean Sauvaget, *op.cit.*, 1941, and his *La mosquée omeyyade de Médine* (Paris, 1947), pp. 101–103, figs. 7, 7 bis; as well as by K.A.C. Creswell, *EMA* I.2 (1969), pp. 484–493, figs. 543–547, pls. 79–80. On the medieval building phase and the interrelation with contemporary mosque architecture influenced by the Umaiyad Friday mosque of Damascus, see Michael Meinecke, "The Great Mosques of the Ḥaurān," *International Colloquium on the History and Archaeology of the Suweida Mohafazat, Suweida 1990* (forthcoming).
11. As outlined by Solange Ory, "Inscriptions de style iranien à Buṣrā," *Mélanges de l'Université Saint-Joseph* 43, 1968, pp. 27–60, pls. 1–3.
12. For the context within the madrasa development: Michael Meinecke, "Rückschlüsse auf die Form der seldschukischen Madrasa in Iran," *Damaszener Mitteilungen* 3, 1988, pp. 185–202, esp. pp. 188–189, fig. 2, pl. 35b.
13. Earlier surveys of both lost structures documented by Abd al-Razzaq Moaz, Les madrasas de Damas et d'al-Salihiyya depuis la fin du V/XIe siècle jusqu'au milieu du VII/XIIIe siècle (unpublished Ph.D. thesis, Aix-en-Provence, 1991), pp. 70–74 nos. 9–10, figs. 16–23.
14. This phenomenon indicated by K.A.C. Creswell, "Fortification in Islam before A.D. 1250," *Proceedings of the British Academy* 38, 1952, pp. 89–125, esp. pp. 122–125, figs. 13–16, pls. 14–16. Some of these fortification systems were already studied in detail, as for instance that of Cairo: K.A.C. Creswell, "Archaeological researches at the Citadel of Cairo," *Bulletin de l'Institut Français d'Archéologie Orientale* 23, 1924, pp. 89–167; extended in *MAE* II (1959), pp. 1–40, figs. 1–15, pls. 1–13; or of Damascus: Paul Edward Chevedden, *The Citadel of Damascus* (unpublished Ph.D. thesis, Los Angeles, 1986); and of Baalbek: Theodor Wiegand, ed., *Baalbek: Ergebnisse der Ausgrabungen und Untersuchungen in den Jahren 1898 bis 1905* III (Berlin and Leipzig, 1925), pp. 41–96: "Die arabische Burg" (Heinrich Kohl), figs. 7–111, pls. 1–13.
15. Evidently this topic will be developed further in the forthcoming monograph of Terry Allen, *Ayyubid Architecture.*
16. Studied prior to the recent clearing measures by Armand Abel, "La citadelle eyyubite de Bosra Eski Cham," *Les Annales Archéologiques de Syrie* 6, 1956, pp. 95–138, pls. 1–11.
17. Revealed during the ongoing restoration; for a preliminary report on a related survey, see Hanspeter Hanisch, "Die Zitadelle von Damaskus: Eine Einführung," Volker Schmidtchen, ed., *Sicherheit und Bedrohung—Schutz und Enge. Schriftenreihe Festungsforschung* 6 (Wesel, 1987), pp. 167–178; and recently *idem, Citadel of Damascus: Investigation of Possible Use* (Damascus [1991]); idem, "Der

Nordwestturm der Zitadelle von Damaskus," *Damaszener Mitteilungen* 5, 1991, pp. 183–233, figs. 1–12, pls. 57–61; idem, "Die seldschukischen Anlagen der Zitadelle von Damaskus," *Damaszener Mitteilungen* 6, 1992, pp. 479–499, figs. 1–7, pls. 79–82; idem, "Der Nordostabschnitt der Zitadelle von Damaskus," *Damaszener Mitteilungen* 7, 1994, pp. 233–296, figs. 1–18, pls. 58–67.

18. For a lengthy account on the history of that period: R. Stephen Humphreys, *From Saladin to the Mongols: The Ayyubids of Damascus, 1193–1260* (Albany, 1977).
19. On Islamic Baalbek, see the volume of final excavation reports quoted in note 14.
20. Though this is definitely not the oldest existing minaret of Islam, as Creswell (*op.cit.*, note 10) claimed, it served as a model for several minarets at Buṣrā, often conspicuously set apart from the religious structures, consequently most, if not all, later additions to earlier foundations.
21. This interpretation was first advanced by Solange Ory, "La mosquée de ʿUmar à Buṣrā," *Actas IV Congresso de Estudos árabes e islâmicos, Coimbra 1968* (Leiden, 1971), pp. 577–580.
22. ʿIzz ad-Dīn Ibn Shaddād, *al-Aʿlāq al-khaṭīra fī dhikr umarā' ash-Shām wa l-Jazīra* II.2, Sāmī ad-Dahān, ed., *Tārīkh Lubnān wa l-Urdun wa Filisṭīn* (Damascus, 1963), p. 64: 8–10.
23. The same officer in 623/1226–27 rebuilt a bridge about 3 km northwest of Buṣrā on the Darb al-Ḥajj, another measure within the improvement program for the pilgrim route; surveyed by H. C. Butler (*op.cit.*, note 1) II.A.5 (Leiden, 1915), p. 304, figs. 273–274. On the inscription, see *RCEA* no. 3946; and Littmann (*op.cit.*, note 7), p. 60 no. 72.
24. Meinecke, *Damaszener Mitteilungen* 3, 1988, p. 189, fig. 4, pl. 34b.
25. Robert Amy, *Mise en valeur de Bosra-Cham: Octobre 1968* (UNESCO Report: Paris, 1969), pl. 2.2.
26. Sulaiman A. Mougdad, *Bosra: Guide historique et archéologique* (Damascus, 1981), illus. p. 63 [a].
27. Excavated 1961 and 1962 in two seasons by Oktay Aslanapa, "Die Ausgrabung des Palastes von Diyarbakir," *Atti del secondo Congresso Internazionale di Arte Turca, Venezia, 1963* (Naples, 1965), pp. 13–29, pls. 5–10; see also Metin Sözen, *Türk mimarisinin gelişimi ve mimar Sinan* (Istanbul, 1975), pp. 132–133, figs. 373–379, color illus. 40–42. Evidently also this small structure is to be interpreted in connection with the adjacent bath chambers.
28. Compare the current situation (*Islamic Bosra, op.cit.*, note 3, illus. p. 38) with the original structure documented in 1904 by Butler (*op.cit.*, note 1), pp. 292–293, fig. 261.
29. According to an unpublished inscription on the west façade (communicated by Solange Ory).
30. Meinecke (1992) II, p. 6 no. 4/2.
31. Meinecke (1992) II, p. 98 no. 9 B/55.
32. On the date and further building activities of the patron, see Viktoria Meinecke-Berg, "The founder of the Ḥammām Manjak in Buṣrā: His works

in Egypt and Syria," in Qāṣim Ṭwair, ed., *New Light on the History and Archaeology of Bilad esh-Sham,* (Damascus, 1989), pp. 209–218 (in Arabic).

33. Michael Meinecke, Sulaimān ʿAbd Allāh al-Muqdād, and Philipp Speiser, "Der Ḥammām Manĝak in Buṣrā. Grabungsbericht 1981–1982," *Damaszener Mitteilungen* 2, 1985, pp. 177–192, figs. 1–5, pls. 56–60; Michael Meinecke and Sulaiman al-Muqdad, "The Hammam Manjak at Bosra," *Les Annales Archéologiques Arabes Syriennes* 33.2, 1983 (1986), pp. 23–25, 44–45, figs. 19–22. For the use as a field museum, a documentation on Islamic Busrā has been prepared, exhibited since May 1993 at the Ḥammām Manjak, after the termination of the extensive restoration; see Michael Meinecke, "Das Islamische Museum zu Bosra/Südsyrien," *Museumsjournal. Berliner Museen,* 5th series 4.2, 1990, pp. 12–14.
34. For the baths at Damascus compare the monograph of Michel Écochard and Claude Le Coeur, *Les bains de Damas*, 2 vols. (Damascus, 1942 and 1943).
35. On this feature see for instance Michael Meinecke, "Der Survey des Damaszener Altstadtviertels aṣ-Ṣāliḥīya," *Damaszener Mitteilungen* 1, 1983, p. 206, and Meinecke (1992), I, pp. 30–31, 86–87, 107, 109.
36. Meinecke (1992) I, pp. 190–193, fig. 138, pls. 105b, 108c, 114a, 131c–d, 135a; II, pp. 328 no. 29/53, 345–346 no. 33/49; see also Michael Meinecke, "Syrian blue-and-white tiles of the 9th/15th century," *Damaszener Mitteilungen* 3, 1988, pp. 203–214, esp. pp. 204–205, fig. 1.
37. Meinecke (1992), II, pp. 336–337, no. 33/9; cf. Écochard and Le Coeur, *op.cit.*, note 34, II (1943), pp. 72–76 no. 49, figs. 72–76. On the other two related examples at Damascus, the Ḥammām az-Zain and the Ḥammām al-Ward, see Meinecke (1992), II, pp. 130 no. 9 C/124, 368 no. 35/43.
38. Meinecke (1992), II, p. 247 no. 22/47; cf. also Meinecke-Berg, *op.cit.*, note 32.
39. Meinecke (1992), II, p. 257 no. 22/98; based on the monographic study by Jean Sauvaget, "Un relais de Barîd mamelouk," *Mélanges Gaudefroy—Demombynes* (Cairo, 1935–1945), pp. 41–48, illus. p. 42, figs. 1–3. The "engineer of Damascus" *(muhandis ash-Shām)* ʿAlī Ibn al-Badrī, who signed the Khān Dannūn, could very well also have designed the earlier building at al-Kiswa, and even the Buṣrā bath.
40. Deducible from the survey documentation of 1904; Butler, *op.cit.,* note 1 (1914), pp. 289–292, figs. 254–258, pl. 18. Since then, the later additions have been removed in the process of restoration.
41. According to the stratigraphy, investigated recently by Sophie Berthier, *op.cit.*, note 7.
42. Meinecke (1992), I, pp. 188–194.
43. The heavily ruined monument, surveyed in 1987/1988, was erected after the Ottoman conquest of 922/1516 by Sultan Selīm I (d.926/1520), as indicated by Karl K. Babir, *Ottoman Rule in Damascus 1708–1758* (Princeton, 1980), pp. 2 map 2, 197.
44. On this period see the illuminating article by Linda Schatkowski Schilcher, "The Hauran conflicts of the 1860s: A chapter in the rural history of modern Syria," *International Journal of Middle East Studies* 13, 1981, pp. 159–179.

45. Cf. note 28. The traditional houses of Buṣrā, though constructed fairly recently, are also determined by the typical features of basalt architecture; Ghada Azar, Giovanni Chimienti, Haytham Haddad, and Helga Seeden, "Busra: Housing in transition," *Berytus* 33, 1985 (1987), pp. 103–142.

CHAPTER 3

Hasankeyf/Ḥiṣn Kaifā on the Tigris: A Regional Center on the Crossroad of Foreign Influences

This chapter is devoted to Hasankeyf (fig. 14), the former Ḥiṣn Kaifā, now a small town of mostly Kurdish-speaking inhabitants in one of the most remote corners of southeastern Anatolia near the area where the Tigris reaches the border of Syria and continues into Iraq toward Mosul. The historic importance of this place is based on the strategic position of a fortified castle on a commanding rock plateau bordering the Tigris, controlling the major caravan route alongside the river from Diyarbakır, the historic city of Āmid, c. 110 km farther west, to the north Mesopotamian center of Mosul, c. 220 km to the southeast, passing Cizre, the former Jazīrat Ibn ʿUmar, just 80 km away, another historic city of the region. Throughout history Hasankeyf protected the access to the Ṭūr Abdīn, the predominantly Christian area to the south, which in turn provided the essential agricultural products to the inhabitants of the town.

Besides the amazingly high artistic quality of the remaining historic fabric, the site is represented in this book also because of romantic memories of the impressive landscape, resulting from the contrast of the steep rock declivity alongside the yellowish Tigris and the green surrounding lands. Even more important is our aim to

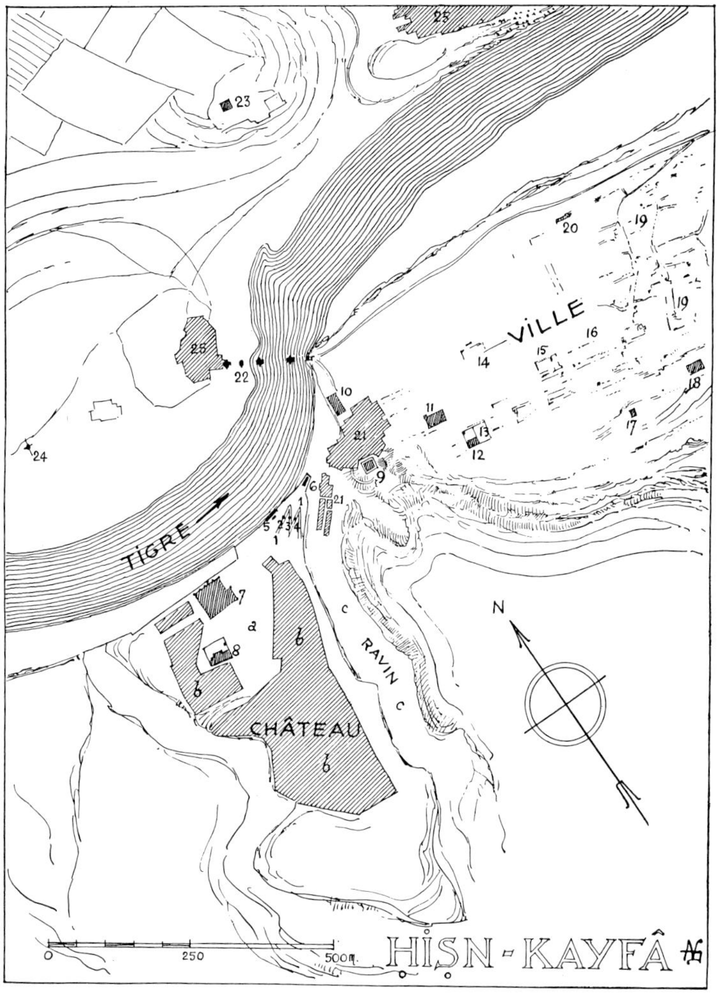

A. Citadel: (a) hippodrome,
(b) inhabited area, (c) ravine

1-1	access ramp
2/3/4	fortified gates
5	staircase to the Tigris
6	Small Palace
7	Great Palace
8	Citadel Mosque

C. Suburb on the left bank of the Tigris:

23	Mashhad Imām Muḥammad b. ʿAbd Allāh aṭ Ṭaiyār
24	Zeynel Bey Türbesi
25-25	modern habitations

B. City

9	donjon
10	Jāmiʿar-Risq
11	Sultan Süleyman Camii/Madrasa of al-ʿAdil Ghāzī
12	Koç Cami/Madrasa of ʿAbd Allāh Ibn al-Mawardī
13	ruins of a madrasa (?)
14	caravanserai (?)
15	bath
16	traces of a mosque (?)
17	Small Mosque
18	Mausoleum
19	ruins of a house
20	part of ancient wall
21	modern shops and houses
22	Tigris Bridge

Fig. 14. Hasankeyf: location map of monuments (situation of 1932), in scale 1:10,000 (after Albert Gabriel, *Voyages archéologiques dans la Turquie orientale* [1940], fig. 44).

attract attention to a doomed historic site, threatened with destruction by projected dam constructions west of Cizre, which will submerge most of its monuments.

The dozen or so Islamic structures surviving at Hasankeyf, mostly in ruinous conditions, date from the mid-sixth/twelfth century to the second half of the ninth/fifteenth century, and thus give testimony of construction activities for over three centuries.

Until the present these monuments remained overshadowed by the rich architectural heritage of the neighboring cities of Diyarbakır/Āmid, Mardin/Mārdīn, Silvan/Mayāfāriqīn, and Kızıltepe/Dūnaisīr, which attracted much scholarly attention.[1] In contrast, knowledge of the Hasankeyf monuments is almost exclusively based on a survey by the eminent French historian of Anatolian architecture, Albert Gabriel, who visited the site twice in 1932, in the company of the historian and epigraphist Jean Sauvaget. Their documentation on findings about Hasankeyf was published jointly in 1940 in the *Voyages archéologiques dans la Turquie orientale,* in a chapter of little more then thirty pages together with twenty-three line drawings and thirty-seven photographs;[2] their proposed dates for the individual buildings are based on altogether fourteen historic inscriptions.[3] Almost nothing new has been added in the meantime.[4] Only very recently, the actual threat caused by the pending development of the area instigated a new architectural survey and the first archaeological rescue measures by a team from Ankara University, headed by Oluş M. Arik.[5]

Also here, in this study, it is neither possible nor intended to present new documentation, which should remain the task of the ongoing research project of Ankara University. Instead I will attempt to indicate the stylistic context of the existing monuments, based on observations during two visits to Hasankeyf, the first on two days in June 1975 en route to Mosul, and the second in May 1989 on a weekend excursion from the Raqqa expedition.

The historic fabric of Hasankeyf falls into four distinct groups corresponding to (1) the Artuqid period of the sixth/twelfth century, (2) a first Aiyūbid period in the middle of the eighth/fourteenth century, (3) a second Aiyūbid period in the early ninth/fifteenth century, and finally (4) the Āq Qoyūnlū period of the later ninth/fifteenth century.

1. ARTUQID PERIOD (SIXTH/TWELFTH CENTURY)

Following the decisive defeat of the Byzantine army at Malazgirt in 463/1071 and the subsequent expansion of the Saljūqs from Iran into Anatolia, several Türkmen families eventually established minor semi-independent principalities in the region bordering the Christian lands in eastern Anatolia. The most important of these east Anatolian principalities is that of the Artuqids at Hasankeyf. The citadel of Hasankeyf together with the adjacent area was handed as a fief to Muʿīn ad-Dīn Sukmān b. Artuq in 495/1102–3 by the Saljūq sultan Rukn ad-Dīn Barkiyāruq (487/1094–498/1105). From that time onward Hasankeyf remained one of the most important family strongholds of the Artuqids for nearly 130 years, until the Aiyūbid conquest of 630/1232. The citadel served as the main residence for the family dynasty until 578/1183, when the court was transferred to the city of Diyarbakır.[6]

TIGRIS BRIDGE (I) At Hasankeyf, artistic activities on a larger scale materialized only around the middle of the sixth/twelfth century—as was the case all over Anatolia and the neighboring region of northern Mesopotamia—when the princely rulers increasingly substituted the courtly pleasures of cultural patronage for the art of warfare. Though only relatively few Hasankeyf monuments can be attributed firmly to this formative period of Anatolian architecture, there is at least one building which definitely is of Artuqid origin, the famous bridge (fig. 14, no. 22) north of the citadel.[7] This most impressive structure remained throughout history the major source for the continued economic prosperity of the town because it not only linked the Artuqid stronghold with the Diyarbakır-Mosul road along the Tigris but also with north-south routes connecting Lake Van with the Euphrates.

According to the local historian Ibn al-Azraq this 200 m long bridge of well-made stone masonry was constructed in 510/1116–17 by the Artuqid ruler Fakhr ad-Dīn Qarā Arslān (579-567/1144–1167) as a replacement for an earlier and more rudimentary bridge. The Hasankeyf bridge with its central arch of c. 40 m and its ascending succession of lateral arches is a unique masterpiece of architectural engineering (fig. 15.1; pl. 16a).[8] The sides were pierced by corridors, providing shelter to the population of the residential

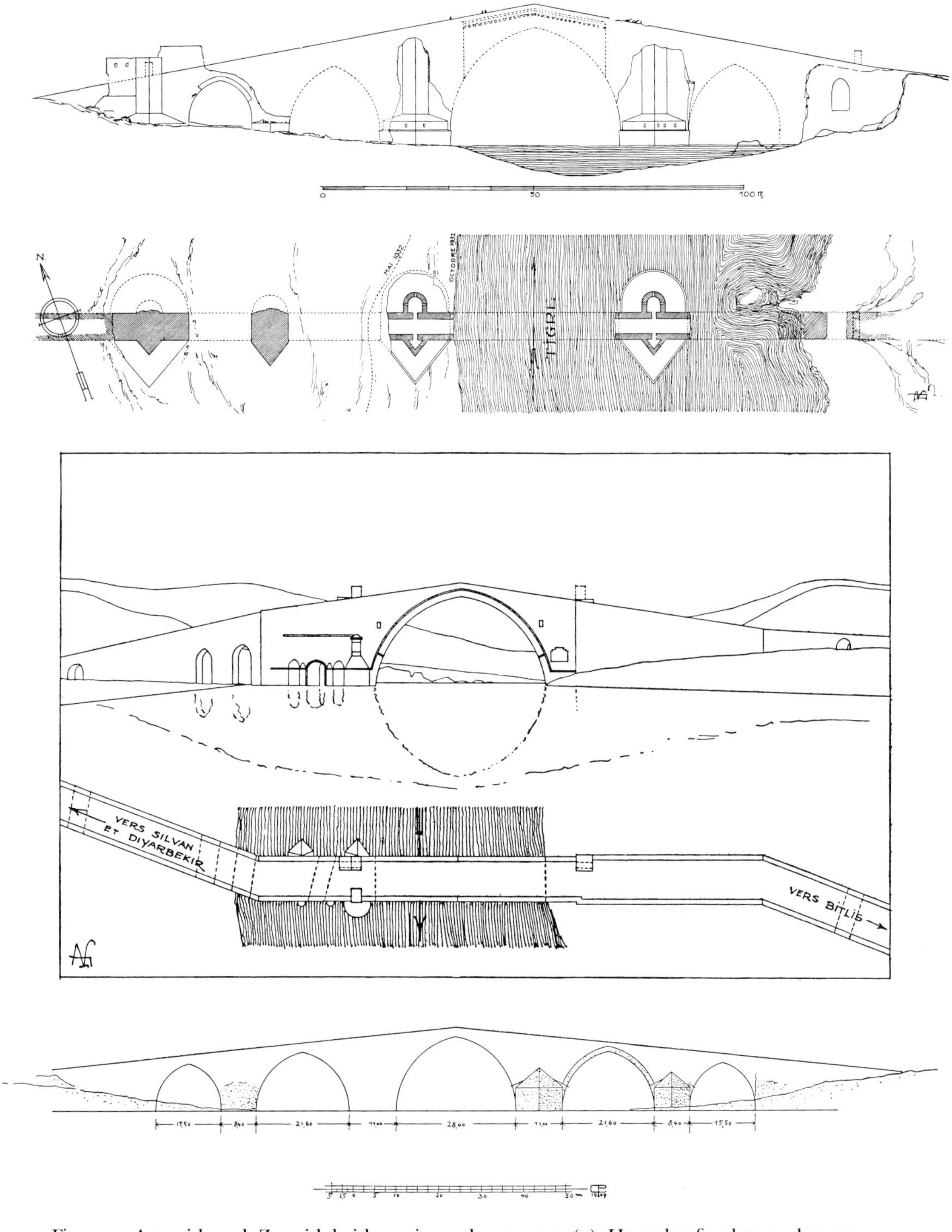

Fig. 15. Artuqid and Zengid bridges, in scale 1:1500: (1) Hasankeyf: plan and reconstructed elevation (after Gabriel [1940], fig. 57). (2) Batman Su Bridge near Silvan: sketch plan and elevation (after Gabriel [1940], fig. 175). (3) Cizre: reconstructed elevation (after Conrad Preusser, *Nordmesopotamische Baudenkmäler* [1911], pl. 39).

quarters on both banks of the river, as well as being used for defensive purposes, as arrow slits clearly indicate. The imperial impact of this majestic monument is proved by a series of reliefs on the triangular buttresses on the western façade, recently interpreted by Estelle Whelan as representing the princely ruler's page corps.[9]

This bridge of Hasankeyf is said by the same Ibn al-Azraq to have been modeled after the bridge on the Batman Su/Sātīdāmē, a tributary of the Tigris, near Silvan/Mayāfāriqīn, another Artuqid stronghold c. 60 km farther northwest on the road to the town of Bitlis.[10] Following the collapse of an older structure, the rebuilding began in 541/1146–47 by the Artuqid ruler of Mardin, Temür Tāsh, and was completed in 548/1153–54 by his son, Najm ad-Dīn Alpī (fig. 15.2; pl. 17a). Though of lesser length, its general layout with the characteristic triangular profile and the almost identical span of its central arch of nearly 39 m, as well as the inclusion of figural representations in the stone decoration, indicates a close relationship with the Hasankeyf bridge.

Almost simultaneously, a third bridge was constructed in the same area near the city of Cizre/Jazīrat Ibn ʿUmar (fig. 15.3; pl. 17b), testifying to the drastic improvement of the road network in the Upper Euphrates region. As this monument, according to contemporary sources, was commissioned by the widely respected *wazīr* of Mosul, Jamāl ad-Dīn Muḥammad al-Iṣfahānī, it must have been erected before his imprisonment in 558/1163 by the Zengid ruler Quṭb ad-Dīn Maudūd (544/1149–564/1169).[11] With a total length of over 140 m and with its triangular contour, this bridge matches that of the Batman Su, though the inclination is considerably lower due to the series of five arches, instead of a single arch, which results in a span of only 28 m for the central arch and consequently in a considerable lesser height. Remarkably, eight figural limestone panels inserted in the black basalt masonry of the southernmost pier (pl. 20b), are identified by inscriptions as zodiac signs.

GREAT PALACE OF THE CITADEL On my first visit to the Cizre bridge in 1984, which now lies within Syrian territory, I noted several mason marks (pl. 17c), a feature also recorded by Albert Gabriel for the Hasankeyf bridge (fig. 16.1). Besides supplying further indications for the close relationship of both constructions, the occurrence of related mason marks (fig. 16.2) also permits the attribution of

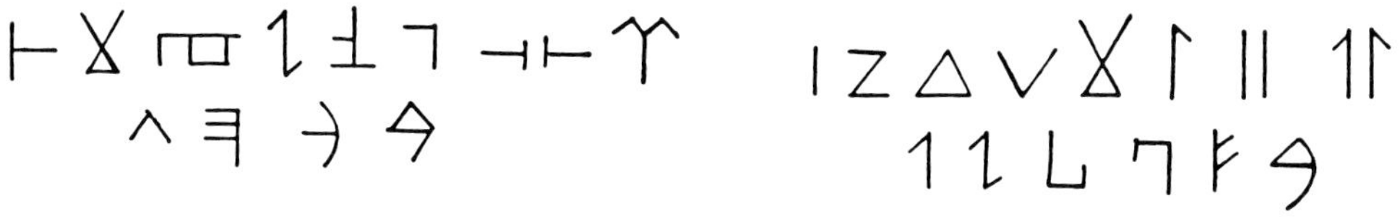

Fig. 16. Hasankeyf, Artuqid mason marks: (1) Bridge. (2) Great Palace of the Citadel (after Gabriel [1940], figs. 62, 48).

another ruin at Hasankeyf to the Artuqid period, the so-called Great Palace of the Citadel (fig. 14, no. 7).[12] Located on the northern edge of the citadel plateau overlooking the Tigris, only the substructures of an important building measuring about 46 × 55 m were still visible in 1932. Though the original room arrangement of this structure unfortunately is not discernible from Albert Gabriel's survey sketch, the northern side evidently was designed as the main façade with a series of round buttresses and a central portal (pl. 16b). This decorated façade, oriented toward the north to be viewed from the opposite bank of the Tigris, rising on top of the impregnable citadel plateau, evidently must have been of imperial importance and therefore might, in fact, be identified with the main residence of the Artuqid rulers of Hasankeyf.

CITADEL MOSQUE (I) Albert Gabriel also tentatively ascribes the mosque of the citadel (fig. 14, no. 8), near the Great Palace, to the Artuqid period.[13] Though a mosque must have existed at that time within the citadel, the original form and date of the initial monument remain to be established. The existing structure on a distorted rectangular plot of c. 28 × 39 m (fig. 19) has been constantly used and consequently successively altered over many centuries. Currently the earliest dates provided by epigraphy point to the last years of the eighth/fourteenth century; the minaret (pl. 16b) was built only in 927/1520, shortly before or after the Ottoman conquest. Nevertheless, the central part, with a rather peculiar T-shaped room arrangement in diminutive scale, definitely in no respect matches the mosque constructions of other towns in the area. In comparison, the Great Mosque of Cizre/Jazīrat Ibn ʿUmar, a Zengid foundation of 555/1160 with a prayer hall divided into several perpendicular aisles and a dominant dome in front of the prayer niche, evidently reflects a much higher standard of architecture.[14] The same is the case with the Artuqid mosques of Silvan/Mayāfāriqīn,[15] built before 575/1179–80, and of Kızıltepe/Dūnaisīr,[16] founded before 597/1201, both characterized by a similar layout and especially rich stone decoration. In a recent comparative study by Tom Sinclair, the dependence of these early Artuqid mosques on the stone architecture of Aleppo, the major urban center of northern Syria, has been convincingly advocated.[17]

ISMĀᶜĪL IBN AR-RAZZĀZ AL-JAZARĪ Altogether there exist only tantalizingly few architectural remains from the Artuqid period at Hasankeyf, where surely one of the most lively courts of that time is known to have been established, famed for the patronage of various artists, creating works of art of the highest aesthetic quality. As an indication of the prevailing artistic climate at the Artuqid residence in Hasankeyf, we can single out the famous universal artist, Abu l-ᶜIzz Ismāᶜīl Ibn ar-Razzāz al-Jazarī, the author of the most famous treatise on automata.[18] By the *nisba* a native of Cizre/Jazīrat Ibn ᶜUmar, al-Jazarī, according to his own testimony, in 570/1174–75 entered the services of the Hasankeyf Artuqid Nūr ad-Dīn Muḥammad b. Qarā Arslān (562/1167–581/1185).[19] At Hasankeyf he passed eight years of his career, until in 578/1183 he moved with his master to Diyarbakır/Āmid farther up the Tigris, where the Artuqid court was transferred. After his arrival at the new residence, al-Jazarī created the monumental door of two wings for the palace built for or at least occupied by and redecorated for Muḥammad b. Qarā Arslān. This door, measuring c. 4.50 × 3 m, as represented in al-Jazarī's treatise, contained eulogies of the ruler Muḥammad b. Qarā Arslān (pl. 18a; see also reconstruction on the back cover), and consequently must have been completed before his death in 581/1185 and the succession of his son Quṭb ad-Dīn Sukmān.[20] The detailed description of this palace door, included in his self-composed oeuvre-catalog, testifies to the elaborate skills of al-Jazarī as a gifted master metalworker who combined cast bronze with metal inlays in several variations. In his own words he lauds this exceptional door in rhymed prose: "It is the chef-d'oeuvre, to view it saddles are strapped on. Truly it is the pearl, the orphan, a priceless possession."[21] This unusual self-esteem seems justified.[22] Most remarkable, for instance, are the two door knockers of cast bronze "in the shape of two connected serpents, the head of one facing the head of the other" (pl. 21a). Nothing remains from the original works of al-Jazarī. But the closest parallel, by chance, is provided by a brass-plated door from the Great Mosque of his hometown Cizre/Jazīrat Ibn ʿUmar, now in the Türk ve Islam Eserleri Müzesi in Istanbul (pl. 18b).[23] On this door, which by comparison makes the mastery of al-Jazarī even more apparent, two door knockers with intertwined pairs of dragons in cast bronze clearly reflect his invention for the palace door at Diyarbakır. That door knockers of this type were widely dispersed is confirmed by a third example, probably from the same mold, discovered in 1912 quite far away, at Tiflis (Tibilisi) in Georgia, which is now in the Berlin Museum of Islamic Art (pl. 21b).[24]

Later in his career, al-Jazarī turned to the creation of a score of mechanical devices, for use at the court of Quṭb ad-Dīn Sukmān (581/1185–597/1201), and after 595/1198–99 for his brother Nāṣir ad-Dīn Maḥmūd, on whose suggestion he compiled and illustrated his treatise, completed in 602/1206. The autograph of al-Jazarī is lost, but within three months a second copy was made by a certain Muḥammad b. Yūsuf b. ʿUṯmān al-Ḥiṣkafī, another artist from Hasankeyf, which is preserved in the library of the Topkapı Saray in Istanbul.[25] This second edition, and a score of later copies, documents al-Jazarī's achievements in detail.[26] Here, in this connection, at least two features should be stressed. The first is his frequent and unprecedented inclusion of human figures in his mechanical devices. Illustrations depicting those devices included in manuscripts of his text often have a lively character (pl. 20a). These illustrations, reminiscent of the zodiac refliefs on the bridge in his home town of Cizre discussed above, inaugurate a new style of painting (pl. 20b). And second, even more informative for the cultural climate of the Artuqid court is his dependence on Greek and early Islamic treatises about mechanical devices, which were not only used, but also further improved.[27]

ARTUQID COINAGE A similar development is in evidence in the coinage of the Artuqids, characterized by seemingly syncretistic images. As Nicholas Lowick indicated in a recent study, minting started in 542/1147–48, shortly after a copper mine had been detected in the vicinity of Silvan/Mayāfāriqīn.[28] Though copying of Byzantine prototypes with Christian iconography (pl. 21c, 3) persisted for some time, royal portraits soon became the main focus, modeled after Hellenistic examples (pl. 21c, 1–6), together with images of the ruler in Oriental fashion (pl. 21c, 7, 10). But from 582/1186–87 onward, astrological motifs were increasingly favored (pl. 21c, 8–9), a result of the same popular belief as the figural stone reliefs on the bridges of the Upper Tigris (pl. 20b).

The same receptivity is reflected by the architecture of the Artuqid period, as represented at Hasankeyf by the monumental Tigris bridge, which can be evaluated as an engineering masterwork of daring design, rivaling its Classical predecessors not only in the remarkable perfection of stone masonry, but also with the human representations incorporated into the architectural decoration.

2. AIYŪBID REVIVAL (SECOND AND THIRD QUARTER OF THE EIGHTH/FOURTEENTH CENTURY)

At Hasankeyf the Artuqid renaissance faded out with the transfer of the court to the neighboring city of Diyarbakır. But this shift of attention only proved to be temporary. The turmoil of the mid-seventh/thirteenth century, caused by the Mongol invasion, was survived by only two principalities centered on the most impregnable fortresses of eastern Anatolia, Mardin and Hasankeyf. At Mardin a branch of the Artuqid family ruled until the conquest by the Türkmen Qarā Qoyūnlū in 813/1410.[29] And at Hasankeyf, an Aiyūbid dynasty of Kurdish origin even outlived the invasion of Tīmūr and the brief Āq Qoyūnlū occupation, until subdued by the Ottoman army in 922/1516.[30]

This particular branch of the Aiyūbid family is directly linked to the prominent sultan of Egypt and Syria, aṣ-Ṣāliḥ Najm ad-Dīn Aiyūb (636/1239–647/1249), who as a prince received the citadel of Hasankeyf as a fief from his father, al-Kāmil Muḥammad, in 630/1232 following its capture from the Artuqids. After 636/1239 Hasankeyf served as the residence of his son al-Muʿaẓẓam Tūrān Shāh until he briefly succeeded his father as Aiyūbid sultan (647/1249–648/1250), only to be murdered during the Mamluk takeover in Egypt. Nevertheless, this unfortunate last Aiyūbid ruler is remembered as the founder of the local dynasty of Hasankeyf, where his son al-Muwaḥḥid ʿAbd Allāh, with considerable political skill, weathered the Mongol incursion and ruled unchallanged for over three decades until 693/1293.[31]

At the site nothing remains visible from this period of relative tranquility. Fortunately the topographer ʿIzz ad-Dīn Ibn Shaddād (d. 684/1285) provides a detailed eyewitness account of the city during the reign of al-Muwaḥḥid ʿAbd Allāh.[32] In the town he lists a Dār as-Salṭana, near the bridge, a mosque, three madrasas, four ḥammāms, mausolea, besides bazaars and caravanserais; and the citadel, where another mosque is mentioned, "had within its enclosure a green *maidān* and fields where enough wheat, barley and grain were grown to feed the inhabitants from year to year."[33] Tellingly, almost nothing of the historic fabric can be attributed to the buildings described. Probably after Ibn Shaddād's last visit to the area in 657/1259 the town fell into disrepair due to the Mongol invasion and the subsequent political instability.

In fact, as a result of the long-lasting conflict between the Mamluk empire of Egypt and the Īl Khānid empire of Iran, the city of Hasankeyf was also impoverished and deteriorated drastically. As described in the local chronicle *Ta'rīkh bait Aiyūb* by the historian Ḥasan Ibn al-Munshiʾ, in the early eighth/fourteenth century most of the inhabitants of the lower town had retreated to the ancient rock caves for safety, and even the Tigris bridge was no longer usable. But eventually, following the peace treaty between the Mamluk sultan an-Nāṣir Muḥammad (698/1299–741/1341 with interruptions) and the Īl Khān Abū Saʿīd (717/1317–736/1335) in 723/1323, prosperity again returned to the region. This is testified by Ibn al-Munshiʾ, who mentions several reconstruction and building projects in this period of revival.[34]

SMALL PALACE OF THE CITADEL Again, almost no traces have survived from this period either, though the new foundations may still be detected in the vast ruin area of the old town. Only in the citadel, a ruinous structure, called the Small Palace by Albert Gabriel (fig. 14, no. 6), can tentatively be associated with the rebuilding program described by Ibn al-Munshiʾ.[35]

Situated on the triangular nose of the rock plateau overlooking the town, this ruin of about 17 × 9 m consists of a single barrel-vaulted room, probably an *īwān,* the last part of a formerly larger complex. Built of rubble masonry with a masking coat of mortar, the smaller side on the exterior features a window frame of cut stone masonry, surmounted by a pair of lions (pl. 22a). Together with the flanking stucco medallions containing arabesque designs, the decoration at this façade transmits an imperial aura, appropriate for a princely resident.

Judging by its commanding location on top of the city, this intriguing ruin might have belonged to the constructions on the citadel commissioned by the Aiyūbid rulers for the improvement of their residence. Besides the restoration of the fortification and the construction of a new palace, even drinking water was piped up to the citadel plateau by specialists engaged from the north Mesopotamian city of Mosul, especially praised by the historian Ibn al-Munshiʾ.[36]

SULTAN SÜLEYMAN CAMII (I) Judging from epigraphy, building activities further accelerated after the middle of the eighth/fourteenth century in the time of the Aiyūbid sultan al-ʿĀdil Ghāzī (742/1341–768/1367). The first extant building inscription at Hasankeyf is situated on a ruinous complex of about 42 × 32 m below the citadel, locally known as Sultan Süleyman Camii (fig. 14, no. 11). Its east portal is dated by an inscription to 752/1351–52.[37] The same imperial patron al-ʿĀdil Ghāzī is also mentioned as founder of the attached cylindrical stone minaret (pl. 23a–b), though the date of 807/1404–5 falls within the reign of his son al-ʿĀdil Sulaimān (779/1377–827/1424). As sources attest to an earthquake shortly before then, it can be assumed that after the collapse of the initial minaret of al-ʿĀdil Ghāzī, the rebuilding was commissioned by the son in his father's name. The last building phase centered on a niched fountain on the east façade near the portal with the minaret, constructed in 181/1416 again by al-ʿĀdil Sulaimān. This imperial monument very probably can be associated with a mosque near the *maidān* of the town mentioned under the year 754/1353–54 in the chronicle *Ta'rīkh bait Aiyūb* of Ḥasan Ibn al-Munshiʾ.[38] In order to ensure an income for the continued upkeep of this building, which incorporated the remains of an old church, an endowment was created based on revenue generated by a village in the Ṭūr ʿAbdīn and by a mill and shops in the bazaar of Hasankeyf itself.

In the confusing mass of collapsed masonry from this structure, still in need of detailed analysis to permit a clearer picture of its complicated building history, two architectural parts can be distin-

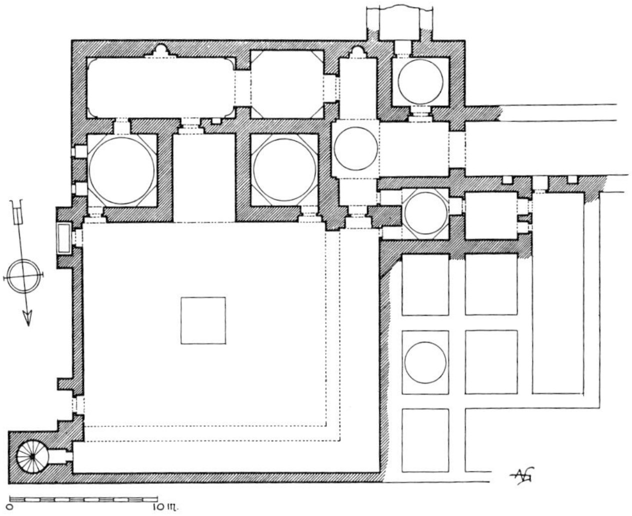

Fig. 17. Hasankeyf, Sultan Süleyman Camii/Madrasa of al-ʿĀdil Ghāzī: sketch plan, in scale 1:500 (after Gabriel [1940], fig. 52).

guished (fig. 17): a central *īwān* flanked by two domed chambers oriented toward an interior courtyard, and, attached on the west, a sophisticated T-shaped arrangement of three *īwāns* with a domed center, where the conspicuous west *īwān* again is flanked by two smaller domed chambers. Both wings are interconnected by an additional dome chamber and a rectangular prayer room featuring a *miḥrāb*. This quite unusual layout evidently is not related to the traditional hypostyle mosques of the region, but obviously represents a mosque-madrasa with integrated mausolea, most probably of the ruling Aiyūbid family.

Most of the structure is built of rubble masonry with thick layers of mortar; only the visible parts of the walls are set up in neat limestone masonry. On the interior the architectural decoration indicates the dominant role of the domed three-*īwān* structure. There the prayer niche of the south *īwān* received an incrustation of colored marble intarsia. But most unexpectedly, the central dome chamber features a lavish stucco decoration, reaching even into the vaulting (pl. 24a): a multifaceted *muqarnaṣ* transition with a sixteen-pointed star pattern fitted into a shallow dome. This truly exceptional stucco decoration of striking aesthetic quality is evidently quite unprecedented for the stone architecture of the region. Instead, it can be grouped with a small series of stylistically rather diverse decorations, probably all from the decade after the middle of the eighth/fourteenth century, marking the brief reappearance of stucco in the Arab countries from Upper Mesopotamia to Egypt.

Geographically the nearest of these contemporary stucco decorations is known from the Dār al-Fakhrī at Aleppo, an earlier structure remodeled some time before 765/1363–64, when one of the *īwāns* received an amazingly elaborate *muqarnaṣ* ceiling (pl. 24b).[39] Further south, at Damascus, the great mosque of the Mamluk governor Yalbughā al-Yaḥyawī, inaugurated in 757/1356, was decorated on the *qibla* wall with a stucco inscription frieze in kufic characters, signed by the craftsman Amrān b. Mahdī.[40] And at Cairo the *qibla īwān* of the monumental madrasa of the Mamluk sultan an-Nāṣir Ḥasan, erected from 757/1356 until 760/1359, shows a similar stucco frieze.[41] All this stucco decoration, created within only a few years, is not rooted in the local artistic tradition, and therefore is evidently the work of migrating artists, most probably of Iranian origin. The dates of the monuments graced by these stucco decorations reveal a movement from north to south, pointing to the Mamluk capital of Cairo as the destination of the artists' journey. En route the stucco specialists seem to have confined themselves to individual contracts commissioned by the local rulers in various locations. In the case of Hasankeyf the foreign specialists passing through were evidently engaged by the ruling Aiyūbid sultan al-ʿĀdil Ghāzī, in a period of political stability for the East Anatolian city-state.[42]

KOÇ CAMI At Hasankeyf the Iranian connection is even more evident in a second monument, the so-called Koç Cami (fig. 14, no. 12), immediately south of the Sultan Süleyman Cami.[43] Within a larger ruined area only the central portion of the structure, measuring about 20 × 35 m, is still visible. As Albert Gabriel documented in a reconstructed and simplified ground plan, prepared in 1932, the central axis of the *qibla* is emphasized by an *īwān* and dome progression which is flanked in turn by barrel-vaulted prayer halls and pairs of domed chambers (fig. 18). The building's exterior is dominated by unimpressive rough stone masonry, designed to be masked by a coat of plaster, which contrasts with the fine limestone masonry of the interior's structural components. The architectural quality of the original structure is only discernible in the rather

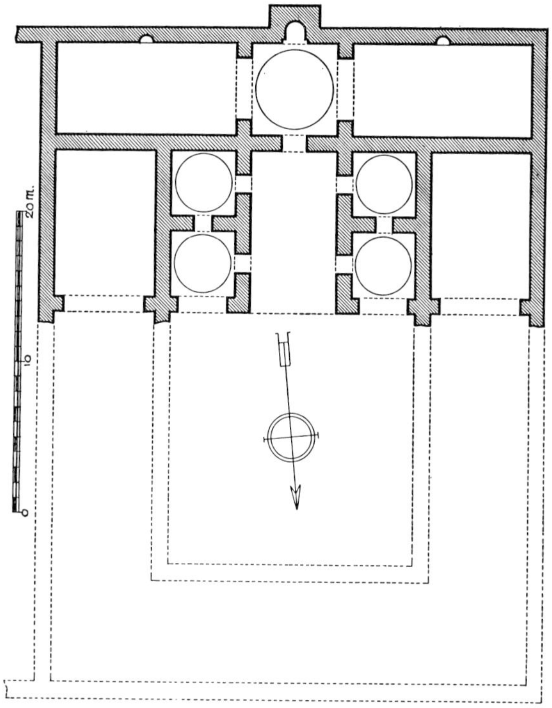

Fig. 18. Hasankeyf, Koç Cami/Madrasa of ʿAbd Allāh Ibn al-Mawardī: sketch plan, in scale 1:500 (after Gabriel [1940], fig. 54).

sophisticated *muqarnaṣ* dome behind the *īwān*. But most unusual are the two elaborate stucco *miḥrābs* on the *qibla* walls of the *īwān* and its attached domed chamber, which seem to have been executed by different although closely related hands.

The prayer niche of the domed chamber (pl. 19a), the less elaborate of the two, features a frame with a *naskhī* inscription on a densely filled scroll background, surmounted by another inscription panel with the *shahāda,* markedly different in style, and therefore probably of a somewhat later date. Rather peculiar is the flamboyant interior arch of the niche, resulting from a curvilinear partition line between a symmetrical arabesque pattern and the tight scrolls of the spandrels.

Even more sophisticated is the second prayer niche in the *īwān* (pl. 19b), where the rectangular frame contains a fine inscription of knotted *kūfī* over a delicate scroll. A similar arabesque scroll reappears in the shallow vault of the niche, while the secondary frame takes up the baroque design of the other *miḥrāb* in an even more flamboyant fashion. Most instructive are the foliated patterns of the spandrels and the upper panel, executed in high-relief stucco, tellingly including perforated secondary ornaments, especially common in Iranian stucco carvings.[44]

Though no exact parallels are known so far, these two neglected masterpieces of stucco work belong stylistically to the same class as the highly complicated stucco decoration of the late Īl Khānid Madrasa Shamsīya at Yazd, in southern Iran, constructed a few years before in 767/1365.[45] Consequently the anepigraphic monument at Hasankeyf must surely be contemporary with that in Yazd and thus also dates from the reign of the Aiyūbid al-ᶜĀdil Ghāzī. On the basis of its characteristic *īwān* and domed chamber sequence, which identifies it as a funerary madrasa rather than as an ordinary congregational mosque, this monument can probably be equated with a building project mentioned in a local chronicle. In the *Taʾrikh bait Aiyūb* Hasan Ibn al-Munshiʾ records that his grandfather *al-ḥājj* ᶜAbd Allāh ibn Muḥammad, known as Ibn al-Mawardī, one of the most influential court officials of the period, erected a madrasa.[46] As *wazīr* of the sultan al-ᶜĀdil Ghāzī he was in charge of administrative affairs from 751/1350–51 until his death in 762/1360–61, when he was buried in his madrasa. According to his grandson, the historian, a *khān* was eventually attached to this funerary madrasa, which was located near another earlier complex of identical function. With high probability the extant remains of the Koç Cami can be identified with Ibn al-Mawardī's madrasa and hence dated before 762/1360–61.

Both *miḥrābs* of this monument therefore can be regarded as additional examples for the previously documented varied group of stucco decorations in Iranian style. Stimulated to migrate by the disintegration of the Īl Khānid empire about the mid-eighth/fourteenth century, Iranian specialists were obviously instrumental in the transplantation of new decorative formulas and artistic media into areas that depended on totally different traditional architectural features.

Nevertheless, at Hasankeyf, as well as in the Arabic countries under Mamluk rule farther south, these stucco cycles did not spawn new traditions. Rather, the few examples of work by these migrating stucco specialists not only underscores the paucity of large-scale construction projects in the second half of the eighth/fourteenth century, but also attests to the devastating effects of the Black Death, which drastically reduced much of the population in the countries from the Tigris to the Nile. It reappeared, for instance, with deathly force in Hasankeyf in 775/1373–74, and was followed by a famine a year later.[47]

3. AIYŪBID ZENITH: REIGN OF AL-ᶜĀDIL SULAIMĀN

Most of the medieval-built fabric of Hasankeyf, according to epigraphy and the architectural style, dates from an even later period, when the town was ruled for nearly half a century by the Aiyūbid sultan al-ᶜĀdil Sulaimān (779/1377–827/1424). In this period, due to the considerable political skills of this ruler, the Aiyūbid city-state survived the invasions of the Mongol conqueror Tīmūr relatively unharmed, which in a marked contrast eventually caused the final collapse of the rivaling Artuqid dynasty in the neighboring city-state of Mardin in 813/1410.

The prevailing economic prosperity created a special cultural climate which finds a visible expression in the architecture of that time. al-ᶜĀdil Sulaimān's intellectual capacity at an early age is attested by the colophon in a volume of Ibn Shaddād's topography of Upper Mesopotamia (which includes a descriptive chapter on Hasankeyf), now in the Bodleian Library, Oxford; it states that he had personally transcribed that book in 789/1387.[48] The ruler's interest in the history of his principality also instigated Ḥasan ibn al-Munshiʾ to compose the *Taʾ rīkh bait Aiyūb,* largely in the course of a year, and to dedicate it to al-ᶜĀdil Sulaimān in 822/1419–20.[49]

CITADEL MOSQUE (II) The earliest of the eleven inscriptions from the time of al-ᶜĀdil Sulaimān, recorded by Jean Sauvaget at Hasankeyf in 1932, survives in the citadel mosque (fig. 14, no. 8), already briefly introduced in connection with the discussion of the Artuqid architecture of the site. From the fragmentary epigraphical information it can be deduced that the building or the rebuilding of the mosque was commissioned by the sultan in 796/1394. With the erection of a wooden minbar two years later in 798/1396, naming a certain Saᶜīd ash-Shāfiᶜī, the construction must have been terminated.[50]

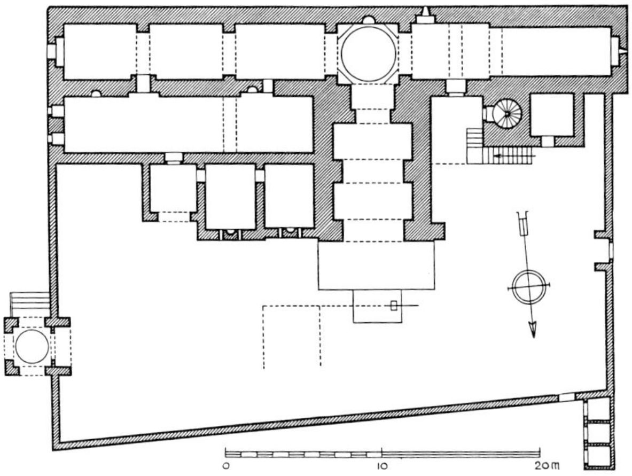

Fig. 19. Hasankeyf, Citadel Mosque: sketch plan, in scale 1:500 (after Gabriel [1940], fig. 46).

Although a detailed analysis might isolate sixth/twelfth century portions of its fabric, this structure's unusual "T-shaped" plan (fig. 19) bears a close resemblance to the central zone of the Koç Cami (fig. 18), identified earlier as the madrasa of Ibn al-Mawardī which was constructed before 762/1360–61. It can, therefore, be assumed that most of extant Citadel mosque belongs to this period of reconstruction.

SULTAN SÜLEYMAN CAMII (II) Next in date, after an interval of nearly a decade, relatively large-scale restoration work followed on the façade of the so-called Sultan Süleyman Cami (fig. 14, no. 11; fig. 17), which obviously served as a funerary complex of his father al-ᶜĀdil Ghāzī, founded in 752/1351–52.[51] First, in 807/1404–5, the minaret was rebuilt with a tall cylindrical shaft of fine stone masonry (pl. 23a–b), probably because of damage caused by the earthquake of 804/1401–2. About a decade later in 818/1416, a fountain was added to the façade. Tellingly identified in its inscription as a *qaṣṭal,* a distinctive term used for identical installations in the north Syrian capital of Aleppo, which lay about 420 km to the southwest, this final example of construction activity at Hasankeyf documents an improvement to its infrastructure through the piping in of drinking water.

JĀMIᶜ AR-RIZQ Evidently the main surviving religious monument of the ruler is the so-called ar-Rizq mosque (fig. 14, no. 10), near the bridge, built on a plot of c. 54 × 27 m and characterized by an arcaded interior courtyard (fig. 20).[52] Though the inscription on the heavily decorated portal of the north façade commemorating its foundation in 811/1409 does not specify this building's function, the tall cylindrical minaret on its northeast corner, rising to a height of almost 30 m clearly testifies to the building's predominant role as a mosque (pl. 23d). A secondary inscription on one of its interior doors identifies a series of rooms attached to its façade as living chambers and water installations.

The sanctuary on the southern side of the courtyard is composed of four interrelated room compartments in a reversed T-shaped arrangement, resulting from the outside projection of the second central room, restored in the sketch plan of Albert Gabriel (fig. 20) with a prayer niche. This particular room configuration, reversing the pattern of previous Aiyūbid mosques at Hasankeyf (figs. 17–19), bears a curious resemblance to almost contemporary early Ottoman *zāwiya*-mosques, as for instance the Muradiye Cami of 839/1435 in Edirne.[53]

The portal of the complex originally contained the signature of the responsible master masons and/or architects, *al-ḥājj* Muḥammad and his brother ᶜUmar, who were also the creators of its elaborately decorated minaret (pls. 23d, 25a–b), a landmark monument of Hasankeyf. The same specialists may well be responsible for the town's only other surviving minaret, at the Sultan Süleyman Cami (pl. 23a), a strikingly similar edifice dated to 807/1404–5 and thus four years older than that of the ar-Rizq mosque. The form and decoration of both monuments signal a close connection to the architectural school of Aleppo. Their cylindrical shafts, for instance, have a close parallel in the minaret of a mosque completed in the 769/1367 for the Mamluk governor Mankalībughā ash-Shamsī (pl. 23e).[54] Even more telling are several details of stone carving: a panel with interlacing bands on the front of the Süleyman Cami minaret's base (pl. 23b) is a faithful replica of a characteristic decorative feature first invented for the Māristān Arghūn of 755/1354–55 at Aleppo, frequently reappearing thereafter on Aleppo monuments (pl. 23c).[55] At the minaret of the Jāmiᶜ ar-Rizq, the richer example of these towers, the dentil pattern and double *muqarnaṣ* frames occur for the first time at Ha-

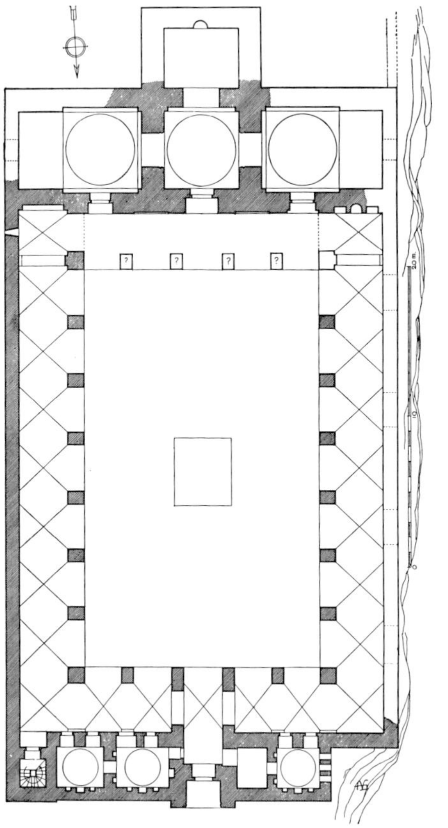

Fig. 20. Hasankeyf, Jāmiᶜ ar-Rizq: sketch plan, in scale 1:500 (after Gabriel [1940], fig. 50).

sankeyf (pl. 25b); they are features especially characteristic for the ornate style of Aleppo, first appearing there at the façades of the Jāmiᶜ al-Uṭrūsh, designed between 801/1399 and 802/1400 by the highly innovative artist Aḥmad al-Kutubī.[56] Though this style was followed at Aleppo by a few more monuments, as for instance by the Jāmiᶜ ad-Darraj with a façade signed by the master *(muᶜallim)* Muḥammad Ibn aṣ-Ṣawwāf (pl. 26c),[57] this development was suddenly interrupted by the conquest of Aleppo by Tīmūr in 803/1400, and therefore it can be assumed that some of the Aleppine construction specialists migrated to the prosperous Aiyūbid principality of Hasankeyf.[58]

But this can explain only part of the decorative program. Other features in turn are closely related to earlier monuments of the neighboring Artuqid city-state of Mardin, about 80 km southwest of Hasankeyf. The portal of the Jāmi^{c} ar-Rizq, for instance, is modeled after the entrance porch of the Sultan Isa Medrese at Mardin (pl. 25c), dated to 787/1385,[59] where the curious tear-shaped medallions of the lowest register of the minaret shaft (pl. 25a) were formulated for the first time. Therefore it can be assumed that construction specialists previously working at Mardin, where the Tīmūrid conquest of 796/1393–94 resulted in a decisive halt of building activities, joined their colleagues from Aleppo for the large-scale architectural projects of the early ninth/fifteenth century at Hasankeyf.

SMALL MOSQUE The extensive building program of that period also included a small *masjid* (fig. 14, no. 17) on an irregular plot, containing a prayer room of only 4 × 9 m and a rather large fountain with a round niche (fig. 21).[60] Its fragmentary inscription, in name of the sultan al-^{c}Ādil Sulaimān, describes this fountain as a *qaṣṭal,* a term used particularly in Aleppo. Ultimately this fountain constitutes another element in a larger water-works project and is linked to the system that channeled drinking water to the Jāmi^{c} ar-Rizq in 811/1409 and to the Sultan Süleyman Cami in 818/1416. Recorded by Albert Gabriel to have been in a ruined state of preservation in 1932, this tiny building seems to have vanished completely in the meantime.

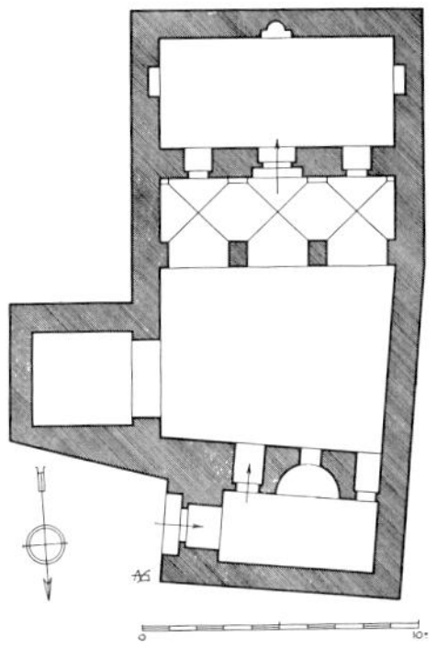

Fig. 21. Hasankeyf, Small Mosque: sketch plan, in scale 1:500 (after Gabriel [1940], fig. 55).

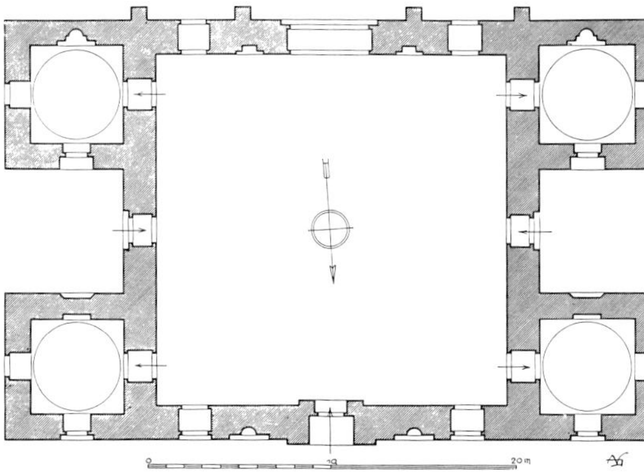

Fig. 22. Hasankeyf, Mausoleum: sketch plan, in scale 1:500 (after Gabriel [1940], fig. 56).

MAUSOLEUM Still another ruin (fig. 14, no. 18), located near the cluster of monuments in the old city center, which is distinguished by a peculiar, strictly symmetrical plan, can be attributed to the same period (fig. 22).[61] Attached to the sides of a square interior courtyard of 19 m, pairs of dome chambers project out, giving the impression that two *īwāns,* oriented toward the exterior and flanked by square domed rooms, were initially intended. By their prayer niches the southern dome chambers attest to the religious function of the monument. Consequently Albert Gabriel suggested that the rooms without *miḥrābs* on the northern side might have been used as mausolea.

The north side, oriented toward the center of the town, was designed as the principal façade of the monument and consequently received an especially rich stone decoration (pl. 26a). The portal, positioned on the central axis, features a kufic inscription frame, resembling the stucco frame of the *miḥrāb* in the *īwān* of the Koç Cami nearby (pl. 19b), as well as the portal frieze of the Sultan Isa Medrese of 787/1385 at Mardin and is flanked by two exterior prayer niches with *muqarnaṣ* vaults and stepped frames with complicated patterns. The windows, surmounted by ornamented lintels, are set into recessed niches (pl. 26b). This special feature relates to the façade style of Aleppo from the time preceding the Tīmūrid conquest. As the decorative program includes the characteristic dentil pattern of Aleppo origin, occurring for the first time at Hasankeyf on the minaret of the Jāmiᶜ ar-Rizq of 811/1409 (pl. 25b), this exceptional monument can also be attributed to the construction atelier from Aleppo employed by al-ʿĀdil Sulaimān for his ambitious building program. But curiously, all walls of the structure survived only up to a maximum height of 3 m, possibly indicating the monument's unfinished state.

CITADEL In addition, much of the effort of al-ʿĀdil Sulaimān was directed toward the improvement of the citadel, which must have served as the residence of the ruling patron. The access to the citadel plateau, a winding ramp (fig. 14, no. 1) near the northeastern spur of the rock, was fortified by three successive gates, of which the second (no. 3), according to an inscription, was constructed in the last years of al-ʿĀdil Sulaimān, between 821/1418 and his death in 827/1424 (pl. 22b).[62] The third gate (fig. 14, no. 2) can also be dated accordingly, as both show integrated buttresses on the outside corners, recalling the cylindrical minarets of the town (pl. 23a, d). The masonry is of very fine quality, matching the slightly earlier monuments of the city center, though the stone decoration, by its rather untectonic and partly floral patterns, attests to a certain degree of decadence.

4. ĀQ QOYŪNLŪ PERIOD (LATER NINTH/FIFTEENTH CENTURY)

The reign of al-ʿĀdil Sulaimān marked the peak of architectural activities at Hasankeyf. The absence of any traceable construction for the following five decades proves that despite the extensive architectural program in the first quarter of the ninth/fifteenth century, the Aleppine construction workshop was not to take root in the Aiyūbid city-state. Consequently, the latest two monuments of Hasankeyf belong to a decidedly different architectural tradition.

After a hiatus of half a century, new constructions were no longer commissioned by the Kurdish rulers from the Aiyūbid family, who still held on to the fortified citadel of Hasankeyf, but by the Türkmen overlords from the Āq Qoyūnlū confederation who held suzerainty in most of Upper Mesopotamia and southeastern Anatolia.[63]

ZEYNEL BEY TÜRBESI Following the final incorporation of Hasankeyf into the empire of the Āq Qoyūnlū ruler Ūzūn Ḥasan in 866/1462, building activities no longer centered on the traditional town but on the opposite side of the ancient bridge. According to an inscription above its entrance executed in multicolored cut-tile mosaic (pl. 27a), a brick mausoleum there with a 9 m diameter and unprecedented faïence decoration (fig. 14, no. 24; pl. 28a) was erected for Zainal, the son of Ūzūn Ḥasan[64] who perished in battle against the army of the Ottoman sultan Meḥmet Fātiḥ (484/1444–886/1481), renowned as the conqueror of Constantinople. The remains of this prince, who died in 878/1473, were eventually brought to Hasankeyf and buried in the newly built mausoleum.

MASHHAD IMĀM MUḤAMMAD B. ᶜABD ALLĀH AṬ-ṬAIYĀR The choice of this very location for the burial of the Āq Qoyūnlū prince seems to have been motivated by the existence of an ancient Shī ᶜite shrine nearby, associated locally with the *imām* Muḥammad b. ᶜAbd Allāh aṭ-Ṭaiyār (fig. 14, no. 23).[65] This rather unpretentious structure of c. 24 × 25 m, which also deserves a detailed architectural survey, is now an agglomerate of loosely connected architectural parts bordering an interior courtyard (fig. 23). An inscription on the entrance porch of the domed funerary chamber, until today closed off by a double wing door of delicate wood carving (pl. 28b), attests to the restoration of the shrine by Khalīl, another son of Ūzūn Ḥasan, in 878/1474.

Consequently it can be assumed that both constructions, the restoration of the shrine and the erection of the mausoleum, were executed simultaneously by the same patron. The major task evidently must have been the building of the mausoleum, commissioned to an imported construction atelier by Khalīl, the elder brother of the deceased prince, Zainal b. Ūzūn Ḥasan.

In form and decoration the mausoleum of Zainal is without parallel in the region. Despite its cylindrical exterior, the interior is octagonal in plan with niches on each side. The dome transition is provided by an intricate system of ascending *muqarnaṣ,* surmounted by an additional double ring of *muqarnaṣ* units. Most exceptional is the faïence decoration of the exterior (pl. 28a). Square *kūfī* inscriptions of "Allah" and "Muḥammad" in brick mosaic arranged in zigzag bands cover the cylindrical body. The entrance on the north (pl. 27a) as well as the opposite window feature cut-tile mosaic in turquoise, cobalt blue, yellow, black, and white of very high quality. The drum, pierced by four additional windows, has a decoration of brick mosaic

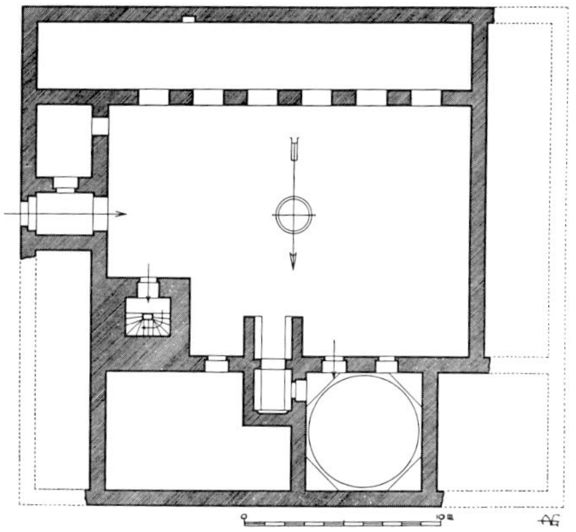

Fig. 23. Hasankeyf, Mashhad Imām Muḥammad b. ʿAbd Allāh aṭ-Ṭaiyār: sketch plan, in scale 1:500 (after Gabriel [1940], fig. 63).

in knotted zigzag design. Also the bulbous dome, probably originally composed of ribs rising from a *muqarnaṣ* transition, was once completely covered by glazed bricks. On the interior there are traces of a dado, with hexagonal turquoise tiles framed by a border of cobalt blue cut tiles. The upper zones of the dome chamber were completely plastered, and structural components were originally decorated with frescos as is evident in the cupola where portions of a star-shaped design are still visible.

As a whole this monument points to a connection with contemporary Iran.[66] Its closest parallels are to be found as far away as Tabrīz, in the Blue Mosque, built before 870/1465 for Ṣāliḥ Khānum, daughter of the Qarā Qoyūnlū Jahān Shāh,[67] or even at Iṣfahān, where the courtyard of the Masjid-i Jumʿa, or at least its south *īwān,* was decorated in 880/1475–76 by order of the Āq Qoyūnlū ruler Ūzūn Ḥasan,[68] father of the prince Zainal buried at Hasankeyf. Farther west only one other monument is also related to the Hasankeyf mausoleum, the Çinili Köşk at Istanbul, a palace commissioned by the Ottoman sultan Meḥmet Fātiḥ in 877/1472 (pl. 27b).[69]

Pīr Ḥasan b. *ustādh* ʿAbd ar-Raḥmān, whose name is inscribed on the entrance niche of the Zeynel Bey Türbe with blue-and-white tiles, may have been one of the leading members of a peripatetic workshop whose work is seen first at Tabrīz, then on a palace in Istanbul. Later they may have paused briefly at Hasankeyf on their return to Iran working on the mausoleum of the Āq Qoyūnlū prince Zainal before moving to Iṣfahān where they embellished the Friday Mosque. During their residence at Hasankeyf this workshop obviously joined forces with stone cutters from the region who built the mausoleum's masonry foundations which curiously also extend to a considerable height into the building's walls.

TIGRIS BRIDGE (II) Possibly a similar joint atelier also reconstructed the Artuqid bridge on the Tigris (fig. 15.1; pl. 16a). According to the testimony of *Ta'rīkh Bait Aiyūb,* by the early eighth/fourteenth century this structure, of prime importance for the city of Hasankeyf, was unusable.[70] Although it had already been restored during the reign of the Aiyūbid sultan al-ʿĀdil Ghāzī, the inclusion of brick masonry, particularly with turquoise glazed bricks, suggests that further repairs were made in 878/1474 when the group of Iranian craftsmen was active in the northern suburb of Hasankeyf, on the left bank of the Tigris.[71]

5. SOUTHWEST VERSUS EAST

The Āq Qoyūnlū, as well as the Iranian workshop, constituted only a brief interlude in the history of Hasankeyf. Although a branch of the Aiyūbid family ultimately continued to rule the town and region until its definitive incorporation into the Ottoman Empire, this continuity does not imply that the area had regained its former importance. For example, the addition, in 927/1520–21, of a minaret, signed by the architect Farabī(?) b. ʿUthmān as-Saʿdī,[72] to the citadel mosque (pl. 16b) suggests it was the only religious structure in use at that time, an obvious sign of the traditional city's decline.

Though only part of the original built fabric of Hasankeyf has been recorded and investigated, it is quite obvious that there were simply insufficient construction tasks to maintain a permanent local community of builders. Therefore, in periods of prosperity, specialized workshops had to be assembled to meet the demands of the local rulers. In the case of Hasankeyf, external factors probably played a greater role in determining which craftsmen were available than did the intent of its patrons.

Only in the formative period of the sixth/twelfth century, when Upper Mesopotamia was one of the main cultural centers, was a local style of architecture formulated for the region, one closely interrelated with the stone architecture of northern Syria. In later periods, there were periodic shifts in the predominate source of influences affecting the area. Thus, a dependence on the skills of craftsmen from Īl Khānid Iran in the mid eighth/fourteenth century was followed in the early ninth/fifteenth century by close links with the architectural traditions of Mamluk Aleppo. Finally, in the later ninth/fifteenth century, an Iranian connection again predominates.

This periodic shifting of stylistic allegiance is the basic feature of Hasankeyf architecture. Its location at the juncture of different artistic traditions finds visual expression in the syncretistic features of the historic fabric in Hasankeyf, which includes some of the most extraordinary monuments within the borders of Turkey. In this respect it is tragic that this important heritage of the Islamic past will eventually be sacrificed to the demands of changing modern society.

Notes

1. On these other cities of the area, see for instance the recent monographs by Ara Altun, *Mardin'de türk devri mimarisi* (Istanbul, 1971); *Anadolu'da Artuklu devri türk mimarisi'nin gelismesi* (Istanbul, 1978); and by Metin Sözen, *Diyarbakır'da türk mimarisi* (Istanbul, 1971).
2. Gabriel (1940), pp. 55–82: "Ḥiṣn Kayfa," figs. 44–66, pls. 34–46.
3. Jean Sauvaget, in Gabriel (1940), pp. 305–310 nos. 23–37, pls. 105/no. 29, 107/no. 31.
4. A description of the current situation of Hasankeyf is included in the reference work of Thomas Alan Sinclair, *Eastern Turkey: An Architectural and Archaeological Survey* III (London, 1989), pp. 230–239, 426, pls. 110–115; IV (London, 1990), p. 368; see also the companion publication of a recent photographic exhibition displayed in 1992 in Stuttgart and Berlin: Gerhard Väth, *Hasankeyf am Tigris: Stiller Untergang einer Stadt in Kurdistan* (Würzburg, 1992), with photographs by Rüdiger Kuhn.
5. According to a lecture by Oluş M. Arık, delivered on 20.6.1989 at the German Archaeological Institute, Berlin, photogrammetric surveys have been conducted together with clearing operations in at least two seasons since 1987. On recent results of this ongoing research project, see Oluş M. Arik, "Hasankeyf kazısı," *9th International Congress of Turkish Art, Istanbul, 1991* (forthcoming).
6. For this period the basic reference work is the recent monograph by Carole Hillenbrand, *A Muslim Principality in Crusader Times: The Early Artuqid State* (Istanbul, 1990); see also her series of articles: "The establishment of Artuqid power in Diyār Bakr in the twelfth century," *Studia Islamica* 54, 1981, pp. 129–153; "The career of Najm al-Dīn Il-Ghāzī," *Der Islam* 58, 1981, pp. 250–292; "The history of the Jazīra, 1100–1250: A short introduction," in Julian Raby,

ed., *The Art of Syria and the Jazīra 1100–1250,* Oxford Studies in Islamic Art I (Oxford, 1985), pp. 9–18.

7. Gabriel (1940), pp. 70–79, figs. 57–62, pls. 39–41; Cevdet Çulpan, *Türk taş köprüleri: Ortaçağdan Osmanlı devri sonuna kadar* (Ankara, 1975), pp. 38–40 no. 23, pls. 29–30, figs. 23.1–6; Altun (1978), pp. 194–195, figs. 258–264; cf. also notes 46, 71, below.
8. The confusing remark by a later annotator of the geography of Ibn Ḥauqal (written about 378/988), discussed by Gabriel (1940), p. 77, note 2, should be interpreted in the light of information supplied by Ibn al-Azraq, quoted by Carole Hillenbrand, *op.cit.,* note 6 (1990), p. 114, note 41; and in *Studia Islamica* 54, 1981, p. 150, note 5. On the historian Ibn al-Azraq, see Claude Cahen, "Le Diyâr Bakr au temps des premiers Urtuḳides," *Journal asiatique* 227, 1935, pp. 219–276; and Carole Hillenbrand, "Some medieval Islamic approaches to source material: The evidence of a 12th century chronicle," *Oriens* 27–28, 1981, pp. 197–225.
9. Estelle Whelan, "Representations of the *Khāṣṣikīyah* and the origins of Mamluk emblems," in Priscilla P. Soucek, ed., *Content and Context of Visual Arts in the Islamic World. Papers from a Colloquium in Memory of Richard Ettinghausen* (University Park and London, 1988), pp. 219–243, esp. p. 222, figs. 9–12.
10. Gabriel (1940), pp. 232–236, fig. 175, pls. 81–83; Çulpan, *op.cit.,* note 7 (1975), pp. 40–44 no. 24, pls. 21–2 figs. 24.1–5. The inscription of 542/1147–48 published by Sauvaget, in Gabriel (1940), p. 345 no. 128; cf. *RCEA* no. 3134 (correcting no. 4 bis). Eventually a certain Abu l-Khair al-Fāsūl, mentioned by Ibn al-Azraq, can be credited for this architectural achievement; Carole Hillenbrand, *op.cit.,* note 6 (1990) 111, 113–115, 188:7–8, 190:9–16; see also Leon Ary Mayer, *Islamic Architects and Their Works* (Geneva, 1956), p. 38.
11. Nothing has been added so far to the survey conducted in 1909 by Konrad Preusser, *Nordmesopotamische Baudenkmäler altchristlicher und islamischer Zeit* (Leipzig, 1911), pp. 26–28, fig. 6, pls. 38–40; repeated by Çulpan, *op.cit.,* note 7 (1975), pp. 44–48 no. 25, pls. 23–4 figs. 25.1–3. The date of this monument and the interpretation are based on Ernst Herzfeld, "Der Thron des Khosrô," *Jahrbuch der Preussischen Kunstsammlungen* 41, 1920, pp. 138–139, note 2, figs. 32–33; supplemented by Willy Hartner, "The pseudoplanetary nodes of the moon's orbit in Hindu and Islamic iconographies," *Ars Islamica* 4, 1938, pp. 114–120, fig. 2.
12. Gabriel (1940), pp. 62–63, figs. 47–48, pl. 36.2; see also Altun (1978), pp. 211, 281, plan 26, figs. 287–290, where the plan layout is linked to Turkestan predecessors.
13. Gabriel (1940), p. 61, fig. 46, pl. 37.4; Sauvaget, in Gabriel (1940), p. 306 nos. 24–26.
14. Orhan C. Tuncer, "Cizre Ulu Camii ve medresesi," *Yıllık Araştırmalar Dergisi* 3, 1981, pp. 95–105, illus. 4–29, 32–52, drawings 1–5, 9.
15. Gabriel (1940), pp. 221–228, figs. 167–172, pls. 77–79; Sauvaget, in Gabriel (1940), pp. 343–344 nos. 123–124, pl. 109 no. 124.
16. Gabriel (1940), pp. 46–51, figs. 37–40, pls. 26–32; Sauvaget in Gabriel (1940), pp. 302–303 nos. 18, 18 bis.

17. Tom (Thomas Alan) Sinclair, "Early Artuqid mosque architecture," in Julian Raby, ed., *The Art of Syria and the Jazīra 1100–1250,* Oxford Studies in Islamic Art I (Oxford, 1985), pp. 49–67, figs. 1–8. For the dependence of the plan type of these mosques on Seljuq models in Iran and their relations to other neighboring regions, see Michael Meinecke, "The Great Mosques of Southeastern Anatolia: A genetic approach," *9th International Congress of Turkish Art, Istanbul, 1991* (forthcoming).
18. Ismāʿīl Ibn ar-Razzāz al-Jazarī, *al-jāmiʿ bain al-ʿilm wa l-ʿamal an-nāfiʿ fi ṣ-ṣināʿat al-ḥiyal,* ed. Aḥmad Yūsuf al-Ḥasan (Aleppo, 1979); facsimile edition of ms. Ahmet III no. 3472, Topkapı Sarayı Library, Istanbul: Kültür Bakan-lığı, ed. *Olağanüstü mekanik araçların bilgisi hakkında kitap* (Ankara, 1990); trans. Donald R. Hill, *The Book of Knowledge of Ingenious Mechanical Devices* (Dordrecht and Boston, 1974).
19. The biography of al-Jazarī was ingeniously defined recently by Rachel Ward, "Evidence for a school of painting at the Artuqid court," in Julian Raby, ed., *The Art of Syria and Jazīra 1100–1250,* Oxford Studies in Islamic Art I (Oxford, 1985), pp. 69–83, figs. 1–8.
20. On the dates of the Diyarbakır door, see Michael Meinecke, "Islamische Drachentüren," *Museumsjournal, Berliner Museen,* new series 3, 4, 1989, pp. 54–58, esp. p. 57, with illus.
21. Quoted after Hill, *op.cit.,* note 18 (1974), p. 191. For the chapter in the treatise, see: ed. al-Ḥasan, *op.cit.,* note 18 (1979), pp. 469–478, figs. 143–149, color plate on p. 524; trans. Hill (1974), pp. 191–195, 274, figs. 142–195; and Eilhard Wiedemann and Fritz Hauser, "Über eine Palasttür und Schlösser nach al-Ĝazarī," *Der Islam* 11, 1921, pp. 214–231, figs. 1–16.
22. For an assessment of the metalwork techniques, see Eva Baer, *Metalwork in Medieval Islamic Art* (New York, 1983), pp. 1–4.
23. Exhibition catalogue, *The Anatolian Civilisations* III (Istanbul, 1983), pp. 60–61 nos. D.95–97, with illus. and color pl. Documented in situ by Preusser, *op.cit.,* note 11 (1911), pp. 25–26, pl. 36. One of the two door knockers was purchased in 1973 by the David Collection, Copenhagen; Kjeld von Folsach, *Islamic Art: The David Collection* (Copenhagen, 1990), p. 184, fig. on p. 185, illus. 323.
24. Inv. no. I.2242. First published by Ernst Diez, "Ein seldschukischer Türklopfer," *Zeitschrift für bildende Kunst* 56, 1921, pp. 18–20, with illus.
25. Topkapı Sarayı Library, Aḥmet III no. 3472; described by Ivan Stchoukine, "Un manuscrit du traité d'al-Jazarī, sur les automates du VIIᵉ siècle de l'hégire," *Gazette des Beaux Arts* 76, 6th series 11, 1934, pp. 134–140; see also the facsimile edition cited in note 18.
26. On the Mamluk copies of the treatise, see Duncan Haldane, *Mamluk Painting* (Warminster, 1978).
27. Kurt Weitzmann, "The Greek sources of Islamic scientific illustrations," in George C. Miles, ed., *Archaeologica orientalia in memoriam Ernst Herzfeld* (Locust Valley, 1952), pp. 244–266. Another example of scientific treatises from the Artuqid context is an illustrated manuscript of the *Catalogue of Fixed Stars* by ʿAbd ar-Raḥmān aṣ-Ṣūfī (d.376/986) in the Fātih Library at Istanbul (no.

3422), copied in 529/1134–35 at Mardin by ʿAbd Allāh al-Jabalī, mentioned by Kurt Holter, "Die islamischen Miniaturhandschriften vor 1350," *Zentralblatt für Bibliothekswesen* 54, 1937, p. 3 no. 3. Also the famous pseudo-Galen manuscript, the treatise on *Theriaca/ Kitāb ad-diryāq* of 595/1199 in the Bibliothèque Nationale in Paris (ms. arabe, no. 2964) would fit especially well into this group; Bishr Farès, *Le Livre de la Thériaque* (Cairo, 1953). On this subject recently, see Nahla Nassar, "Saljuq or Byzantine: Two related styles of Jazīran miniature painting," in Julian Raby, ed., *The Art of Syria and the Jazīra 1100–1250,* Oxford Studies in Islamic Art I (Oxford, 1985), pp. 85–98. The existence of a large library at Hasankeyf is also proved by the Syrian prince Usāma Ibn Munqid (d.594/1188), who on the invitation of Qarā Arslān lived for a decade at the Artuqid court, where he compiled, among other works, an anthology of old Arabic poetry; for this see his *Kitāb al-iʿtibār,* trans. and ed. Philip Khûri Hitti (New York, 1929; Princeton, 1930).

28. Nicholas Lowick, "The religious, the royal and the popular in the figural coinage of the Jazīra," in Julian Raby, ed., *The Art of Syria and the Jazīra 1100–1250,* Oxford Studies in Islamic Art I (Oxford, 1985), pp. 159–174; on the same topic see also the more recent study by William F. Spengler and Wayne G. Sayles, *Turkoman Figural Bronze Coins and their Iconography* (Lodi, Wisconsin, 1992); cf. also Lutz (Ludger) Ilisch, "Die älteste artuqidische Kupferprägung," *Münstersche Numismatische Zeitung* 6/69, 1976, pp. 1–2, with illus.
29. Ludger Ilisch, Geschichte der Artuqidenherrschaft von Mardin zwischen Mamluken und Mongolen 1260–1410 A.D. (Ph.D. Münster, 1984); see also Gerhard Väth, *Die Geschichte der artuqidischen Fürstentümer in Syrien und der Ĝazīra'l-Furātīya (496–812/1002–1409)* (Berlin, 1987).
30. The history of the Aiyūbids at Hasankeyf has yet to be researched in detail. The only basic study so far is Claude Cahen's "Contribution à l'histoire du Diyâr Bakr au quatorzième siècle," *Journal Asiatique* 243, 1955, pp. 65–100. Information on the local mint is available in the catalog of Paul Balog, *The Coinage of the Ayyūbids* (London, 1980), pp. 267–283 nos. 886–926, pls. 45/888–47/926. See also the general surveys by Besim Darkot, "Hisn Keyfâ," *İslâm Ansiklopedisi* V (Istanbul, 1950), pp. 452–454, with 9 illus.; Nazmi Sevgen, *Anadolu kaleleri* I (Ankara, 1960), pp. 132–136, with 2 figs.; and Solange Ory, "Ḥiṣn Kayfā," *Encyclopaedia of Islam* III (Leiden and London, 1971), pp. 506–509, with map.
31. For the initial decades of Aiyūbid rule at Hasankeyf, see R. Stephen Humphreys, *From Saladin to the Mongols: The Ayyubids of Damascus, 1193–1260* (Albany, 1977).
32. ʿIzz ad-Dīn Ibn Shaddād, *al-Aʿlāq al-khaṭīra fī dhikr Umarāʾ ash-Shām wa l-Jazīra* III/2, ed. Yaḥyā ʿAbbāra (Damascus, 1978), pp. 529–535; summarized by Claude Cahen, "La Djazira an milieu du treizième siècle d'après ʿIzz ad-din ibn Chaddâd," *Revue des Études Islamiques* 8, 1934 (1937), pp. 109–128, esp. 115–116.
33. Quoted after Carole Hillenbrand, *op.cit.*, note 6 (1985), p. 16.
34. The building information from the chronicle, of which only the first part until the year 778/1376–77 has survived in the Vienna Nationalbibliothek, is listed

without further specification by Cahen, *Journal Asiatique* 243, 1955, pp. 95–96. For the identification of the author, see Ilisch, *op.cit.*, note 29 (1984), pp. 13–14.

35. Gabriel (1940), p. 63, fig. 49, pl. 36/1. Gabriel argues for a later date in the early ninth/fifteenth century on the basis of a technical detail, the bottle-like pottery elements used for the vault construction. But as the other monuments of Hasankeyf characterized by this method of construction can again be attributed to the eighth/fourteenth century—also because of the rubble masonry with plaster coating—an earlier date seems much more probable.
36. Probably also part of the Mashhad Imām Muḥammad b. ʿAbd Allāh aṭ-Ṭaiyār, discussed below, belongs to this period. The shrine was desecrated by the Artuquid army from Mardin in 736/1335; see Ilisch, *op.cit.*, note 29 (1984), pp. 94–95. The curious tower of rubble masonry, featuring a ring of large size mortar *muqarnaṣ* in a rather archaic fashion, may prove to belong to the subsequent restoration.
37. Gabriel (1940), pp. 66–67, figs. 52–53, pls. 37/1, 44/3, 45/1, 46/5–7; Sauvaget, in Gabriel (1940), pp. 307–308 nos. 30–33, pl. 107 no. 31; *RCEA* no. 6173.
38. This identification was already suggested by Cahen, *Journal Asiatique* 243, 1955, p. 95.
39. The stucco decoration was recently destroyed together with the mosque; Meinecke (1992), I, pp. 93–94, note 170, pl. 55c; II, p. 238 no. 22/2.
40. Meinecke (1992), II, pp. 225–226 no. 19 B/15, pl. 80 c–d.
41. Meinecke (1992), I, pp. 121–122, pls. 80a, 82c; II, pp. 224–225 no. 19 B/13; see also II, pp. 235–236 no. 21/8.
42. For a discussion of the whole group of Mamluk stucco decorations and their connection with Hasankeyf, see Meinecke (1992), I, pp. 129–130. In addition, the relations of the Hasankeyf dome (pl. 24a) with the strikingly close formal parallels at the monastery of Mār Behnām/Khiḍr Eliā, about 35 km southeast of Mosul, attributed to the mid-seventh/thirteenth century, remain to be researched; documented by Preusser, *op.cit.* note 11 (1911), pp. 5–6, pls. 5, 6.2; cf. J. M. Fiey, *Assyrie chrétienne: Contribution à l'étude de l'histoire et de la géographie ecclésiastiques et monastiques du nord de l'Iraq* (Beirut, 1965), I, pp. 565–609, esp. pp. 605–606.
43. Gabriel (1940), pp. 68–69, fig. 54, pls. 37/2, 45/3–4.
44. *SPA* II (1939), figs. 473–475. The small medallion above the apex of the niche contains the undeciphered signature of the stucco worker (Richard Brotherton, pers. comm.).
45. Donald N. Wilber, *The Architecture of Islamic Iran: The Il Khānid Period* (Princeton, 1955), p. 186 no. 107, pls. 205–207.
46. Cahen, *Journal Asiatique* 243, 1955, p. 95. According to his grandson-historian, this personality also reactivated the ruinous Tigris bridge (see notes 7, 71) and personally designed the wooden center part (Lutz Ilisch, pers. comm.). Consequently the timber construction mentioned by later travelers, and indicated on the reconstructed elevation by Albert Gabriel, does not belong to the original Artuqid design.
47. Ilisch, *op.cit.*, note 29 (1984), pp. 128, 183.

48. Following Ilisch p. 14.
49. Ilisch (1984), p. 15.
50. Cf. note 13.
51. Cf. note 37.
52. Gabriel (1940), pp. 64–66, figs. 50–51, pls. 44/2, 46/1–3; Sauvaget apud Gabriel (1940), pp. 306–307 nos. 27–29; see also Gertrude Lowthian Bell, *Palace and Mosque at Ukhaiḍir: A Study in Early Mohammadan Architecture* (Oxford, 1914), p. 133, pl. 84/1.
53. Ayverdi II (1972), pp. 405–415, figs. 706–723. On the architectural type, see Ahmet Işık Doğan, *Osmanlı mimarisinde tarikat yapıları: Tekkeler, zaviyeler ve benzer nitelikteki fütuvvet yapıları* (Istanbul, 1977); and for the role in the mosque development of the Ottoman period, see Aptullah Kuran, *The Mosque in Early Ottoman Architecture* (Chicago and London, 1968), pp. 71–136.
54. Meinecke (1992), I, pp. 133–134, fig. 43, pl. 90a; II, p. 236 no. 21/9.
55. Meinecke (1992), I, pl. 70a; II, pp. 220–221 no. 20/20. On this decorative detail, *op. cit.*, I, p. 114, pl. 70b–e.
56. Meinecke (1992), I, pp. 134–135, fig. 88, pls. 91b, 92a, 99b, 128b, 140d; II, pp. 295–206 no. 26A/2, 308 no. 26B/24.
57. Meinecke (1992), I, p. 135, pls. 91d, 99d; II, p. 297 no. 26A/9.
58. For a discussion of the impact of Mamluk architecture on Hasankeyf, see Meinecke (1992), I, pp. 149–150, where also the identification of one of the responsible architects of the Jāmiʿ ar-Rizq, *al-ḥājj* Muḥammad, with the architect of the Jāmiʿ ad-Darraj at Aleppo (see note 57), Muḥammad Ibn aṣ-Ṣawwāf, has tentatively been proposed.
59. Gabriel (1940), pp. 28–33, figs. 22–25, pls. a–b, e/1, 8/3, 12–15, 18/1, 19/2–3, 20/1–3; Sauvaget in Gabriel (1940), pp. 300–302 nos. 14–17. On the connection of the late Artuqid architecture of Mardin with the development of Mamluk Aleppo, see Meinecke (1992), I, pp. 143–149.
60. Gabriel (1940), p. 69, fig. 55; Sauvaget, in Gabriel (1940) pp. 308–309 no. 34.
61. Gabriel (1940), pp. 69–70, fig. 56.
62. Gabriel (1940), pp. 59–60, fig. 45, pls. 34/2, 35/1, 38/1–3; Sauvaget, in Gabriel (1940), p. 305 no.23.
63. John E. Woods, *The Aqqoyunlu: Clan, Confederation, Empire* (Minneapolis and Chicago, 1976). On the preserved monuments of this period in Anatolia, see Metin Sözen, *Anadolu'da Akkoyunlu mimarisi* (Istanbul, 1981).
64. Gabriel (1940), pp. 80–81, figs. 65–66, pls. 42–44/1; Sauvaget, in Gabriel (1940), pp. 309–310 nos. 36–37; building inscription republished by Jaques Jarry, "Inscriptions syriaques et arabes inédites du Ṭur ʿAbdīn," *Annales Islamologiques* 10, 1972, p. 232 no. 53, pl. 67/no. 53; see also Sözen (1981), pp. 148–152, fig. 48, illus. 114–119.
65. Gabriel (1940), pp. 79–90, figs. 63–64, pls. 38/4, 45/2, 4; Sauvaget, in Gabriel (1940), p. 309 nos. 35, 35 bis.; cf. Sözen (1981), pp. 140–142, fig. 44, illus. 104–106. The complete name of the venerated *imām* is mentioned by Ibn al-Munshiʾ in connection with events in 736/1335; see Ilisch, *op.cit.*, note 29, (1984), p. 95. For older parts of the structure, see note 36.

66. On the Iran connection of the Zeynel Bey Türbe see Meinecke (1976), I, pp. 96–98; II, pp. 153–155 no. 43.

67. Lisa Golombek and Donald Wilber, *The Timurid Architecture of Iran and Turan* (Princeton, 1988), pp. 407–409 no. 214, fig. 140, pls. 415–426, color pl. 15b: see also Robert Byron, "Timurid architecture: General trends," *SPA* II (1939), pp. 1130–1131; IV (1938), pls. 452–456.

68. André Godard, "Historique du Masdjid-é Djumʿa d'Iṣfahān," *Aṯhār-é Īrān* 1, 1936, pp. 246–256, figs. 164–169.

69. Ayverdi IV (1974), pp. 736–775, figs. 1056a–z. This relation already indicated by Meinecke (1976), 1, pp. 114–118; and lately by Walter B. Denny, "Points of stylistic contact in the architecture of Islamic Iran and Anatolia," *Islamic Art* 2, 1987, pp. 33–34, figs. 10–11, pl. 2/B; followed by Nurhan Atasoy and Julian Raby, *Iznik: The Pottery of Ottoman Turkey* (London, 1989), p. 89, attributing the decoration of the Çinili Köşk to tile cutters from Khurāsān.

70. Cahen, *Journal Asiatique* 243, 1955, p. 95; Ilisch, *op.cit.*, note 29 (1984), p. 86; on the buildings see note 7, above.

71. To this period also belongs an anonymous madrasa at Cizre/Jazīrat Ibn ʿUmar, locally called the Red Madrasa because at the brick masonry; published by Orhan C. Tuncer, "Mardin-Cizre Kırmızı Medrese," *Vakıflar Dergisi* 10, 1978, pp. 425–434, figs. 1–26, drawings 1–3. Despite the attribution to the early eighth/fourteenth century, the network vaulting definitely indicates to the ninth/fifteenth century.

72. The minaret seems to have been rather unimpressive, as was the artist's signature, carved in plaster; Sauvaget, in Gabriel (1940), p. 306 no. 26.

CHAPTER 4

Mamluk Architecture and the Ottoman Empire: The Formation of New Architectural Styles

The discussion in this chapter centers on the phenomenon of the emergence of a new style of architecture in the Ottoman empire, the most recent climax of Islamic architecture from an international perspective. Ottoman architecture is almost inevitably associated in our memories with towering mosque constructions on the seven hills of Istanbul, gracing the townscape with their ascending domes and slender pairs of minarets, and characterized on the interior by sumptuous multicolored tile revetments. That these architectural masterpieces originate mostly from the golden age of the Ottoman empire in the tenth/sixteenth century is, by now, common knowledge, and names like Sulaimān the Magnificent (926/1520–974), the most influential of all imperial patrons, or the dominant architectural genius Sinān (d. 996/1588), his chief architect, immediately come to mind.[1]

Less evident, in contrast, remains the process of formation of the distinctive Ottoman style of architecture. Previous research has rightly stated that the monumental Hagia Sophia, one of the few truly influential world monuments, created by the architects Anthemios of Tralles and Isidorus of Miletus between 532 and 537 for the Byzantine emperor Justinian,[2] set the standard for Ottoman mosques as a constant source of inspiration. But for any response to the challenge posed by the Hagia Sophia, the most able and inventive architect had to depend on a specialized labor force trained to implement his daring designs. Much new information in this respect was recently made available by Turkish scholarship, especially by Ömer Lütfi Barkan, permitting intriguing insights into the organization of large-scale building operations of the period and the actual management of the huge labor force involved.[3]

On the other hand, Turkish scholarship also provided detailed catalogs of building projects in the lands ruled by the Ottoman family, to underline the continuity of architectural traditions from the time of the Saljūq empire in seventh/thirteenth-century Anatolia until the tenth/sixteenth century. Most important for this aspect is the series of folio volumes on early Ottoman architecture by Ekrem Hakki Ayverdi, where in five definitive installments published between 1966 and 1983 all traceable construction projects from the ʿUthmān (680/1281–726/1326) until the death of Selīm the Grim (918/1512–926/1520), the father of Sulaimān the Magnificent, are painstakingly described and documented. Covering a period of two and a half centuries, altogether 2530 monuments and construction projects are presented on over 2600 pages and illustrated with about 4100 drawings and photographs—a truly exceptional mine of information.[4] Serving as a continuation of these cataloging efforts, extensive monographs on the immense oeuvre of the famous architect Sinān have appeared more recently, especially those by Aptullah Kuran, listing and analyzing the nearly 480 building projects attributed to his long term of office as royal architect, from 945/1539 until his death in 996/1588.[5] In addition, surveying has recently reached an unprecedented level of perfection with two oversized portfolios measuring 52 – 73 cm, containing drawings by Ali Saim Ülgen devoted to the oeuvre of Sinān, presented on 266 plates.[6]

Despite this huge mass of basic information, now easily accessible, relatively little attention has been directed toward the hereditary component of Ottoman architecture. Though construction projects commissioned in the area of Ottoman rule in a long and continuous chain, in fact, apparently reach back into the time of the Saljūq sultanate of Anatolia in the seventh/thirteenth century, the role of outside influence from neighboring cultural areas in the formation of the Classical Ottoman style of architecture still remains to be determined.[7]

When the founder of the Ottoman dynasty, ʿUthmān (680/1281–726/1326), in the period of disintegration of the Saljūq empire settled down together with his Tūrkmen clansmen in the northwestern corner of Anatolia on the border of Byzantium, supremacy over the lands of Turkey was contested by two major powers: the Mamluk empire of Egypt and Syria, and the Īl Khānids of Iran. This geopolitical rivalry continued over the centuries, during which the Mamluk state maintained a relatively stable presence, while Iran was dominated by a succession of dynasties, including the Tīmūrids and finally the Ṣafawids. In between these late medieval superpowers, the Ottomans, first centered around their early capitals of Iznik and Bursa, enlarged their dominion in the western direction, into the Balkans, and consequently moved their capital to Edirne, the former Adrianople, in 767/1366. The capture of Constantinople in 857/1453 by Sultan Meḥmet Fātiḥ can be considered the turning point, when the Ottomans emerged as one of the major forces of the Islamic world. Enlarging their empire systematically further east, they eventually dominated all the various principalities of Anatolia. Finally even the Ṣafawids of Iran were subdued in 920/1514 and shortly later, in 923/1517, the Mamluk state was also incorporated into the Ottoman empire.[8]

To date the Iranian contribution has occasionally received scholarly attention;[9] whereas the strong bonds between Ottoman architecture and the Mamluk architecture in Egypt and Syria, to be discussed below, have so far been largely overlooked.[10]

1. FORMATIVE PERIOD OF OTTOMAN ARCHITECTURE (LATE EIGHTH/FOURTEENTH AND FIRST HALF OF NINTH/FIFTEENTH CENTURIES)

Architecture in the emirates, which had emerged after the dissolution of the Anatolian Saljūq state, manifests a marked decline in ambition and artistic quality when compared to the numerous impressive constructions of the previous period. In general, new foundations are characterized by rather limited dimensions, use of brick and rubble masonry in place of refined stone-work, and an absence of sophisticated decorative programs. When, during the later decades of the fourteenth century, a few exceptional monuments were erected in the important cities of several emirates which transcended this modest level of construction, such buildings were not produced by the local work-force alone but with the assistance of specialists drawn from neighboring regions. Though occasionally Iranian influences are also in evidence, the main contribution was made by migrating construction specialists from Mamluk Syria.[11] The first in date, and ultimately the most influential of these outstanding constructions, is the Ulu Cami, or Great Mosque at Manisa, capital of the Ṣarūkhān dynasty, commissioned by the local ruler Isḥāq Chelebi in 768/1366–67.[12] Rising on a comparatively small plot of c. 37 – 33m, the building is subdivided into two parts: a courtyard and a prayer hall, both roughly of equal dimensions. Access is provided by three axial portals leading to a rather small interior court, surrounded by arcades on three sides (pl. 30a). The prayer hall, accessible from the courtyard through a central gate, shows peculiar design of four perpendicular aisles and a central dome of about 11 m in front of the *miḥrāb*.

Though reminiscent of the Artuqid mosques of the distant Tigris region, created about two hundred years before, its characteristic combination of prayer hall and arcaded courtyard, which links it with a closely related group of Friday mosques in the Mamluk capital, was first employed in the palace mosque of Sultan an-Nāṣir Muḥammad at the Cairo citadel founded in 718/1318 and rebuilt with taller proportions, but on the original foundations, in 735/1334–35 (fig. 25). [13] The Friday mosque at Damascus founded by the Mamluk viceroy of Syria, Yalbughā al-Yaḥyāwī constitutes the only example of this imperial mosque type outside Cairo (fig. 27). Although begun in 747/1346 it was completed only in 757/1356, due to a temporary halt in construction.[14] Tellingly, the domes of the Cairo prototype and the Damascus example, both measuring about 12 m in diameter, are only slightly larger than that of the Manisa mosque. In addition to the similarities of the plan layout, several decorative features of the Manisa monument also point to a dependence on Mamluk models, for instance the medallions above the lateral niches of the north portal, composed of two knotted trefoils (pl. 29.). The pattern echoes more complicated medallions appearing on several Mamluk monuments, as for instance about 698/1299 at the Turba at-Takrītīya at aṣ-Ṣāliḥīya near Damascus.[15]

A close kinship with Mamluk architecture is even more evident on a monument c. 70 km farther south at Selçuk, ancient Ephesus, capital of the neighboring Aidīn emirate.[16] A signature on the main portal of its Friday mosque, erected before 776/1375 for the local ruler ʿĪsā Bey, identifies it as the work of a Damascus architect, ʿAlī b. Mushaimish ad-Dimashqī. This building, with dimensions of c. 56 × 52 m—markedly larger than the Manisa mosque—reflects the traditional mosque type of Damascus, established for posterity by the venerable early Islamic Friday mosque in the Syrian capital (fig. 26).[17]

As is true in the only slightly earlier Manisa mosque, space in the ʿĪsā Bey mosque is divided into a prayer hall and an attached forecourt with entrances and arcades on three sides, though instead of a central dome the middle axis of the sanctuary is emphasized by two consecutive domes, reflecting the characteristic transept of the Umaiyad prototype at Damascus.[18] Most remarkable of all, the western façade is adorned with a surprisingly rich marble decoration (pls. 29b, 31a). The repertoire of patterns includes interlacing bands on the interior windows (pl. 29b), a feature also common at Damascus, for instance on a building commissioned by the Mamluk sultan an-Nāṣir Ḥasan in 762/1361 (pl. 29c),[19] as well as at Aleppo, for example on one of the portals of the mosque of the governor, Mankalībughā ash-Shamsī, inaugurated in 769/1369 (pl. 29d).[20] The prayer niche of this Aleppo mosque, originally framed by inlaid marble in contrasting colors, is especially close to the decoration in the ʿĪsā Bey mosque.

Both southwest Anatolian mosques are of paramount importance for the genesis of Ottoman architecture—on two accounts: for the reintroduction into Turkey of stone masonry combined with relief decoration, and for their plan layout. Initially their innovative technical and decorative features found wide distribution. They reappeared again slightly later at the Yeşil Cami, or Green Mosque, at Iznik (fig. 24.2), one of the early centers of the Ottoman emirate.[21] This influential building from the reign of Murād I (761/1360–791/1389), commissioned in 780/1378–79 by the wazīr Khair ad-Dīn Pāshā (d.789/1387), but completed only in 794/1391–92, thus several years after the patron's death in the reign of Yıldırım Bāyazīd (791/1389–804/1402), can be regarded as the first large-scale example of Ottoman centralized dome construction. This structure with its inte-

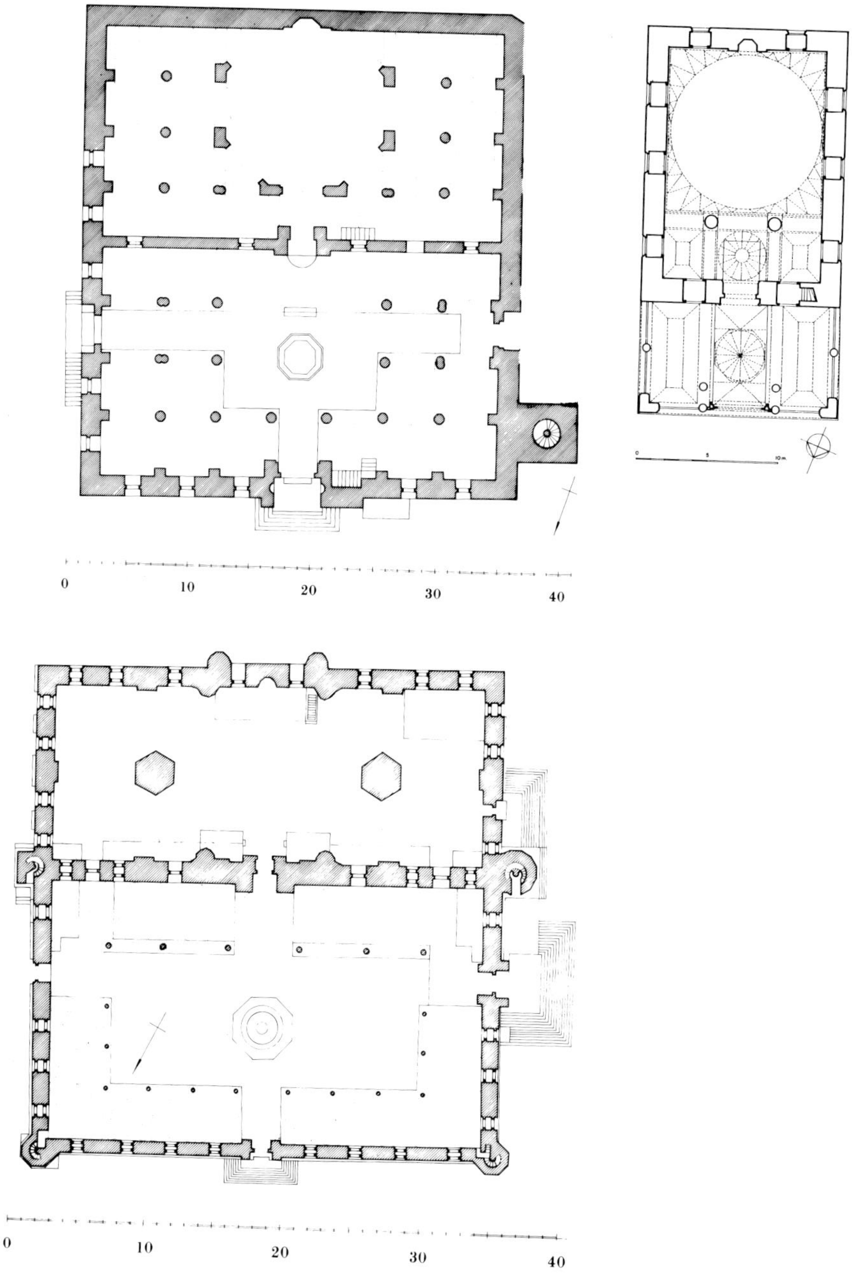

Fig. 24. (1) Manisa, Ulu Cami: plan (after Michael Meinecke, *Die mamlukische Architektur* [1992], I, fig. 89). (2) Iznik, Yeşil Cami: plan (after Aptullah Kuran, *The Mosque in Early Ottoman Architecture* [1968], fig. 54). (3) Edirne, Üç Şerefeli Cami: plan (after Meinecke [1992], I, fig. 90), all in scale 1:500.

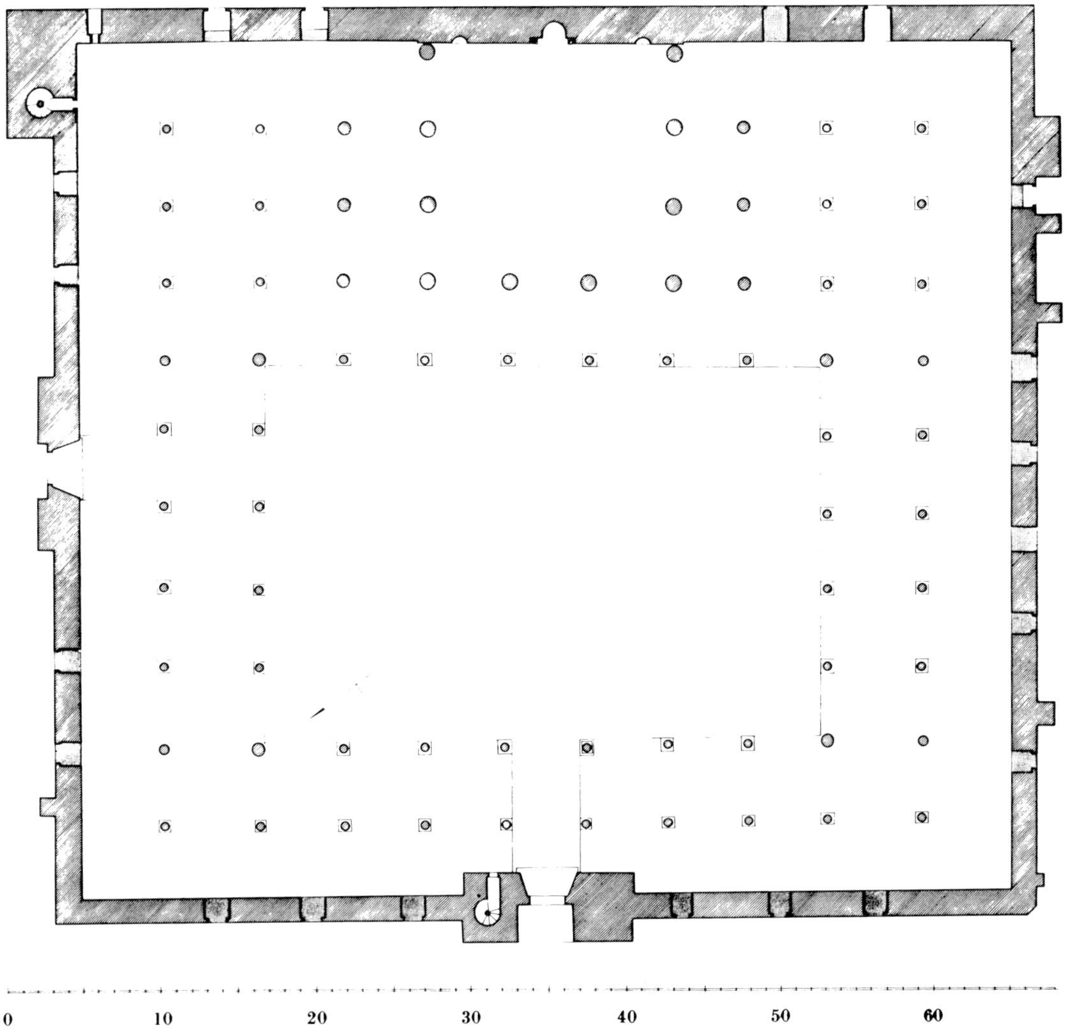

Fig. 25. Cairo Citadel, Mosque of an-Nāṣir Muḥammad: plan, in scale 1:500 (after Meinecke [1992], I, fig. 28).

rior portico appears to be a quotation from the central zone of the Manisa mosque (fig. 24.1), where too the 11 m diameter of its dome finds an exact parallel. Most notable is the use of marble, accentuating the exterior and reaching up to a height of 3.30 m on the interior walls. The rich stone carvings, a mixture of vegetal and geometric patterns, together with variations of script, also include some features first introduced at the Isa Bey Cami at Selçuk, as for instance

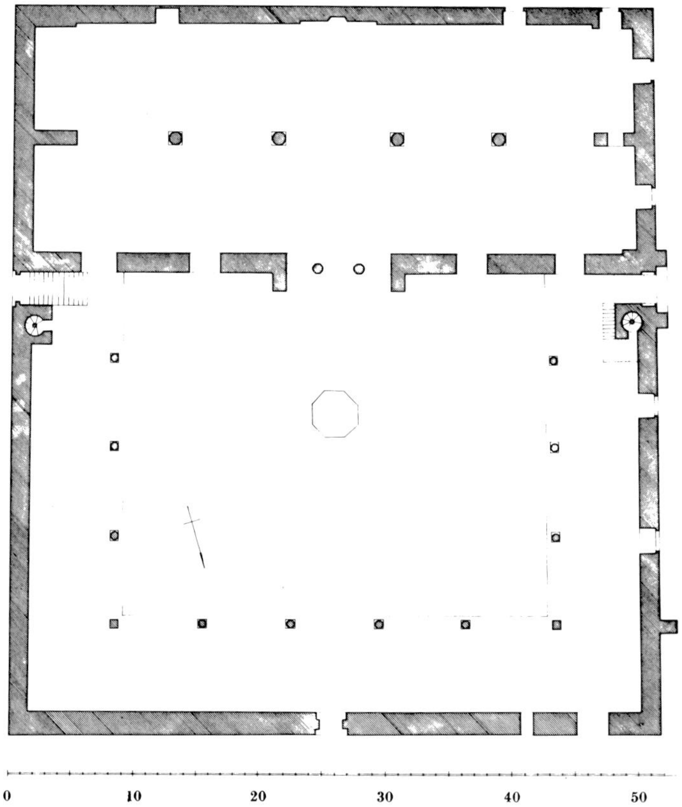

Fig. 26. Selçuk, Isa Bey Camii: plan, in scale 1:500 (after Meinecke [1992], I, fig. 91).

at the false door of the exterior portico (pl. 31b), signed by the architect Ḥājjī b. Mūsā. There the door opening is framed by a *muqarnaṣ* frieze of four registers, which, on the upper corners, the meeting points of the horizontal and vertical portions of the frieze, shows rather oddly distorted *muqarnaṣ* fragments. As this characteristic detail already occurred on the Selçuk mosque (pl. 31a), it can be assumed that part of the labor force previously active in southwestern Anatolia had since moved some 350 km farther northeast to the city of Iznik to participate in this Ottoman construction project. There they were also joined by another workshop of Iranian origin, who executed the exceptional multicolored decoration in glazed bricks and cut-tile mosaic of the minaret, which inspired the local appellation of the monument as the "Green Mosque".[22]

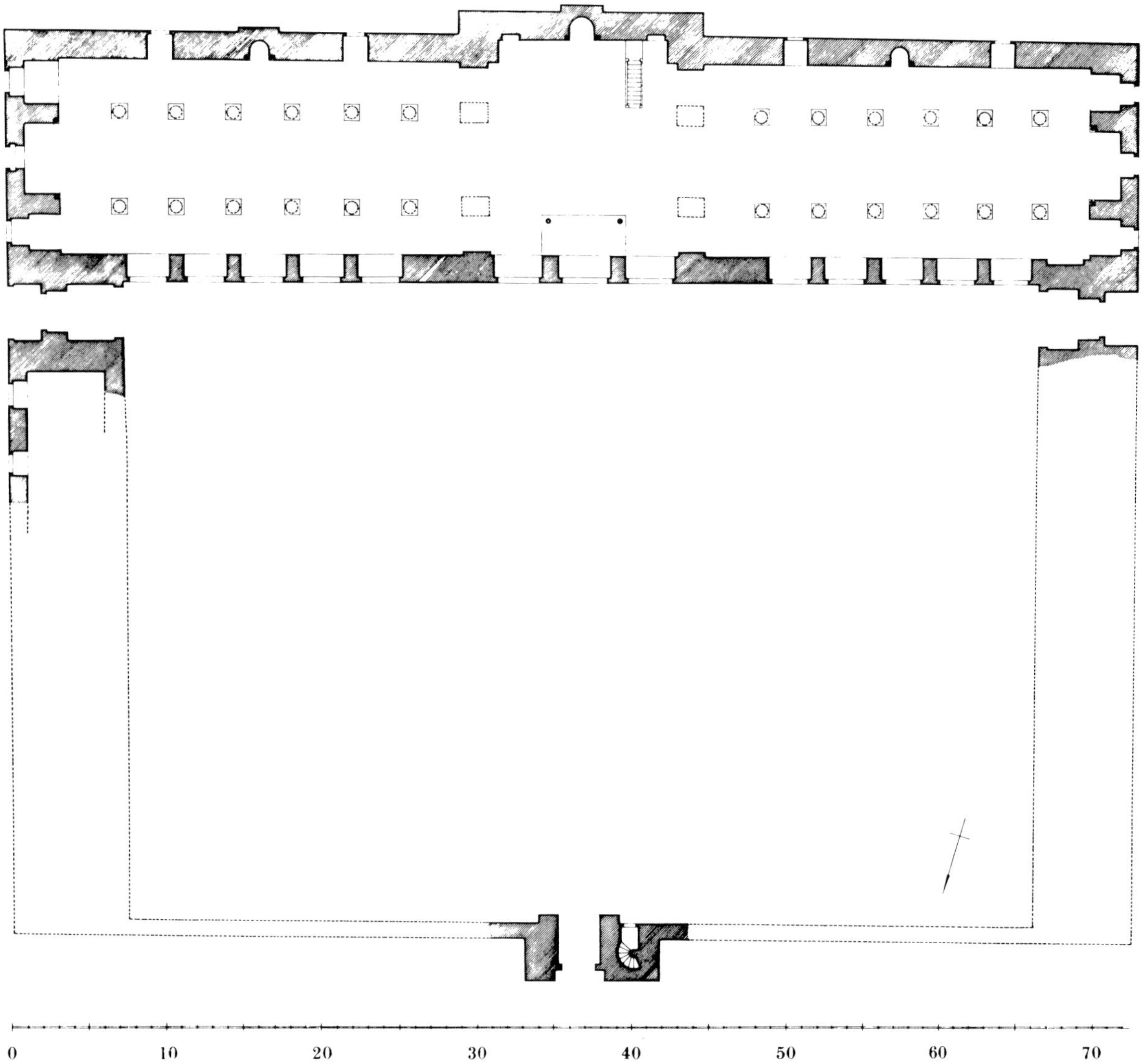

Fig. 27. Damascus, Mosque of Yalbughā al-Yaḥyāwī: reconstructed ground plan, in scale 1:500 (after Meinecke [1992], I, fig. 68).

In the last two decades of the eighth/fourteenth century, this special type of marble decoration, concentrated on doors, windows and prayer niches, was spread widely in the Ottoman emirate. Quotations from the decorative repertoire of the Selçuk mosque reappear, for instance, simultaneously in 797/1394–95 at Bursa on the mosque of

Yıldırım Bāyazīd,[23] and, about 330 km away, at Milas on the Piruz Bey Cami,[24] both executed by two former members of the Mamluk workshop previously employed on the Isa Bey Cami at Selçuk. Later on, after a short interruption caused by the Tīmūrid invasion of Anatolia in 805/1402, the dependence on Mamluk ornamental prototypes decreases as new patterns were invented, stressing vegetal aspects of the decoration. An example for the new independence of architectural decorations, only distantly echoing the Mamluk ancestors, can be seen on the Ilyas Bey Cami in Balat, ancient Miletus, founded in 806/1406 by the ruler of the local Menteshe emirate (fig. 30.2).[25]

Increasingly the new stonework decorations were incorporated in buildings belonging entirely to the emerging local tradition of architecture. At the same time, another structural change gradually accelerated: the replacement of brick and rubble masonry by finely cut stone masonry, which is to be credited to the immigrant construction specialists from Mamluk Syria and was further distributed by migrating workshops. But eventually Syrian artists and artisans were assimilated by the local early Ottoman school of architecture. This seems to be the case with the descendants of the Mamluk architect of the Selçuk mosque, ᶜAlī b. Mushaimish ad-Dimashqī: the two known works of the master mason *(muᶜallim)* Abū Bakr b. Muḥammad named Ibn al-Mushaimish ad-Dimashqī, probably a grandson of the Selçuk architect, the Beyazit Paşa Cami at Amasya,[26] and the madrasa of Meḥmet Chelebī at Merzifon near Amasya,[27] both dated to 817/1414, as well as the Karaca Bey Cami of 831/1427–28 in Ankara,[28] signed by his son Sinān ad-Dīn Aḥmad b. Abī Bakr al-Mushaimish, are firmly rooted in the Ottoman architectural tradition, at that time increasingly characterized by a high quality of stone masonry.

The impact of both the Manisa and the Selçuk mosques is not limited to their contribution toward the reintroduction and further distribution of stone masonry and decoration in Anatolia and Rumelia. Probably even more decisive was the challenge posed by their plan layout, based on Mamluk prototypes, but quite innovative within the Anatolian environment. Only after the engineering techniques to implement more daring designs became available, were the architectural features of the southwest Anatolian mosques further developed in the Friday mosque of Sultan Murād II, the Üç Şerefeli

Cami, at his capital Edirne (fig. 24.3).[29] Though foundation work had already started in 841/1437–38, the building was not yet completed when the sultan decided to leave the throne to his son Meḥmet in 848/1444 and to retire to Manisa to pursue religious studies. Nevertheless, construction work was again taken up when Murād II returned to the sultanate two years later, in 850/1446, sending his son to Manisa instead. The Üç Şerefeli Cami, inaugurated soon after, in 851/1447, reveals an intimate acquaintance especially with the Great Mosque of Manisa (fig. 24.1), which is about eighty years older. Closely related in proportions, as well as in the general layout, two innovations are of special importance for later Ottoman mosque architecture: the inclusion of a fourth arcade on the interior courtyard in front of the prayer hall façade (pl. 30b), and the greater dominance of the central dome of 12 m in diameter, spanning the whole depth of the sanctuary. The building's exterior is emphasized by four minarets rising from the corners of the courtyard (pl. 32a). With their enormous height of 67 m and their three superimposed spiral staircases leading to three balconies, the pair of minarets contiguous with the prayer hall façade give vivid testimony to the engineering mastery of this remarkable limestone structure. Remarkably, two tympana of the courtyard windows are decorated by delicately designed tiles in blue-and-white contrast, the last works of a migrating atelier of Iranian origin.[30]

This early Ottoman masterpiece, constructed just a few years before the conquest of Constantinople, prepares the path for the future development of mosque architecture. By the express intent of the imperial patron, Sultan Murād II, an innovative mosque design, based on Mamluk models, was taken up and further improved. Thus the Üç Şerefeli Cami at Edirne is to be interpreted as a late descendant of the imperial mosques in the Egyptian capital, Cairo, constructed about a century earlier for the Mamluk sultan an-Nāṣir Muḥmmad (fig. 25).

2. OTTOMAN ARCHITECTURE AFTER THE CONQUEST OF CONSTANTINOPLE

In contrast to the early Ottoman period, there are no indications that Mamluk construction specialists contributed significantly to the extensive building program following the conquest of Constantino-

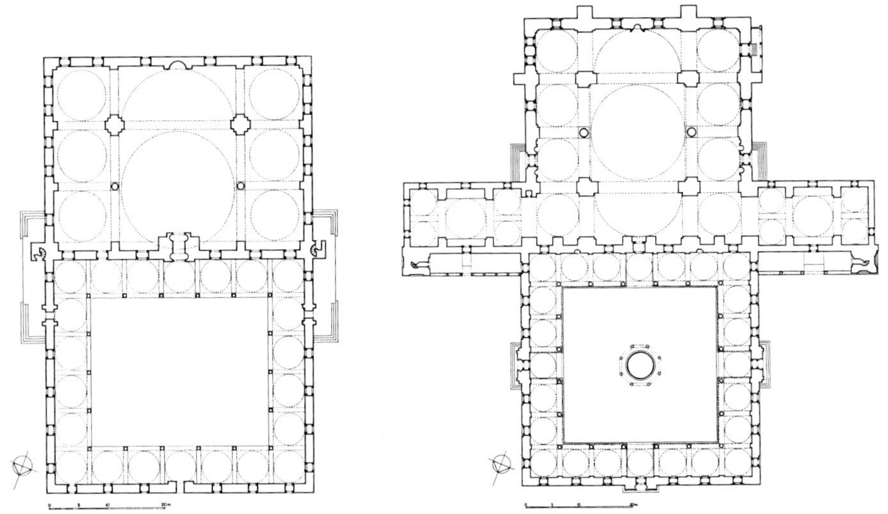

Fig. 28. Istanbul: (1) Mosque of Meḥmet Fātiḥ: plan. (2) Mosque of Bāyazīd II: plan, both in scale 1:500 (after Aptullah Kuran, *The Mosque in Early Ottoman Architecture* [1968], figs. 216, 218).

ple in 857/1453. The Islamization of the Byzantine city remained the major task until the tenth/sixteenth century, when the royal architect Sinān embellished the townscape of Istanbul with daring mosque designs. Initially the efforts of the victorious conqueror Meḥmet Fātiḥ, who in his youth, as already mentioned, was exiled by his father Murād II to Manisa, crystallized in two main projects: the construction of a congregational mosque, and the foundation of the imperial residence. A huge mosque complex, which became the largest social organization of the Ottoman empire, was constructed between 867/1463 and 875/1470 to replace the church of the Hagia Sophia, used as a mosque since the fall of Byzantium.[31] The mosque, set on atop one of the hills of Istanbul for visibility, is positioned at the center of a nearly square exterior courtyard about 210 m on each side, which is bordered on two sides by madrasa quarters, each comprising four structures with arcaded courtyards and fronting dependencies; on the *qibla* side two additional square enclosures of 100 m each were constructed with large-size buildings, one used as a hospital and the other as a kitchen for charity. The mosque proper (fig. 28.1) utilizes the characteristic division into courtyard and sanctuary, introduced into Ottoman architecture by the quarter of a century older Üç Şerefeli Cami at Edirne (fig. 24.3), and therefore

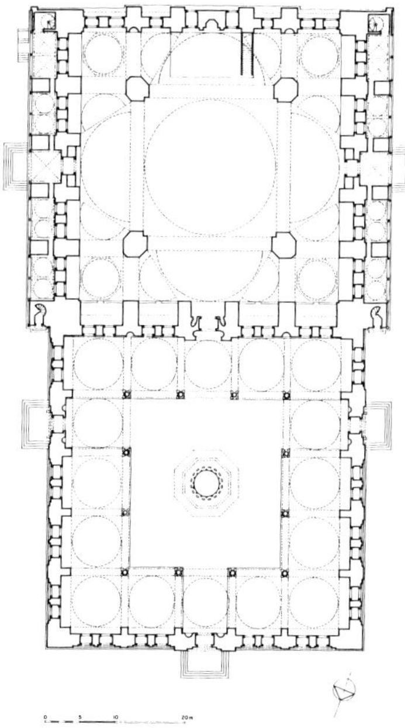

Fig. 29. Istanbul, Şehzade Cami: plan, in scale 1:500 (after Kuran [1968], fig. 222).

indirectly it is still linked to the distant Mamluk architectural tradition. The prayer hall, altered after destruction caused by the earthquake of 1179/1766, according to old representations originally featured a dome of over 24 m. Typologically this mosque closely follows the pattern of the Edirne model but, emphasizing the longitudinal axis, the depth of the courtyard is enlarged by the incorporation of an additional arch on the lateral arcades; similarly, the prayer hall was also enlarged on the *qibla* side by a huge semi-dome supporting the high-rising central dome. The evident increase in volume, as well as the ascending sequence of semi-dome and full dome is to be understood as a first response to the Hagia Sophia, though the dimensions of the earlier dome of about 31 m were not yet reached. The avant-garde position of the Fātiḥ Mosque in Ottoman mosque architecture is underlined by the fact that another twenty years had to pass before this design was further improved at the imperial mosque of Bāyazīd II (886/1481–918/1512) in Istanbul (fig. 28.2), constructed from 906/1501 until 911/1505–6 with two axial semi-domes,[32] and then, after another long interval, again at the first masterpiece of the architect Sinān, the Şehzade Cami (fig. 29), founded in 950/1543,[33] which features four semi-domes supporting the central cupola.

Parallel efforts centered on the residence of the imperial court, the Topkapı Saray, which was to be enlarged by the succeeding sultans to form a huge enclosed palace city.[34] Construction work was started by Meḥmet Fātiḥ about 873/1468, when construction activities were in full swing at the sultan's mosque; the enclosure wall was completed in 883/1478, according to a building inscription on the main exterior gate. So far the origin of the sizable labor force implementing these double construction projects has not been investigated and remains a fascinating topic for future research. But in general it can be assumed that the majority of the construction specialists were brought from all over the Ottoman empire. Nevertheless, workshops from more distant regions outside the Ottoman lands were also attracted by the vast construction program at the new capital of Istanbul. This is proved by the famous garden pavilion near the Topkapı Saray, the Çinili Köşk, constructed before 877/1472 in the Persian manner and decorated with a tile and cut-tile mosaic decoration by a specialized atelier from Iran (pl. 27b), as already briefly indicated in the earlier chapter on Hasankeyf.[35] Again, masons or other trained specialists from the Mamluk empire might have been active in the building projects at Istanbul without exerting any visible influence on the architectural style.

But in turn, toward the end of the reign of Meḥmet Fātiḥ, who died in 886/1481, most probably when the construction boom at Istanbul slowed down, the impact of Ottoman architecture can be witnessed on a few contemporary monuments of the Mamluk empire. The first in date is a tiny mausoleum at Aleppo, built in 881/1476–77 by the local dignitary ʿUthmān Ibn Ughulbak for his family (fig. 30.1), the last remains of a larger complex of two courtyards and important water installations.[36] The niched west façade, only 8 m in length (pl. 33a), documents the revival of the ornate style invented at Aleppo shortly before the Tīmūrid conquest of 803/1400 (pl. 26c), reappearing here for the first time after a hiatus lasting for the first three quarters of the century, with double *muqarnaṣ* frames, dentil patterns, and ornamented lintels. Even more remarkable is the interior, a simple square room of 4.40 m, enlarged by an *īwān* extension with a prayer niche, which features a perfect little dome on pendentives (pl. 33b) of that type common in the Ottoman architecture, but hitherto unknown in the Mamluk lands. This transitional design betrays an intimate knowledge of contemporary Ottoman building techniques. But it appears that the architect of this fascinating small monument did not work at Aleppo only for the rather ephemeral patron ʿUthmān Ibn Ughulbak. It seems more likely that this architect was occupied mainly with the reconstruction of the Aleppo Citadel carried out between 877/1472–73 and 880/1475 for the Mamluk sultan al-Ashraf Qaitbāy (872/1468–901/1496).[37] There the nine-domed audience hall built over the main gate has a window framed by knotted columns in the center of its main exterior wall, an innovation also used on the façade of the Aleppo mausoleum (fig. 30.1–4).

It seems doubtful that this anonymous construction specialist should be identified with a craftsman *(ṣāniʿ)* from Rūm, Anatolia, or even Constantinople, who, according to the historian-topographer al-ʿUlaimī (writing in 901/1495), renewed the lead roof of the Masjid al-Aqṣā in Jerusalem in 884/1479–80. His work, anyhow, did not find the approval of the inspector *(nāzir)* of the holy precinct, the *amīr* Muḥammad Ibn Nashāshibī, who consequently decided not to also commission the restoration of the Dome of the Rock from the same Ottoman building specialist.[38] Nevertheless, this amusing anecdote attests to the activities of Ottoman construction workers in the Mamluk empire.

The impact of the distant architectural developments in the Ottoman homelands also extended to Cairo, the center of power of the Mamluk empire. There, on the northern outskirts of the city an exceptional building, the Qubbat al-Fadāwīya (fig. 30.3), was founded in 884/1480 by the imperial major-domo Yashbak min Mahdī (d.885/1480); completed only after the patron's death by order of the ruling sultan al-Ashraf Qaitbāy, the structure was inaugurated in 886/1481.[39] This remarkable monument, a high-rising structure on a shallow ground floor, consists of a single square room of over 14 m each side, surmounted by a dominant dome (pl. 34a). Contrary to local practice, the dome transition is composed not of the customary *muqarnaṣ* pendentives but from a combination of corner squinches and spherical triangles (pl. 34b). In addition, the squinches received an intricate secondary vaulting system, resembling a halved folded vault of the local decorative repertoire, resulting in a trefoil profile. This rather curious single-unit structure of religious func-

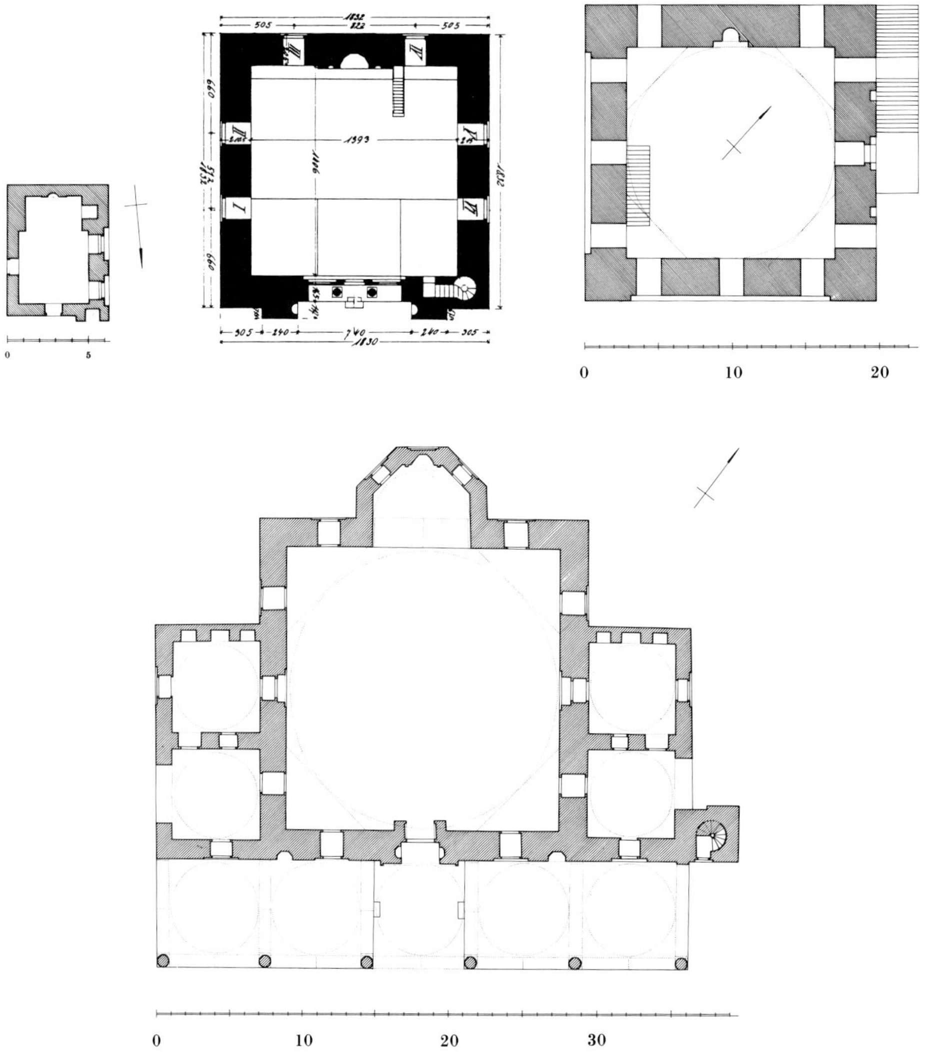

Fig. 30. (1) Aleppo, Mausoleum of ʿUthmān Ibn Ughulbak: plan, in scale 1:500 (after Michael Meinecke, *Die mamlukische Architektur* [1992], I, fig. 133). (2) Balat, Ilyas Bey Camii: plan, in scale 1:500 (after Theodor Wiegand, ed., *Das islamische Milet* [1935], pl. 23). (3) Cairo, Qubbat al-Fadāwīya, plan of upper story, in scale 1:500 (after Meinecke [1992], I, fig. 129). (4) Istanbul, Davut Paşa Camii: plan, in scale 1:500 (after Meinecke [1992], I, fig. 130).

tions, as defined by the prayer niche, remarkably resembles contemporary Ottoman mosque constructions.

Notably, this peculiar architectural design was not followed, at least not on the same monumental scale, in Mamluk Cairo, but reappears shortly thereafter on major Ottoman foundations. Three years after the inauguration of the Cairo monument, in 889/1484, construction work started at the mosque complex of the Ottoman sultan Bāyazīd II at Edirne.[40] This multifunctional unit, completed in 893/1487–88, also comprises a hospital, a madrasa, stables, kitchen facilities, and other charitable institutions, and features rather unusual decorative designs, worthy of further investigation to determine their artistic pedigree. The sanctuary of the centrally positioned mosque (fig. 31) is confined to a single square room surmounted by a high-rising dome of over 20 m in diameter, resting on pendentives. Remarkably, as is well known, the layout and elevation of this mosque together with its immediate dependencies were faithfully repeated on a larger scale a generation later at Istanbul, in the mosque of Sultan Selīm I (918/1512–926/1520), completed posthumously by his son Sulaimān the Magnificent in 929/1525 (fig. 32).[41]

That the Qubbat al-Fadāwīya in Cairo has to be interpreted in connection with this second line of development of Ottoman mosque architecture is attested by another contemporary monument at Istanbul, the Dawut Paşa Cami of 890/1485–86 (fig. 30.4).[42] This building again centers on a square dome chamber of 18 m. But its transition zone, instead of using the pendentives which are employed in the contemporary Edirne building, features a *muqarnaṣ* squinch with a trefoil façade similar, although not identical, to those which had been used four years earlier in the Cairo monument. These similarities indicate a close and direct connection. Most probably Ottoman construction specialists active in the Mamluk empire, at Aleppo, Jerusalem, and finally at Cairo, had returned to their country of origin after only a few years, and there they drew on experience gained from another architectural tradition.

These new inventions were not incorporated into the local repertoires, either at Istanbul or at Cairo, but remained isolated experiments. But probably as a last reflection of these distant Ottoman developments, a small group of buildings at Cairo, all founded shortly before the downfall of the Mamluk empire, manifest a new

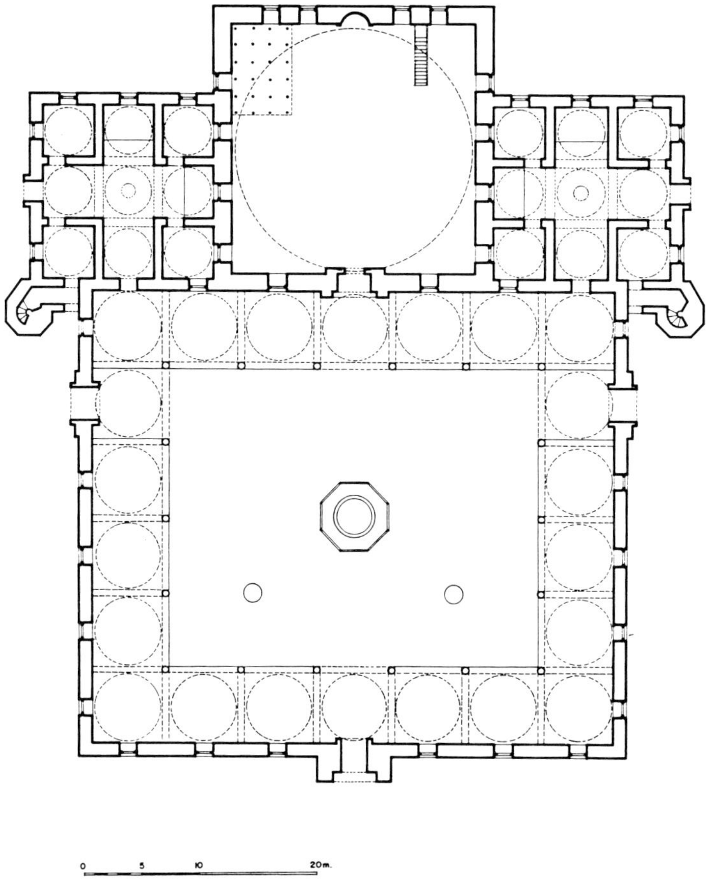

Fig. 31. Edirne, Mosque of Bāyazīd II: plan, in scale 1:500 (after Aptullah Kuran, *The Mosque in Early Ottoman Architecture* [1968], fig. 46).

use of vaulting. For instance, in the funerary madrasas of Khāʾīrbak al-Ashrafī (fig. 33.7, pl. 35a),[43] or of Qānībāy Qarā ar-Rammāḥ (fig. 33.2, pl. 35b),[44] both dating from the same year 908/1502–3, all parts of the buildings customarily covered by wooden ceilings, and even the interior courtyards, are completely vaulted. The varieties of vaults and even hanging domes recall the formal character of Ottoman pendentive domes but depend structurally on earlier inventions in Mamluk architecture.

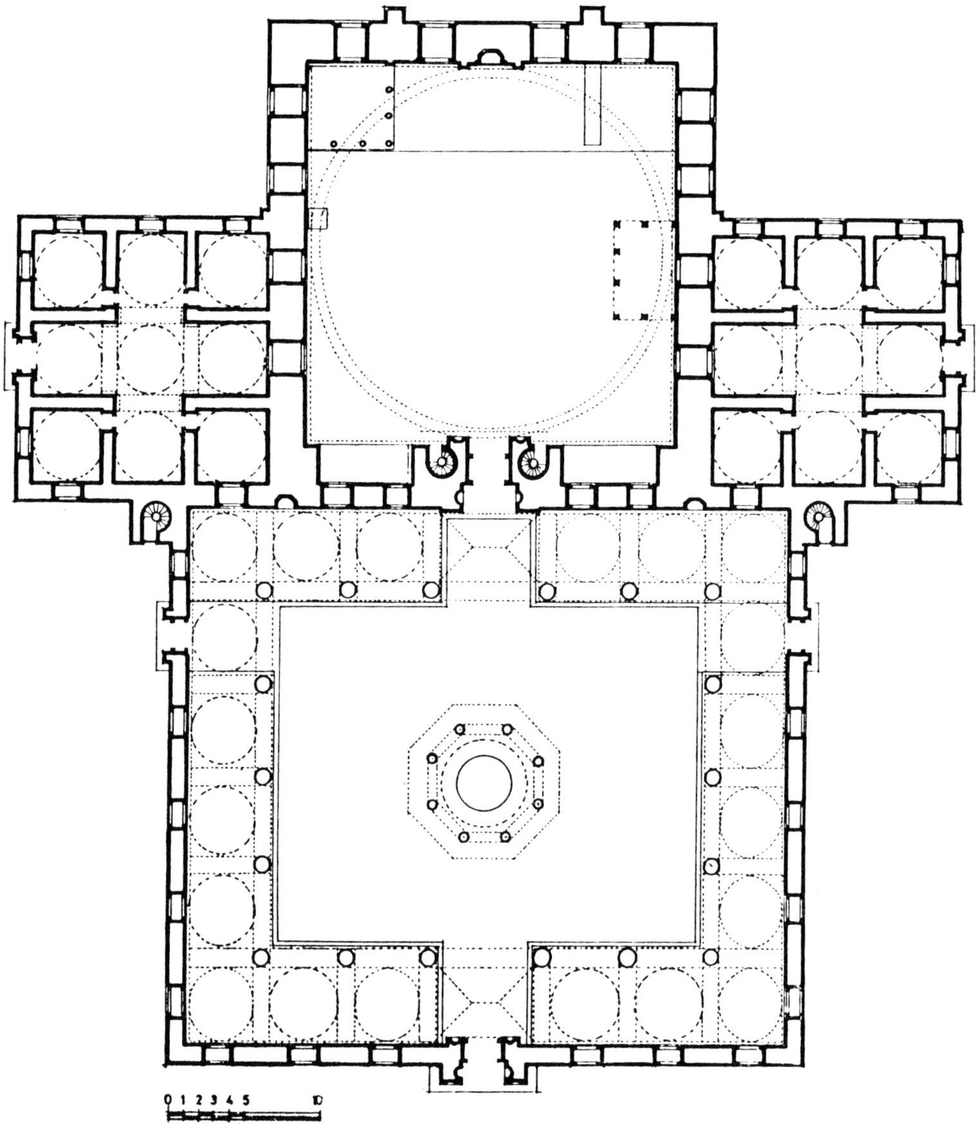

Fig. 32. Istanbul, Mosque of Selīm I: plan, in scale 1:500 (after Metin Sözen, *Türk mimarisinin gelişimi ve mimar Sinan* [1975], fig. 154).

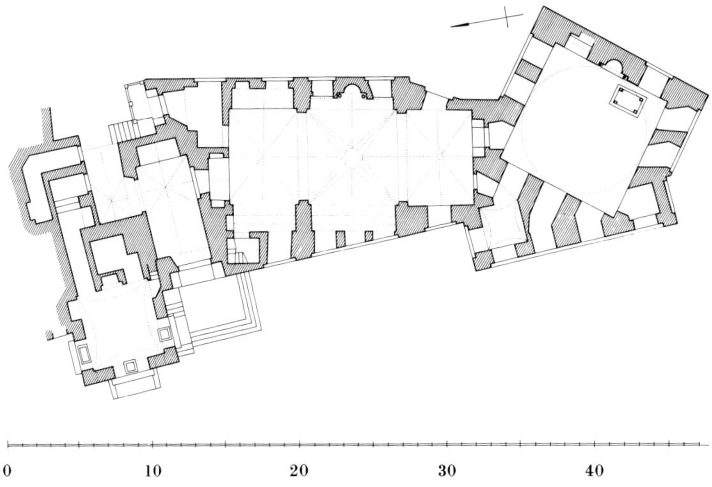

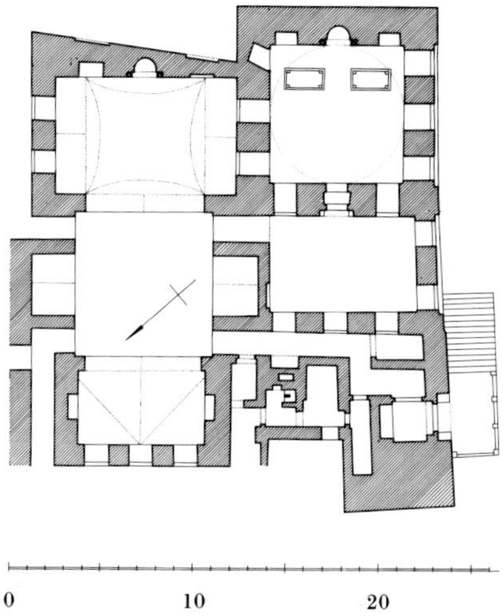

Fig. 33. Cairo: (1) Madrasa of Khāʾīrbak al-Ashrafī: plan. (2) Madrasa of Q̣ānībāy Q̣arā ar-Rammāḥ: plan, both in scale 1:500 (after Michael Meinecke, *Die mamlukische Architektur* [1992], I, figs. 131, 132).

3. OTTOMAN SUPREMACY AFTER THE CONQUEST OF CAIRO

A last phase of mutual exchange between these schools of architecture began after the dramatic downfall of the Mamluk empire. The medieval system of the Mamluks proved powerless against the mighty military machine of the Ottomans. After the decisive defeat of the Mamluk forces in northern Syria in 922/1516, the Mamluk state as a whole was incorporated into the Ottoman empire with the conquest of Cairo in 923/1517. According to the eyewitness account of Ibn Iyās (writing in 928/1521–22), the victorious Ottoman sultan Selīm the Grim was so deeply impressed by the Mamluk monuments of Cairo, especially by the sumptuously decorated madrasa-mausoleum complex of Sultan al-Ashraf Qānṣūh al-Ghaurī, built between 907/1501 and 910/1504 (see the illustration on the front cover),[45] that he decided to erect a similar complex at Istanbul. For this future project, not only the marble revetments of the Cairo monuments were systematically requisitioned, but a complete construction atelier, headed by the last Mamluk chief architect *(muʿallim al-mu ʿallimīn)* Shihāb ad-Dīn Aḥmad b. Ḥasan Ibn aṭ-Ṭūlūnī, was brought to Istanbul as well.[46]

These specialists most probably never participated in the construction of Sultan Selīm's mosque at Istanbul (fig. 32), which was not finished until three years after his death and closely followed, as mentioned previously, the design of his father's mosque at Edirne (fig. 31). But shortly after his return from Cairo, the sultan also commissioned the construction of a palace pavilion in Istanbul near the Topkapı Saray in 924/1518, for which evidently some of the marble imported from the Mamluk capital was used; it consequently received the name "Mermer Köşk," the Marble Kiosk.[47] As this building disappeared long ago, and therefore is known only from old descriptions, it is impossible to determine the dependence on Mamluk prototypes. The sole surviving example of the re-use of Mamluk marble revetments in Istanbul is the rather insignificant façade of the Hırka-i Saadet Dairesi, the series of rooms at the imperial palace, constructed to house the holy relics carried off from Cairo as well.[48] But altogether the impact of Mamluk decoration on Ottoman architecture was only marginal.

On the death of Sultan Selīm in 926/1520, the deported construction specialists are shown by the contemporary chronicle of Ibn Iyās to have reappeared in Cairo, which explains the conspicuous absence of further related works in the Ottoman capital.[49] Nevertheless, only a few years later a last attempt to transplant Mamluk features to Turkey was instigated by the influential Ottoman court official Muṣṭafā Pāshā (d.935/1529), who during his short term of office as governor of Egypt from 928/1522 until 929/1523 had developed a taste for Mamluk art and architecture. Immediately after his return from Cairo, Muṣṭafā Pāshā ordered the construction of a funerary complex at Gebze, about 70 km southeast of Istanbul, which was inaugurated soon after in 930/1523–24.[50] The centerpiece of the complex is a mosque, clearly echoing the Qubbat al-Fadāwīya in Cairo in its proportions, which has sometimes, rather implausibly, been described as one of the earliest works of the architect Sinān (fig. 30.3).

Trying to emulate Mamluk interiors, the patron not only furnished the mosque with objects collected at Cairo, as for instance two brass chandeliers which in 1910 reached the Berlin Museum of Islamic Art (pl. 36b–c),[51] but also ordered a complete set of wooden furniture, including two Koran boxes signed by the woodworker Aḥmad *al-miʿmār;*[52] and most impressive of all, he also commissioned a marble decoration in Mamluk style.[53] Though the marble revetment of extremely refined quality is expertedly integrated into the built fabric on the interior walls (pl. 36a) and on the façade, in appearance the building also clearly reflects the contemporary mode of Ottoman architecture. The appreciation for this type of decoration is vividly expressed by the traveler Ewliyā Chelebī (d.1095/1684), who remarks with characteristic exaggeration that this revetment "has no equal in the world" and then rightly concludes that similar decorations are "not to be seen in any other mosque in the capital".[54] This most ambitious decorative program modeled in the Mamluk manner in fact remains an isolated example in imperial Ottoman architecture. Restricted to the dados, evidently this type of marble revetment could not be adjusted to the dynamic three-dimensional treatment of space in Ottoman mosques. In this respect the horizontal marble decorations were outlived by tile revetments, first in blue-and-white, then of color glazes, and finally of underglaze painted multicolored pattern tiles, more easily adaptable to larger wall surfaces.[55] Tellingly early examples of blue-and-white pattern tiles were used even in the mausoleum of Muṣṭafā Pāshā, situated behind his mosque within the charitable complex at Gebze.[56] Altogether it reflects a certain degree of structural logic that the Mamluk fashion of decoration never took root in the Classical period of Ottoman architecture, which was to be characterized eventually by the exquisite tile revetments of the famous Iznik production.

4. PATTERNS OF CHANGES IN ARCHITECTURAL STYLES

The changing course of architectural interrelations between the Mamluk and the Ottoman empires, to be deduced from the historic fabric of one and a half centuries, provides ample indication about the patterns of stylistic changes. In general, it should be evident that cultural developments never prospered in isolation, but usually benefited from a wide range of inspiration, occasionally even from far distant areas. Even political rivalry did not necessarily exclude the infusion of new ideas, transported by various means but mostly along commercial routes. Artistic influences in most cases have to be credited to migrating artisans and specialists, though occasionally the sheer presence of challenging masterpieces alone gave reason for the adaptation and transformation of forms and designs.

The dynamics of artistic exchange often reflect the current international political situation. When the descendants of Mamluk architecture first appeared in Anatolia, the Mamluk empire was still at the zenith of its power whereas the Ottoman principality was in a formative period. Consequently Mamluk impact remained relatively strong, until the Ottomans gained political momentum. Later, when the Ottoman empire increasingly reached international stature, the Mamluk state was in eclipse, and therefore the direction of interrelations was reversed, resulting in the influence of Ottoman architecture on Mamluk architectural traditions. Subsequently, when Ottoman power extinguished the Mamluk state, despite the intrinsic quality of Mamluk decoration, and the admiration for it voiced by Ottoman observers, Ottoman architecture was already almost self-dependent and was no longer readily assimilating outside influence.

Similar tendencies also constituted the formative force for the architecture of the three cities discussed in the earlier chapters: ar-Raqqa on the Euphrates in early Islamic times depended on the interrelations with Baghdād, the cultural center of that period; Buṣrā in turn benefited from the artistic exchange with the nearby

Syrian capital, Damascus; and the historic fabric of Hasankeyf on the Tigris over the centuries reflects varying alliances with either Iran or northern Syria.

Scaled down to a human perspective, in most cases the stylistic changes were brought about by migrating artists. In the last analysis, it was of no stylistic consequence for the newly created works of art whether these artists were brought through forced labor or whether they were traveling of their own accord seeking new patrons and projects in distant places. What matters most, probably also for the artists themselves, is that they were able to exercise their skills in the creation of new masterpieces. And it can be assumed that especially the innovative minds preferred mobility to the routine of permanent local employment.

Notes

1. The most stimulating and detailed survey of this chapter of architectural development was written by Godfrey Goodwin, *A History of Ottoman Architecture* (London, 1971); see also the recent reference work by Oktay Aslanapa, *Osmanlı devri mimarisi* (Istanbul, 1986). Recently a series of international exhibitions has pointed to the artistic refinement of Ottoman art in the Classical period, documented in a series of catalogues: Esin Atil, *The Age of Sultan Süleyman the Magnificent* (Washington and New York, 1987); Michael J. Rogers and Rachel M. Ward, *Süleyman the Magnificent* (London, 1988); idem, *Schätze aus dem Topkapı Serail. Das Zeitalter Süleyman des Prächtigen* (Berlin, 1988); Marthe Bernus Taylor, ed., *Soliman le Magnifique* (Paris, 1990).
2. For the position of this major monument of Istanbul within architectural evolution, see Richard Krautheimer, *Early Christian and Byzantine Architecture* (Harmondsworth, U.K., 1965), pp. 153–160, figs. 61–62, pls. 68–74a, 76, 78b; for an example of the many monographs on this building, see for instance Heinz Kähler, *Die Hagia Sophia* (Berlin, 1967).
3. Most important are the documents concerning the mosque of Sulaimān the Magnificent in Istanbul: Ömer Lütfi Barkan, *Süleymaniye cami ve imareti inşaatı (1550–1557)* I-II (Ankara, 1972/1979); see also the analyses by Michael J. Rogers, "The state and the arts in Ottoman Turkey," *International Journal of Middle East Studies* 14, 1982, pp. 71–86, 283–313.
4. Ayverdi I–IV (1966–1974); the fifth volume of the series was compiled by I. Aydın Yücel (1983). In a parallel series of four volumes all Ottoman monuments in Europe were listed and catalogued as well: Ekrem Hakkı Ayverdi, in collaboration with I. Aydın Yücel, Gürbüz Ertürk, and Ibrahim Nûman, *Avrupa'da Osmanlı mimârî eserleri* I: *Romanya, Macaristan* (Istanbul, [1978]);

II–III: *Yugoslavya* (Istanbul, 1981); IV: *Bulgaristan, Yunanistan, Arnavudluk* (Istanbul, 1982).

5. The projected comprehensive monograph on Sinān, commissioned in 1937 to the French architect-historian Albert Gabriel, eventually found its conclusion just in time for the 300th anniversary of the architect's death: Aptullah Kuran, *Sinan: The Grand Old Master of Ottoman Architecture* (Istanbul, 1987); see also the richly illustrated study edited by Metin Sözen, *Türk mimarisinin gelişimi ve mimar Sinan* (Istanbul, 1975). For the relevant documents, see Rıfkı Melûl Meriç, *Mimar Sinan—hayatı, eseri I: Mimar Sinan'ın hayatına, eserlerine dair metinler* (Ankara, 1965).
6. Ali Saim Ülgen, *Mimar Sinan yapıları. The Buildings of Mimar Sinan* (Ankara, 1989), two portfolios with catalog, prepared posthumously by Filiz Yenişehirlioğlu and Emre Madran. In size this documentation drastically surpasses the previous collection of survey drawings by Sedat Çetintaş, *Türk mimari anıtları—Osmanlı devri* I: *Bursada ilk eserler* (Istanbul, 1946); II: *Bursada Murad I ve Bayezid I binaları* (Istanbul, 1952).
7. For a penetrating analysis of the formative period, see Aptullah Kuran, *The Mosque in Early Ottoman Architecture* (Chicago and London, 1968).
8. On the history of the period, see for instance Claude Cahen, *Pre-Ottoman Turkey: A General Survey of the Material and Spiritual Culture and History c. 1071–1330* (London, 1968); and Halıl Inalcık, *The Ottoman Empire: The Classical Age 1300–1600* (London, 1973).
9. On the Iran connection of Ottoman architectural decoration, see Meinecke (1976), I, pp. 98–120; idem, "Early Ottoman tile decoration: The Iznik contribution," *International Symposium on Iznik Ceramics and Tiles, Istanbul 1989* (forthcoming). Lately, further interrelations between the Tīmūrid architecture of Iran and the Ottoman architectural development have increasingly been pointed out: Walter B. Denny, "Points of stylistic contact in the architecture of Islamic Iran and Anatolia," *Islamic Art* 2, 1987, pp. 27–35; Lisa Golombek and Donald N. Wilber, *The Timurid Architecture of Iran and Turan* (Princeton, 1988), pp. 334–336 no. 95, 407–409 no. 214; Thomas W. Lentz and Glenn D. Lowry, *Timur and the Princely Vision: Persian Art and Culture in the Fifteenth Century* (Los Angeles, 1989), pp. 317–319.
10. Outlined in greater detail in my recent monograph on Mamluk architecture: Meinecke (1992), I, pp. 135–143, 168–72, 183–184, 202–204; cf. also the summary "Mamluk architecture. Regional architectural tradition: Evolution and interrelations," *Damaszener Mitteilungen* 2, 1985, pp. 163–175.
11. This point is also advanced in two forthcoming articles, "The mosque of sultan an-Nāṣir Ḥasan at Cairo: Origins and influences," *Festschrift ʿAbd ar-Raḥmān ʿAbd at-Tawwāb;* and "The Ulu Cami at Manisa and the Isa Bey Cami at Selçuk: Seljuk revival versus Mamluk influences," *The 8th International Congress of Turkish Art, Cairo 1987.*
12. Meinecke (1976), II, pp. 400–403 no. 97; see also the relevant article quoted in the preceding note.
13. Meinecke (1992), II, pp. 122 no. 9C/78, 167 no. 9C/324; further examples of

this group of imperial mosques: II, pp. 110 no. 9C/18, 155 no. 9C/261, 178 no. 9C/373; cf. I, pp. 59–62, figs. 27–30.

14. Meinecke (1992), I, pp. 109–10, fig. 68; II, pp. 206 no. 18/2, 225–226 no. 19B/15. The mosque was recently cleared away to give way for an office building; previously documented by ʿAbd al-Qādir ar-Riḥāwī, "Jāmiʿ Yalbughā fī Dimashq," *Les Annales Archéologiques Arabes Syriennes* 24, 1974, Arabic section, pp. 125–138, figs. 1–6, pls. 1–12.
15. Meinecke (1992), I, pl. 16b; II, p. 88 no. 9B/3; further examples: *op. cit.* I, pl. 16a,c.
16. Meinecke (1976), II, pp. 414–417 no. 103; see also the forthcoming analysis quoted in chapter 3 note 10. Already some time ago two monographic articles were devoted to this important monument: Katharina Otto-Dorn, "Die Isa Bey Moschee in Ephesos," *Istanbuler Forschungen* 17, 1952, pp. 115–131; Aziz Ogan, "Aydın Oğullarından İsa Bey Camiʾi," *Vakıflar Dergisi* 3, 1956, pp. 73–80.
17. Creswell, *EMA* I (1969), pp. 151–210, figs. 79–94, 96, 99–100, 118, 127, pls. 40–62A.
18. The impact of the Umaiyad Mosque at Damascus on Damascene architecture was brilliantly demonstrated by Ernst Herzfeld, "Damascus: Studies in architecture," IV, *Ars Islamica* 13–14, 1948, pp. 118–138, figs. 1–38.
19. Meinecke (1992), I, p. 131, fig. 139, pls. 69d, 73b, 94d; II, pp. 232 no. 19B/53, 244–245 no. 22/34, 329 no. 29/58.
20. Meinecke (1992), I, pp. 132–133, fig. 43, pl. 66d; II, p. 236 no. 21/9.
21. Ayverdi I (1966), pp. 309–319, figs. 463–495; and also Katharina Otto-Dorn, *Das islamische Iznik* (Berlin, 1941), pp. 20–33, figs. 7–11, pls. 6/3, 7–17.
22. Meinecke (1976), I, pp. 101–102.
23. Ayverdi I (1966), pp. 419–440, figs. 721–757/a–b; see also Albert Gabriel, *Une capitale turque: Brousse, Bursa* (Paris, 1958), pp. 67–72, figs. 27–29, pls. 22–26 bis.
24. Ayverdi I (1966), pp. 514–523, figs. 876–895/a; previously surveyed by Karl Wulzinger, "Die Piruz-Moschee zu Milas, ein Beitrag zur Frühgeschichte osmanischer Baukunst," *Festschrift anläβlich des 100-jährigen Bestehens der Technischen Hochschule Fridericiana zu Karlsruhe* (Karlsruhe, 1925), pp. 161–187, figs. 1–11; idem, "Die Piruz-Bej-Moschee zu Milas," in Theodor Wiegand, ed., *Das islamische Milet* (Berlin and Leipzig, 1935), pp. 60–68, figs. 33–41.
25. Extensively documented by Wulzinger, in Wiegand, ed., *op.cit.* note 24 (1935), pp. 12–37, figs. 2–25, pls. 1–10, 23–34.
26. Ayverdi II (1972), pp. 4–25, figs. 1–37; first surveyed by Albert Gabriel, *Monuments turcs d'Anatolie* II: *Amasya—Tokat—Sivas* (Paris, 1934), pp. 25–31, figs. 11–14, pls. 4/1–2.
27. Ayverdi II (1972), pp. 185–190, figs. 311–323; Gabriel, *op. cit.*, note 26, pp. 72–73, fig. 48, pl. 19/1–2.
28. Ayverdi II (1972), pp. 255–263, figs. 440–450; compare also Gönül Öney, *Ankara'da Türk devri dini ve sosyal yapıları* (Ankara, 1971), pp. 52–54, figs. 91–96, plans 24a–b.

29. Ayverdi II (1972), pp. 422–461, figs. 736–794. On the relations of the Edirne mosque with Manisa, see also Kuran, *op.cit.* note 7 (1968), pp. 175–181, figs. 197–202.
30. On this workshop recently, see Michael Meinecke, "Syrian blue-and-white tiles of the 9th/15th century," *Damaszener Mitteilungen* 3, 1988, pp. 203–214, esp. p. 214, pl. 40e; and the forthcoming article quoted in note 9.
31. Ayverdi III (1973), pp. 356–406, figs. 567–639, color pl. after p. 368.
32. Yücel (1983), pp. 191–204, illus. 64–67, figs. 271–302.
33. Kuran, *op.cit.* note 5 (1987), pp. 64–68, figs. 32, 37–40, 44; cf. Goodwin, *op.cit.*, note 1 (1971), pp. 206–211, figs. 196–202.
34. Recently a detailed architectural survey was published by Sedat Hakkı Eldem and Feridun Akozan, *Topkapı Sarayı: Bir mimari araştırma* (Istanbul, [1981]). On the foundation period extensively Ayverdi IV (1974), pp. 682–736, figs. 1038/a–1055/e; see also Tahsin Öz, *Topkapı Sarayında Fatih Sultan Mehmet II. ye ait eserler* (Ankara, 1953).
35. See chapter 3, note 69.
36. Meinecke (1992), I, pp. 183–184, fig. 133, pls. 106b, 110c, 125b; II, pp. 409–410 no. 42/73.
37. Meinecke (1992), I, p. 184, pls. 119a, 125a; II, p. 402 no. 42/39.
38. Mujīr ad-Dīn al-ᶜUlaimī, *al-Uns al-jalīl bi-tārīkh al-Quds wa l-Khalīl,* Muḥammad Baḥr al-ᶜUlūm, ed. (an-Najaf, 1968) II, p. 321; Henry Sauvaire, trans., *Histoire de Jérusalem et d' Hébron, depuis Abraham jusqu'a la fin du XV*ᵉ *siècle* (Paris, 1876), p. 285; cf. Meinecke (1992), I, p. 168; II, p. 417 no. 42/111.
39. Meinecke (1992), I, pp. 168–170, fig. 129, pls. 106a, 108a, 116c; II, p. 419 no. 42/118. On this monument and a few similar though definitely smaller buildings: Doris Behrens-Abouseif, "Four domes of the late Mamluk period," *Annales Islamologiques* 17, 1981, pp. 191–201, pls. 11–14; and on the related urban development, idem, "The north-eastern extension of Cairo under the Mamluks," *loc.cit.*, pp. 157–189, pls. 8–10.
40. Yücel (1983), pp. 103–127, illus. 40–45, figs. 137–179.
41. Goodwin, *op. cit.*, note 1 (1971), pp. 184–187, figs. 178–180.
42. Ayverdi III (1973), pp. 327–334, figs. 534–543, color pl. after p. 336; Yücel (1983), pp. 235–238, illus. 79–80, figs. 351–361; on the Mamluk features: Meinecke (1992), I, p. 169, fig. 130, pl. 108b.
43. Meinecke (1992), I, pp. 170–172, fig. 131, pls. 106c, 107a–b; II, p. 450 no. 47/6.
44. Meinecke (1992), I, p. 172, fig. 132, pls. 107d, 113a, 117b; II, p. 450 no. 47/7.
45. Meinecke (1992), I, pp. 166–167, fig. 128, pls. 113d, 117c, 118c; II, pp. 451–452 nos. 47/9–11.
46. Muḥammad Ibn Iyās, *Badāʾ iᶜ az-zuhūr fī waqāʾ iᶜ ad-duhur,* Muḥammad Muṣṭafā, ed., V (Cairo, 1961), pp. 162, 179, 182, 188; Gaston Wiet, trans., *Journal d'un bourgeois du Caire* II (Paris, 1960) pp. 156, 173–174, 176; see Meinecke (1992), I, pp. 202–203.
47. Sedad Hakkı Eldem, *Köşkler ve kasırlar* I (1969), pp. 93–98, figs. 60–63; Yücel (1983), p. 440 Ist. 29.

48. On the building: Eldem and Akozan, *op.cit.* note 34 (1981), p. 77, pls. 77–84, 184–188; on the holy relics on exhibit: Kemal Çığ, *Relics of Islam* (Istanbul, 1966); and on the marble decoration: Michael Meinecke, "Mamlukische Marmordekorationen in der osmanischen Türkei," *Mitteilungen des Deutschen Archäologischen Instituts—Abteilung Kairo* 27/2, 1971, pp. 207–220, esp. 210–213, pls. 52a–b, 54a, 55a.
49. Ibn Iyās V, p. 336, trans. Wiet, p. 324; cf. Meinecke (1992), I, p. 203.
50. Ülgen, *op.cit.* note 6 (1989), pls. 1–5; Ikaur Aktuğ, *Gebze Çoban Mustafa Paşa Külliyesi* (Ankara, 1989); see also the following notes.
51. Both objects (inv.nos. I.4500 and 4502) were acquired in 1910: Almut Hauptmann von Gladiβ and Jens Kröger, *Berlin, Staatliche Museen Preuβischer Kulturbesitz—Museum für Islamische Kunst: Metall, Stein, Stuck, Holz, Elfenbein, Stoffe*, Klaus Brisch, ed., *Islamische Kunst: Loseblattkatalog unpublizierter Werke aus deutschen Museen* (Mainz, 1985), pp. 127–128 no. 315, 129–30 no. 316, with illus.
52. Both since 1931 in the Türk ve Islam Eserleri Müzesi in Istanbul (inv.nos. 4669–4670): Ernst Kühnel, *Die Sammlung türkischer und islamischer Kunst im Tschinili Köschk* (Berlin and Leipzig, 1938), pp. 19–20, pl. 17[a]; Leon Ary Mayer, *Islamic Woodcarvers and Their Works* (Geneva, 1958), p. 27. A Koran table, probably of Mamluk origin, said to originate from the Gebze mosque, is now also in the Istanbul museum (inv.no. 4667): Kühnel, (1938), p. 20, pl. 19[a].
53. Discussed in my article quoted in note 48, 1971, pp. 214–220, pls. 53, 54c, 55c, 56a, 57a–b, 58a,c, 59a, 60d, 61a,c.
54. Quotation from the translation by Joseph von Hammer, *Evliya Efendi: Narrative of Travels in Europe, Asia and Africa in the Seventeenth Century* II (London, 1850), p. 90.
55. For the process of development from cut-tile mosaic to wall tiles, see the works mentioned in note 9.
56. Atasoy and Raby, *op.cit.* note 69, chapter 3 (1989), p. 102, fig. 129.

Plates

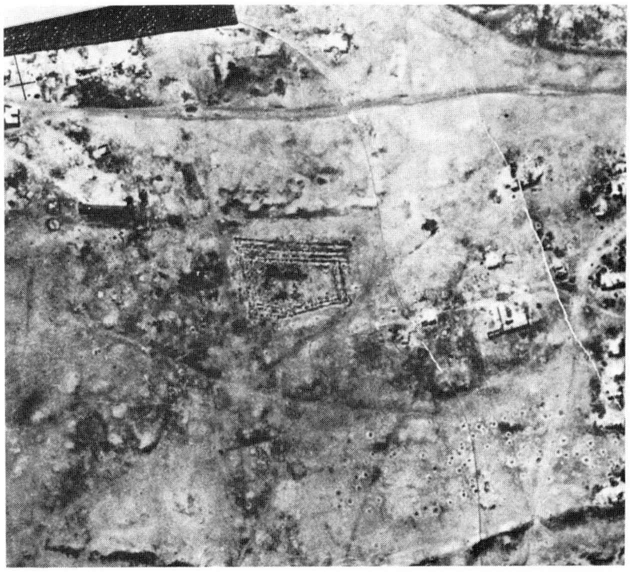

a

b

c

Plate 1. (a) ar-Raqqa/Nikephorion, Great Mosque: aerial view of 1942 (courtesy Directorate General of Antiquities and Museums, Damascus). (b) ar-Raqqa/Nikephorion, Great Mosque—Maᶜdhānat al-Munaiṭir: minaret in February 1909 (photo Gertrude L. Bell, 181; courtesy Gertrude Bell Photographic Archive: Department of Antiquities, The University of Newcastle upon Tyne). (c) ar-Raqqa/ar-Rāfiqa, city walls and palace area: aerial view of 1929 (courtesy of Institut Français d'Archéologie de Proche Orient, Damascus).

(a) Aerial view of 1961 before the removal of advance fortifications (photo Marwan Musselmany and Ahmed Kurumli; courtesy Kassem Toueir).

(b) North Gate after excavation (photo Meinecke 84/IX-11).

Plate 2. ar-Raqqa/ar-Rāfiqa, city walls.

(a) View of ruin in 1973 before excavation (photo Meinecke 73/LXXXII-11).

(b) Stucco decoration of prayer niche (photo Muhammad Faris, 1986).

Plate 3. ar-Raqqa/ar-Rāfiqa, Great Mosque.

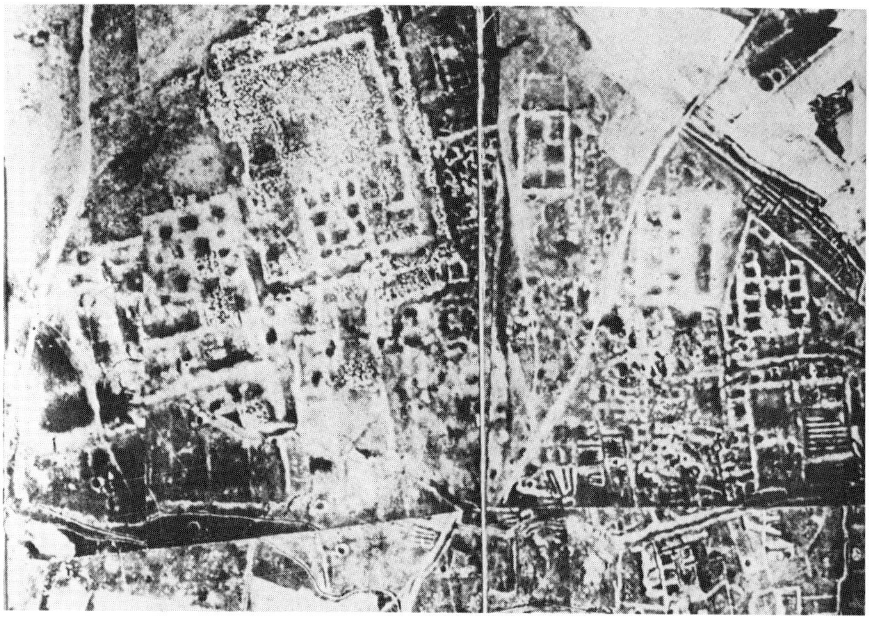

(a) Central palace of Hārūn ar-Rashīd and adjacent residences; aerial view of c. 1930 (after Maurice Dunand, *De l'Amanus au Sinai* [1953], fig. p. 97).

(b) Excavation Site East-Eastern Palace, after partial reconstruction in 1989 (photo German Archaeological Institute, Damascus, no. 89/535: Andreas Wegner).

Plate 4. ar-Raqqa/ar-Rāfiqa, Palace City.

(a) View from southwest during excavation (photo German Archaeological Institute, Damascus, no. 86/1250a: Klaus Anger).

(b) Stucco frieze (photo Meinecke 83/IV-11).

(c) Stucco frieze (photo Meinecke 83/VI-33).

Plate 5. ar-Raqqa/ar-Rāfiqa, Palace City, Excavation Site East-Western Palace.

(a) Aerial view of c. 1930 (after Maurice Dunand, *De l'Amanus au Sinai* [1953], fig. p. 97).

(b) Main building, south façade with central entrance during excavation in 1989 (photo German Archaeological Institute, Damascus, no. 89/650: Michael Meinecke).

Plate 6. ar-Raqqa/ar-Rāfiqa, Palace City, Northeast Complex.

(a) ar-Raqqa/ar-Rāfiqa, Palace City: Excavation Site East-Western Palace, stucco friezes of central reception room (photo German Archaeological Institute, Damascus, no. 85/750: Peter Grunwald).

(b) Hiraqla near ar-Raqqa: aerial view of 1935 (courtesy Institut Français d'Archéologie de Proche Orient, Damascus).

Plate 7.

(a) Citadel: Saljūq northwest tower, interior of upper part (photo Meinecke 86/VI-36).

(b) Madrasa of Kumushtakīn at the al-Mabrak Mosque: ceiling of main *īwān* (photo German Archaeological Institute, Damascus, no. 88/13: Peter Grunwald).

Plate 8. Buṣrā.

(a) Madrasa of Kumushtakīn at the al-Mabrak Mosque: interior courtyard with façade of north *īwān* (photo Meinecke 73/CXXXI-25).

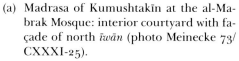

(b) Citadel: Aiyūbid southwest tower, interior (photo German Archaeological Institute, Damascus, no. 86/200: Peter Grunwald).

Plate 9. Buṣrā.

a

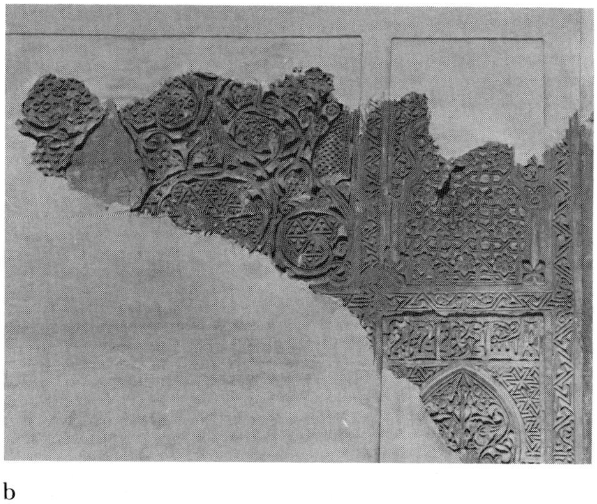

b

c

Plate 10. Buṣrā, al^cUmarī Mosque: (a) Prayer hall (photo German Archaeological Institute, Damascus, no. 83/1161: Klaus Anger). (b) Stucco decoration of *miḥrāb* (photo German Archaeological Institute, Damascus, no. 83/1186: Klaus Anger). (c) Fragment of stucco frieze on *qibla* wall (photo German Archaeological Institute, Damascus, no. 83/1190: Klaus Anger).

(a) al-Fāṭima Mosque: interior (photo Meinecke 73/CXXXI-4).

(b) Dār al-Qurʾān of ʿAbd al-Wāḥid ash-Shāfiʿī: view from east (photo Meinecke 84/XVI-3).

Plate 11. Buṣrā.

(a) Buṣrā, Ḥammām Manjak: reception room after restoration (photo German Archaeological Institute, Damascus, no. 89/1569: Peter Grunwald).

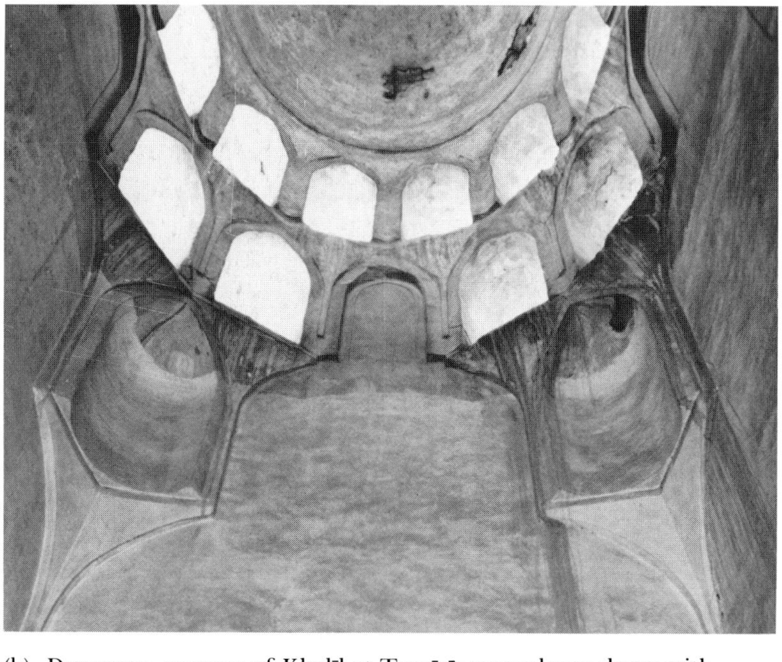

(b) Damascus, mosque of Khalīl at-Taurīzī: mausoleum dome with *muqarnaṣ* pendentives (photo Meinecke 73/C-1).

Plate 12.

(a) Buṣrā, Ḥammām Manjak: bath chambers during excavation (photo Meinecke 87/V-14).

(b) Damascus, Ḥammām at-Taurīzī: central bath chamber (photo Meinecke 73/XCVI-2).

Plate 13.

(a) Buṣrā, Ḥammām Manjak: fragment of corner transition in bath chamber (photo German Archaeological Institute, Damascus, no. 87/2315: Peter Grunwald).

(b) Damascus, Ḥammām at-Taurīzī: stucco *muqarnaṣ* vault of bath chamber (photo Meinecke 73/XCVI-4).

Plate 14.

(a) al-Kiswa, Zāwiyat Manjak: *qibla īwān* (photo Meinecke 84/IV-5).

(b) al-Muzairīb, Khān: entrance (photo Meinecke 88/I-9).

Plate 15.

(a) Tigris Bridge: general view with Citadel plateau (photo Meinecke 75/LII-20).

(b) Citadel-Artuqid palace and Aiyūbid mosque: view from the left bank of the Tigris (photo Meinecke 75/LIV-22).

Plate 16. Hasankeyf.

(a) Batman Su Bridge near Silvan (photo Meinecke 75/LII-17).

(b) Cizre, Bridge: general view (photo Meinecke 84/VI-36).

(c) Cizre, Bridge: mason marks on south pier (photo Meinecke 84/VI-25).

Plate 17.

(a) Istanbul, Topkapı Sarayı Library ms. Aḥmet III no. 3472, pp. 328–329: double page miniature of palace door at Diyarbakır by al-Jazarī (museum photograph; courtesy Filiz Çağman).

(b) Cizre, Ulu Cami: bronze door on middle entrance of prayer hall façade (after Conrad Preusser, *Nordmesopotamische Baudenkmäler* [1911], pl. 36).

Plate 18.

(a) Stucco *miḥrāb* in main domed chamber (photo Meinecke 75/LIII-18).

(b) Stucco *miḥrāb* in central *īwān* (photo Meinecke 75/LIII-16).

Plate 19. Hasankeyf, Koç Cami.

(a) Washington, D.C., Freer Gallery of Art inv.no. 30.77: figural scene from a miniature page of a Mamluk copy of al-Jazarī's treatise, dated 715/1315 (museum photograph neg.no. 2271 B; courtesy Esin Atıl and Freer Gallery of Art, Smithsonian Institution, Washington, D.C.).

(b) Cizre, Bridge: zodiac relief of Saturn and Libra on south pier (photo Meinecke 84/VI-1).

Plate 20.

a

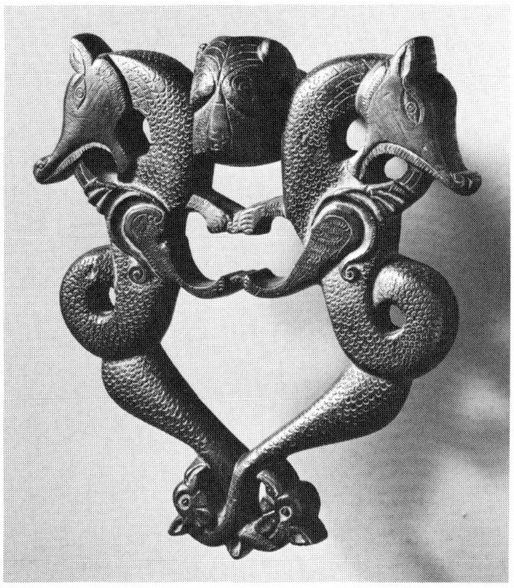

b

c

Plate 21. (a) Istanbul, Topkapı Sarayı Library ms. Aḥmet III, no. 3472, p. 335: door knocker of palace door at Diyarbakır by al-Jazarī (museum photograph; courtesy Filiz Çağman). (b) Berlin, Museum of Islamic Art inv.no. I.2242: bronze door knocker from Tiflis (museum photograph pl. 516: Dietrich Graf). (c) Berlin, Museum of Islamic Art: coins of the sixth/twelfth and seventh/thirteenth centuries from Southeast Anatolia and North Mesopotamia, in scale 1:1 (museum photographs nos. 8307, 8311–12: Petra Stüning); for identification see appendix.

(a) Small Palace: exterior façade (photo Meinecke 75/LII-26).

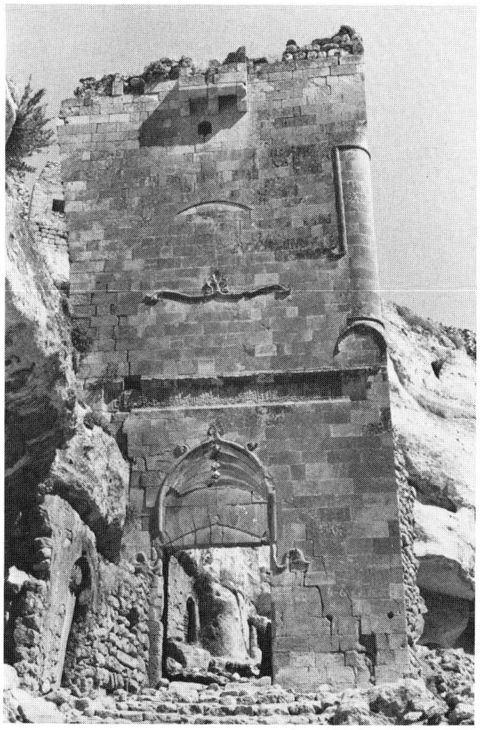

(b) Second gate (photo Stefan Heidemann 1982).

Plate 22. Hasankeyf, Citadel.

b

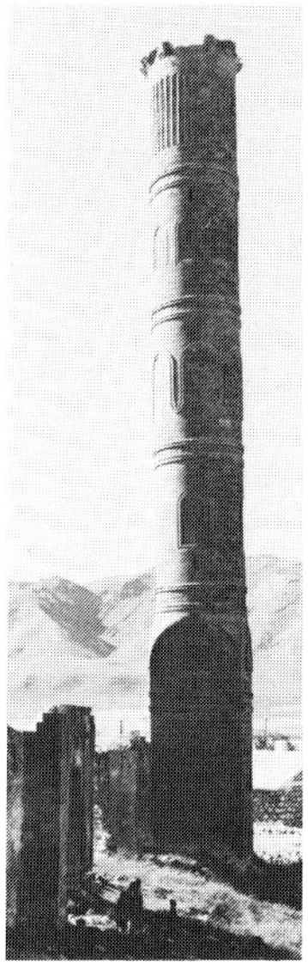

a

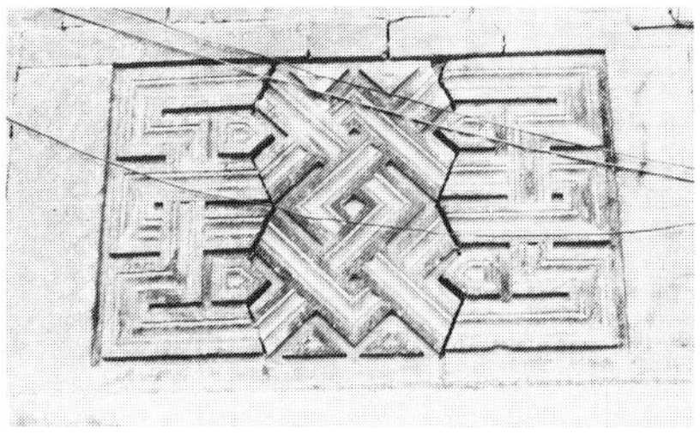

c

d

e

Plate 23. (a–b) Hasankeyf, Sultan Süleyman Camii: minaret and base with inscription of 807/1404–5 and decorative panel (photos Meinecke 75/LIII013 and 9). (c) Aleppo, Madrasa aṣ-Ṣāḥibīya of 765/1363–64: window panel (photo Meinecke 71/CXXXIII-13). (d) Hasankeyf, Jāmiʿ ar-Rizq: minaret (photo Stefan Heidemann 1982). (e) Aleppo, mosque of Mankalībughā ash-Shamsī: minaret (after Jean Sauvaget, *Alep* [1941], pl. 39).

(a) Hasankeyf, Sultan Süleyman Camii: domed courtyard of three-*īwān* structure (photo Meinecke 75/LIV-15).

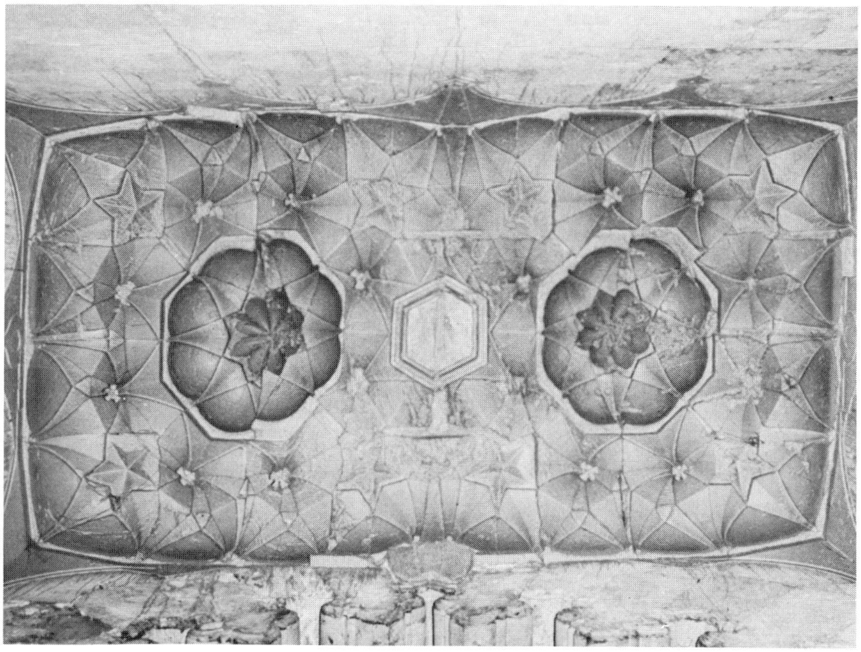

(b) Aleppo, Dār al-Fakhrī: stucco ceiling of *īwān* (photo Meinecke 73/LXXI-10).

Plate 24.

a

b

c

Plate 25. (a–b) Hasankeyf, Jāmiᶜ ar-Rizq: minaret shaft and base (photos Meinecke 75/LII-29, LIII-1). (c) Mardin, Sultan İsa Medresesi: entrance porch (photo Meinecke 75/LVII-31).

a

b

c

Plate 26. (a–b) Hasankeyf, Mausoleum: façade and window niche (photos Meinecke 75/LIII-24,28). (c) Aleppo, Jāmiʿ ad-Darraj: window niche of façade (photo Meinecke 71/CXLI-12).

(a) Hasankeyf, Zeynel Bey Türbesi: building inscription on portal in cut tile mosaic (photo Meinecke 75/LIV-31)).

(b) Istanbul, Çinili Köşk: cut tile mosaic decoration of portico (photo Meinecke 70/LXI-31).

Plate 27.

(a) Zeynel Bey Türbesi: exterior view (photo Meinecke 75/LIV-23).

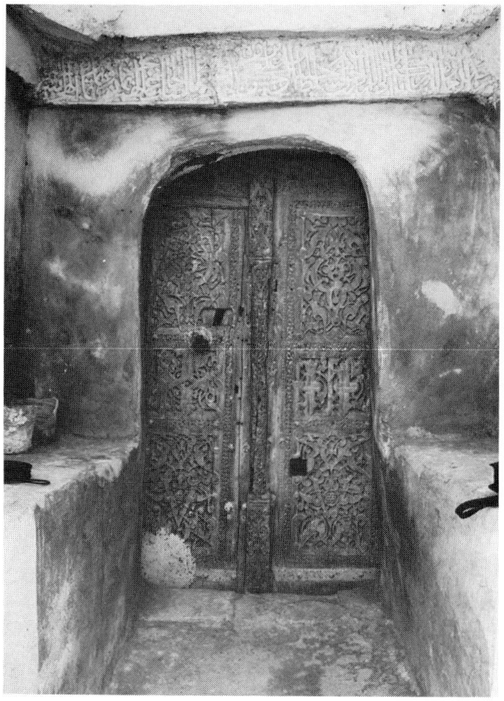

(b) Mashhad Imām Muḥammad b. ʿAbd Allāh aṭ-Ṭaiyār: entrance of mausoleum (photo Meinecke 75/LV-1).

Plate 28. Hasankeyf.

c

a b d

Plate 29. (a) Manisa, Ulu Cami: lateral niche of north portal (photo Meinecke 75/XXV-22). (b) Selçuk, İsa Bey Camii: courtyard window (photo Meinecke 75/XXVI-6). (c) Damascus, madrasa of Jaqmaq al-Arghūnshāwī: prayer niche (photo Meinecke 71/CXI-10) (d) Aleppo, mosque of Mankalībughā ash-Shamsī: east portal (photo Meinecke 73/XLVI-25).

(a) Manisa, Ulu Cami: courtyard (photo Meinecke 75/XXV-1).

(b) Edirne, Üç Şerefeli Cami: courtyard (photo Meinecke 72/XXXI-6).

Plate 30.

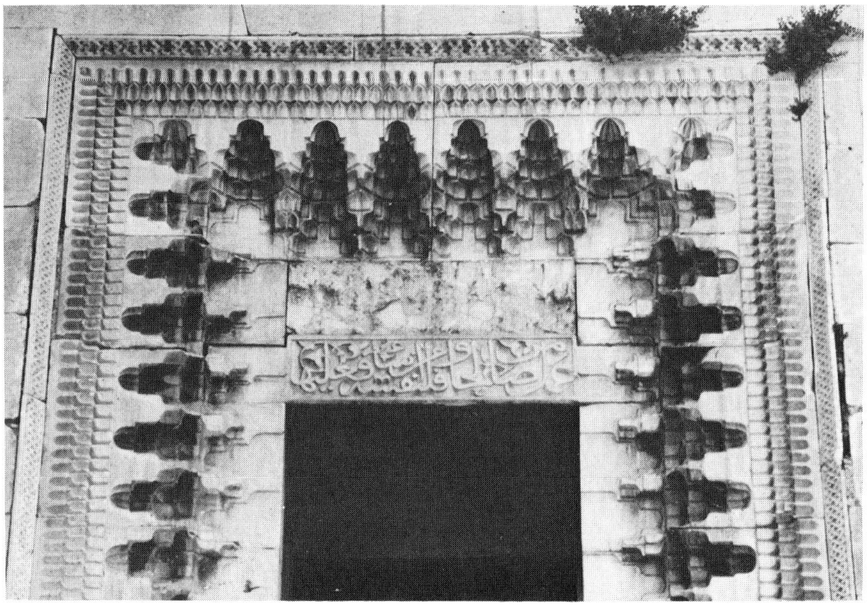

(a) Selçuk, İsa Bey Camii: window of façade (photo Meinecke 75/XXVII-25).

(b) Iznik, Yeşil Cami: door of exterior portico (photo Meinecke 1989).

Plate 31.

(a) Üç Şerefeli Cami: exterior view (photo Meinecke 72/XXX-14).

(b) Mosque of Bāyazīd II: exterior view (photo Meinecke 72/XXXIII-31).

Plate 32. Edirne.

(a) Exterior view (photo Meinecke 73/XLI-16).

(b) Interior dome (photo Meinecke 71/CXXX-17).

Plate 33. Aleppo, Mausoleum of ʿUthmān Ibn Ughulbak.

(a) Façade (photo K. A. C. Creswell, neg. no. 3712/E.7A.14; courtesy Creswell Archive, Ashmolean Museum, Oxford).

(b) Interior (photo German Archaeological Institute, Cairo, no. 4357: Dieter Johannes).

Plate 34. Cairo, Qubbat al-Fadāwīya.

(a) Madrasa of Khāʾirbak al-Ashrafī: interior (photo Meinecke 77/XXVIII-16).

(b) Madrasa of Qānībāy Qarā ar-Rammāḥ: main *īwān* (photo Meinecke 71/XIV-31).

Plate 35. Cairo.

(a) Gebze, Çoban Mustafa Paşa Camii: interior (photo Meinecke 70/XLVIII-11).

(b–c) Berlin, Museum of Islamic Art inv.nos. I.4500 and 4502: Mamluk brass chandeliers from the Mustafa Paşa Camii at Gebze (museum photographs pl. 491: Karl-Heinz Paulmann; and diapositive: Petra Stüning).

Plate 36.

Appendix

Key to coins in the Berlin Museum of Islamic Art represented on pl. 21c:

1.	Inv.no. I.1989.18:	Ḥusām ad-Dīn Tīmūr Tāsh, Artuqid of Mardin (516/1122–547/1152), with two countermarks of Najm ad-Dīn Alpī (see below, no. 2); Hennequin no. 936
2.–3.	Inv.nos. I.1989.19–20:	Najm ad-Dīn Alpī, Artuqid of Mardin (547/1152–572/1176); Hennequin nos. 957, 1016
4.	Inv.no. I.1989.26:	Fakhr ad-Dīn Qarā Arslān, Artuqid of Hasankeyf (539/1144–562/1167), minted at Hasankeyf in 560/1164–65; Hennequin no. 862
5.	Inv.no. I. 1989.29:	ʿIzz ad-Din Masʿūd, Zengid of Mosul (572/1176–589/1193), minted at Cizre in 577/1181–82; Hennequin no. 323

6. Inv.no. I.1989.23: Ḥusām ad-Dīn Yūluq Arslān, Artuqid of Mardin (580/1184–c.597/1201), minted in 582/1186–87; Hennequin no. 1079
7. Inv.no. I.1990.11: Nūr ad-Dīn Muḥammad b. Qarā Arslān, Artuqid of Hasankeyf and Diyarbakır (562/1167–581/1185), minted in 576/1180–81; Hennequin no. 881
8. Inv.no. I.1989.27: Rukn ad-Dīn Maudūd, Artuqid of Diyarbakır (619/1222–629/1232), minted at Āmid/Diyarbakır in 621/1224–25; Hennequin no. 927
9. Inv.no. I.1989.20: Nāṣir ad-Dīn Maḥmūd, Zengid of Mosul (616/1219–631/1233), minted at Mosul in 627/1229–30; Hennequin no. 909
10. Inv.no. I.1989.25: Nāṣir ad-Dīn Artuq Arslān, Artuqid of Mardin (c.597/1201–637/1239), minted in 628/1230–31; Hennequin no. 1357

The identification of these coins by Stefan Heidemann is gratefully acknowledged; bibliographical indications are restricted to the standard reference work by Gilles Hennequin, *Catalogue des monnaies musulmanes, Asie pré-Mongole: Les Salǧūqs et leur successeurs. Bibliothèque Nationale, Departement des Monnaies, Médailles et Antiques* (Paris, 1985).

Index

ᶜAbbāsid, xviii, 8, 9, 11–13, 16, 18, 22–25, 38
ᶜAbd Allāh ibn Muḥammad. *See* Ibn al-Mawardī
ᶜAbd al-Wāhid ash-Shāfiᶜī, 42
Abu l-ᶜAbbās as-Saffāḥ, 9
Abū Sa'īd, 65
ᶜĀdil Abū Bakr, 38, 39
ᶜĀdil Ghāzī, 66, 68, 70, 72, 80
ᶜĀdil Sulaimān, 66, 71, 75, 77
Aiyūb b. Majd ad-Dīn ᶜĪsā an-Najrānī, 43
Aiyūbid(s), 24, 31, 33, 38, 39, 41–43, 49, 57, 58, 64, 66–68, 70, 71, 73, 74, 77, 80
Aḥmad al-kutubī, 74
Aḥmad al-miᶜmār, 110
Aleppo, xviii, 5, 24, 38, 62, 68, 72–77, 81, 93, 105; Bāb Qinnasrīn, 13; Citadel, 103; Dār al-Fakhrī, 68; Jamiᶜ ad-Darraj, 74; Jamiᶜ al-Uṭrūsh, 74; Māristān Arghūn, 73; Mausoleum of ᶜUthmān Ibn Ughulbak, 102, 103
ᶜAlī, 8
ᶜAlī b. Mushaimish ad-Dimashqī, xviii, 93, 98
ᶜAlī Ibn Abi Ṭālib, 8
Ali Saim Ulgen, 90
Amasya, Beyazit Paşa Camii, 98; Meḥmet Chelebī Madrasa at Mezzifon, 98
Āmid. *See* Diyarbakīr
Amīn ad-Daula Abū Manṣūr Kumushtakīn, 35, 37–39
ᶜAmmūrīya, 13
Amorion. *See* ᶜAmmūrīya
Amrān b. Mahdī, 68
Anatolia(n), xviii, xix, 13, 23, 55, 58, 64, 68, 77, 90, 91, 93, 96, 98, 103, 111
Ankara, Karaca Bey Camii, 98
Ankara University, 57

Āq Qoyūnlū, 57, 64, 77–80
Arik, Oluş M., 57
Artuqid(s), 42, 57, 58, 60–64, 71, 75, 80, 92
Ashraf Qaitbāy. *See* Qaitbāy
Ashraf Qānṣūh al-Ghaurī. *See* Ghaurī
Atābeks, 31, 33
Ayverdi, Ekrem Hakki, 90

Baalbek, 38, 40
Baghdād, 9, 11, 12, 15–17, 23–25, 111
Balat, Ilyas Bey Camii, 98
Balikh River, 7
Balkans, 91
Barkan, Ömer Lauutfi, 90
Baṣra, 9, 11
Bāyazīd, 101, 105
Berlin Museum of Islamic Art, 110
Birkat al-Ḥajj cistern, 41, 42
Bitlis, 60
Būrid, 35
Bursa, Mosque of Yildirim Bāyazīd, 93, 97, 98
Buṣrā, xviii, 3, 31–33, 35, 38, 39, 42–44, 46, 48, 49, 111; Citadel, 39, 41; Directorate of Antiquities, 33; Great Mosque, 35, 37, 40, 43, 46, 48; Hammām Manjak, 44, 46, 50n. 5; Madrasa Dār al-Qur'ān, 42; Madrasa of Abū Hanīfa an-Nu'mān, 37, 38; Masjid Yāgūt, 42; Mosque of al-Fātima, 42, 43, 48; Mosque of al-Mabrak, 42; Mosque of 'Unarī, 46
Byzantium (Byzantine), 2, 7, 11–13, 23, 58, 63, 90, 91, 100; Emperor Justinian, 7, 90; Hagia Sophia, 89, 90, 100, 101; Heraclea/Ereğli, 23

Cairo, 38, 68, 92, 99, 103, 105, 109, 110; Citadel, 13; Complex of Ashraf Qānṣūh al-Ghaurī, 109; Madrasa of Khā'īrbak al-Ashrafi, 106; Madrasa of Qānībāy Qarā ar-Rammāḥ, 106; Mosque of Aḥmad Ibn Ṭūlūn, 15; Mosque of 'Amr Ibn al-'Āṣ, 26n. 9; Qubbat al-Fadāwīya, 103, 105, 110
Chelebī, Ewliyā, 110
Cizre. *See* Jazīrat Ibn 'Umar
Constantinople. *See* Istanbul
Creswell, K. A. C., 2, 9
Crusader, 35, 38

Damascus, xviii, 3, 7–9, 13, 17, 31–33, 35, 38, 39, 41, 46, 48, 49, 68, 93, 112; Citadel, 13, 39; Friday Mosque, 92; Great Mosque, 2, 15, 36–38, 44, 93; Madrasa al-Amīnīya, 38; Mosque, Mausoleum, and Ḥammām of Khalīl at-Taurīzī, 44; Turba at-Takrītīya at aṣ-Ṣāliḥīya, 92
Damascus, German Archaeological Institute of, 5, 18, 33
Dār as-Salṭana, 65
Darb al-Ḥajj, 32, 46
Diyarbakır, 42, 55, 57, 58, 62, 64
Dūnaisīr, 57, 62

Edirne, 91, 109; Complex of Bāyazīd II, 105, 109; Muradīye Camii (Üç Şerefeli), 73, 98–101
Egypt(ian), xviii, xix, 38, 64, 65, 68, 91, 99, 110
Euphrates River, xvii, 2, 5, 7, 13, 16, 18, 24, 58, 60

Fakr ad-Dīn Qarā Arslān, 58
Farabī (?) b.'Uthmān as-Sa'dī, 80
Fatimid, 35
Fusṭāṭ. *See* Cairo

Gabriel, Albert, 57, 60, 61, 65, 68, 73, 75, 76
Gebze, Funerary complex of Muṣṭafā Pāshā, 110, 111
Ghaurī, 109

Hādī, 16
Hajjaj b. Arṭāt, 11
Hājji b. Mūsā, 96
Hamdānid, 13
Hārūn ar-Rashīd, 15–19, 22–24
Hasankeyf. *See* Ḥiṣn Kaifā

Hāshimīya, 9
Ḥaurān Province, 32, 33, 35, 37–39, 41, 42, 46–49
Ḥijāz, 32
Ḥīra, 9
Ḥiṣkafī, Muḥammad b. Yūsuf b. ᶜUthmān, 63
Ḥiṣn al-Qādisīya. *See* Qāṭūl
Ḥiṣn Kaifā, xviii, 3, 55, 57, 58, 61–66, 68, 70–81, 102, 112; Bridge, 60; Citadel, 77; Great Palace of the Citadel, 60, 61; Jāmiᶜ ar-Rizq, 73, 75, 76; Koç Camii, 68, 70, 72, 76; Mausoleum, 76; Mosque of the Citadel, 61, 71, 72; Muwahhīd ᶜAbd Allāh, 64, 65; Shrine of imām Muḥammad b. ᶜAbd Allāh aṭ-Ṭaiyār, 78; Small Mosque, 75; Small Palace of the Citadel, 65; Sultan Süleyman Camii, 66, 68, 72, 73, 75; Zeynel Bey Türbesi, 77–79
Herzfeld, Ernst, 5, 7–9, 23

Ibn al-Azraq, 58, 60
Ibn al-Mawardī, 70; Madrasa, 70, 72
Ibn al-Munshiʾ, Ḥasan ("Taʾrīkh bait Aiyūb"), 65, 66, 70, 71, 80
Ibn al-Mushaimish ad-Dīmashqī (Abū Bakr b. Muḥammad), 98
Ibn Iyās, 109, 110, 112
Il-Khanid, 65, 70, 81, 91
Iran(ian), xviii, 58, 65, 68, 70, 79–81, 91, 92, 96, 99, 102
Iraq, 55
Iṣfahān, 80; Masjid-i Jumᶜa, 2, 79, 80
Istanbul, 91, 99–103, 109, 110; Çinili Köşk, 79, 102; Dawut Paşa Camii, 105; Hirka-i Saadet Dairesi, 109; Mermer Köşk, 109; Mosque of Bāyazīd II, 101; Mosque of Meḥmet Fātiḥ, 101; Mosque of Selīm I, 105, 109; Şehzade Camii, 101
ᶜIyād Ibn Ghanm, 7
Iznik, 91, 96, 111; Yeşil Camii, 93
ᶜIzz ad-Dīn Ibn Shaddād, 41, 65, 71

Jahān Shah (Qarā Qoyūnlū), 79
Jamāl ad-Dīn Muḥammad al-Iṣfahānī, 60
Jazarī, Ismāᶜīl ibn ar-Razzāz, 62, 63
Jazira, 5
Jazīrat Ibn ᶜUmār, 55, 57, 60, 62; Bridge, 60; Great Mosque, 61–63
Jerusalem, 105; Dome of the Rock, 2, 103; Masjid al-Aqṣā, 103

Khalīl (Āq Qoyūnlū), 78
Khān Dannūn, 46
Khiḍr, Mosque, 37
Khurāsān, 16, 24
Kiswa, 46
Kiziltepe. *See* Dūnaisīr
Koran, 37, 42
Kūfa, 8, 9, 11
Kuran, Aptullah, 90
Kurd(ish), 55, 64, 77

Lassner, Jacob, 9
Lowick, Nicholas, 63

Maᶜdhānat al-Munaiṭir, 8
Mahdī, 11, 16
Mamluk(s), xviii, xix, 3, 13, 33, 43, 44, 46, 64, 65, 68, 70, 73, 81, 89, 91–93, 98–100, 102, 103, 105, 106, 109–11
Manisa, 99, 100; Great Mosque, 92, 93, 95, 98, 99
Manjak al-Yūsufī, 44, 46
Mankalībughā ash-Shamsī, 73; Mosque, 93
Manṣūr, 9, 11, 12, 16, 17
Mārdīn, 57, 60, 64, 71, 75; Sultan Isa Medrese, 75, 76
Mayāfāriqīn. *See* Silvan
Mecca, 31
Medina, 31
Meḥmet, 99
Meḥmet Fātiḥ, 78, 79, 91, 100, 102
Mesopotamia(n), 5, 7, 8, 11, 13, 16, 18, 22, 24, 55, 58, 66, 68, 71, 77, 80
Milas, Piruz Bey Camii, 98
Mongol(s), 13, 24, 43, 64, 65, 71

Mosul, 5, 9, 24, 55, 58, 60, 66
Mount Tabor, 38
Muᶜāwiya Ibn Abī Sufyān, 8
Muᶜaẓẓam ᶜIsā, 41
Muᶜaẓẓam Tūrān Shāh, 64
Muḥammad, 37
Muḥammad, al-ḥājj, 73
Muḥammad b. Qarā Arslān, 62
Muḥammad Ibn aṣ-Ṣawwāf, 74
Muᶜīn ad-Dīn Sukmān b. Artuq, 58
Murād I, 93
Murād II, 98–100
Muṣtafā Pāshā, 110
Muᶜtaṣim, 13, 17, 19
Muzairīb Lake, Khān, 48

Najm ad-Dīn Alpī, 60
Nāṣir ad-Dīn Maḥmūd, 42, 63
Nāṣir Ḥasan, 68, 93
Nāṣir Muḥammad, 43, 65, 92, 99
Nikephorion. *See* Raqqa
Nile River, 71
Northedge, Alastair, 17
Nūr ad-Dīn Maḥmūd, 15
Nūr ad-Dīn Muḥammad b. Qarā Arslān, 62

Ottoman, xviii, xix, 3, 48, 64, 73, 78–80, 89–91, 93, 96–103, 105, 106–11

Persia, 9, 24
Pīr Ḥasan b. ustādh ᶜAbd ar-Raḥmān, 79
Pseudo-Dionysius, 11

Qaitbāy, 103
Qalᶜat Najm, 38
Qarā Qoyūnlū, 64, 79
Qāṭūl, 17, 24
Quṭb ad-Dīn Maudūd, 60
Quṭb ad-Dīn Sukmān, 62, 63

Rabaḥ, 11
Rāfiqa, 8, 11–13, 18; Bāb Ḥarrān (Ḥarrān Gate), 12; Baghdād Gate, 16; Great Mosque, 12, 13, 15, 22; Qaṣr al-Banāt (Girls' Palace), 16
Raqqa, xvii, xviii, 3, 5, 7–9, 11, 13, 16–18, 23–25, 111; Friday Mosque, 15; Hiraqla, 23; Qaṣr as-Salām (Palace of Peace), 18
Roman, 35
Rukh ad-Dīn Barkiyāruq, 58
Rūm, 103

Ṣafawid, 91
Saif ad-Daula ᶜAlī, 13
Saᶜīd ash-Shāfiᶜī, 71
Saᶜīd ibn ᶜĀmir Ibn Ḥidhyam, 7
Ṣaliḥ Ismāᶜīl, 39–41
Ṣāliḥ Khānum, 79
Ṣaliḥ Najm al-Dīn Aiyūb, 64
Saljūq, 2, 31, 33, 35, 37, 38, 58, 90, 91
Sāmarrāʾ, 13, 17, 22, 24; Bāb al-ᶜĀmma, 13; Great Mosque, 15; Mosque of Abū Dulaf, 28n. 33
Sarre, Friedrich, 5
Ṣarūkhān Dynasty, Isḥāq Chelebi, 92
Sassanian, 2, 7; Ctesiphon, 9; Emperor Khusrau I, 7, 9
Sauvaget, Jean, 57, 71
Selçuk, xviii, 93; Friday Mosque (Isa Bey Camii), 93, 95–98
Selīm I, the Grim, 90, 105, 109
Shams ad-Dīn Sunqur al-Hakīmī, 41
Shīᶜa, 8, 78
Shihāb ad-Dīn Aḥmad b. Ḥasan Ibn at-Ṭūlūnī, 109
Silvan, 57, 60, 62, 63
Sinān, 89, 90, 100, 101, 110
Sinān ad-Dīn Aḥmad b. Abī Bakr al-Mushaimish, 98
Sinclair, Tom, 62
Sulaiman the Magnificent, 89, 90, 105
Syria(n), xviii, 3, 5, 7–9, 13, 15–17, 22, 24, 25, 31, 35, 37–39, 43, 44, 46, 48, 49, 55, 60, 62, 64, 72, 81, 91, 92, 98, 109, 112
Syrian Antiquities Organization, 5, 18

Ṭabarī, 11, 16, 17
Tabrīz, Blue Mosque, 79
Temür Tāsh, 60
Tigris River, xviii, 3, 5, 9, 17, 42, 55, 58, 60–62, 64, 65, 71, 92; Bridge, 64, 80
Timūr(id), 48, 64, 71, 74–76, 91, 98, 102
Ṭughtakīn, Atābak, 35
Ṭūr Abdīn, 55
Turkey (Turkish), xviii, 81, 90, 91, 110
Türkman, 58, 64, 77, 91

ᶜUlaimī, 103
Umaiyad, 7–9, 11, 15, 25, 31, 35, 93
ᶜUmar, 73
ᶜUmar Ibn al-Khaṭṭāb, 7, 37
ᶜUmarī Mosque, 35
ᶜUthmān, 90, 91
Uwais al-Qaranī, 8
Ūzūn Ḥasan, 77–79

Van Lake, 58

Wāsiṭ, 9
Whelan, Estelle, 60

Yalbughā al-Yaḥyawī, 68, 92
Yaᶜqūbī, 9
Yazd, Madrasa Shamsīya, 70

Ẓāhir Baibars, 13, 43
Zainal, Mausoleum of, 78, 79
Zengid, 15, 24, 31, 60, 61
Zeynel Bey Türbesi, 77